Science Development

International Development Research Center
William J. Siffin, Director
Indiana University
Bloomington, Indiana

Science Development

The Building of Science in Less Developed Countries

by

Michael J. Moravcsik

 PROGRAM FOR ADVANCED STUDIES IN INSTITUTION BUILDING AND TECHNICAL ASSISTANCE METHODOLOGY

This publication was financed by a grant from MUCIA's Program for Advanced Study in Institution Building and Technical Assistance Methodology, which is funded by a 211(d) grant from USAID. Contractors undertaking projects under government sponsorship are encouraged to express freely their professional judgment in the conduct of the project. Points of view of opinions stated do not, therefore, necessarily represent official AID position or policy.

First Printing 1975
Second Printing 1976

ISBN 0-89249-008-X
Printed in the United States of America

The way in which man has come to understand celestial matters appears to me hardly less wonderful than the nature of the celestial events themselves.

—*Johannes Kepler*

Dedicated to all who devote themselves to the often difficult, lonely, frustrating, and complex task of creating opportunities for the pursuance of science.

Contents

FOREWORD TO THE SECOND PRINTING   ix

FOREWORD   xi

PREFACE   xvii

A WORD ON FORMAT   xxi

ABBREVIATIONS AND ACRONYMS   xxiii

ACKNOWLEDGMENTS   xxix

1 WHY SCIENCE IN LDCS?   1
Background and Comments   9

2 EDUCATION AND SCIENCE   17
Background and Comments   26

3 MANPOWER   41
Background and Comments   49

4 SCIENTIFIC COMMUNICATION   69
Background and Comments   80

5 SCIENTIFIC RESEARCH   93
Background and Comments   103

6 PLANNING, POLICY, AND MANAGEMENT   121
Background and Comments   135

7 INTERNATIONAL ASPECTS   161
Background and Comments   174

8 THE BIG INTANGIBLE   199
Background and Comments   205

9 WHERE DO WE GO FROM HERE?   209

REFERENCES   215

SUGGESTED INITIAL READINGS   253

SUBJECT INDEX   255

AUTHOR INDEX   260

Foreword to the Second Printing

About a year ago the Program for Advanced Studies in Institution Building and Technical Assistance Methodology (PASITAM), a program of the Midwest Universities Consortium for International Activities, issued this provocative book. We felt that it presented a significant statement on a central issue of institution building for national development.

The first edition was quickly exhausted. Copies were ordered from 62 countries; and 1200 complimentary copies were sent to individuals in 42 of the "less-developed" countries on the basis of personal requests. There remains a backlog of demand.

So we have decided, with considerable pleasure, to issue another edition of this work. The text remains basically unchanged. A substantial index has been prepared to replace the briefer version in the first issuance.

It is our hope that this volume makes a number of worthy contributions to an important concern. It is the most comprehensive and systematic summation of the "state of the art" that we know. It is also a provocative argument for a certain line of action. That argument is advanced by the author, not as truth, but as food for thought, and stimulus for the development of variations and alternatives. We welcome comments and reactions.

William J. Siffin
Director
PASITAM
7 July 1976

ix

Foreword

Development is both urgent and difficult, a situation which has understandably led to much frustration. One of the causes of disappointment has been the failure of "science and technology" to sharply raise standards of living in most developing countries. The magic machine which has produced such dazzling results in advanced countries has too often malfunctioned when assembled in a developing country, and its output has seldom been dazzling. The reasons range from problems encountered by the individual scientist to shortcomings of the entire international scientific community. They involve the nonscientific community as well—governments in developing countries, donor agencies in advanced countries, and society as a whole. The fostering of science and its applications in a developing country is a subtle and complex process.

Is science necessary to development? Is it possible to improve the standard of living in a developing country without establishing a formal scientific community? The second question differs from the first, and there is no simple answer to either. It is obviously possible to achieve some economic improvement in a developing country in the absence of a domestic science capability, for a number of countries have done so. But can a developing country achieve the status of an advanced country without the participation of its own scientists?

There is much disagreement, frequently involving a distinction between basic science and applied science. (Basic science is done for its own sake with the intended result a scientific paper. Applied science is done on a problem imposed "from the outside" with a view to specific technical application. Some who concede the necessity of indigenous *applied* science in development maintain that basic science is a luxury which developing countries cannot afford. Others argue that an effective applied science capability cannot be developed in the absence of a basic science capacity—that applied scientists must have thorough backgrounds in basic science if they are to do competent work—and must be able to interact with basic scientists in the course of their work.

The problem is made more difficult by the long-range nature of science development. Between the initial stage, when students are sent abroad for advanced education, and the final stage, when a self-sustaining scientific community can apply itself to problems of national development, there is a lapse of several decades (about fifty years, for example, in the case of Japan). A government trying to cope with widespread famine is understandably uninterested in an activity whose dimly perceived benefits will only materialize in a future which may never arrive. Science development often requires a long-term investment at a time of short-term crisis.

Can't a developing country import the scientific knowledge which it needs without having to conduct its own research? Experience seems to indicate that it cannot. A vast amount of scientific knowledge is continually being generated by the world's scientists; the only persons capable of selecting from the flood of information what is useful for local purposes are *practicing* scientists. They alone can comprehend what is being done and keep abreast of scientific advances. However, they can perform that service only if they are familiar with local needs and conditions. Scientists isolated from their society, however competent they may be, can contribute little to the development effort.

The same is true in importing technology. The bewildering array of possible solutions to any technical problem requires both technical expertise and extensive knowledge of local conditions if the recipient is to make a satisfactory choice. Technologies devised in an advanced country to deal with problems there must usually be adapted to local conditions if they are to function at all in a developing country. Differences of scale, infrastructure labor, and management must be taken into account. The necessary adjustments are frequently so fundamental that applied scientists must be involved. And those scientists must be familiar with the local conditions to which the imported technology is to be adapted.

It therefore appears that a developing country must have indigenous applied scientists even if it intends only to import the scientific and technical knowledge necessary for development. Whether the applied scientists *must* be linked with an indigenous community of basic scientists is a matter of some dispute. At any rate, it is clear that applied scientists do better work when they have strong backgrounds in basic science and can consult basic scientists.

Expenditures on research and development vary considerably. Among advanced countries the average figure is 2-3% of the gross national product (GNP). For most developing countries the average is about 0.2% of GNP, though there are notable exceptions (such as Brazil). The latter figure is small, but in the context of a developing country it is significant. The magnitude of these sums justifies efforts to improve the policy-making process which determines how they are spent.

This book is concerned with the deliberate and systematic development of scientific capability in developing countries. Some science development probably occurs under other names in the context of various development efforts. For example, attempts to increase agricultural productivity involve research of a very specific nature—research for which support can be obtained without having to establish the intrinsic importance of all science. However, it is still necessary to produce the scientists who will do the research, and that entails problems of the sort discussed in this volume.

The author, a physicist, has been much involved in the processes of science development. Since his personal experience has been mainly independent of "official" programs, he is free to express his views. He believes strongly that science is important in its own right (an attitude which colors his presentation). His purpose is to convince his readers that science development has been neglected and "to suggest very specific ideas which, if implemented, would help to remedy this neglect." The book is a "summary of the state of the art in science development," a collection, distillation, and generalization of an accumulated body of experience. It appears to be the first *book* on the subject, though the literature on science development has become quite extensive. A valuable feature of this book is the list of 500 publications on various aspects of science development, many of them summarized in the text.

Moravcsik argues that science must be developed in developing countries if the desirable goals of a higher standard of living, an independent economy, political and military power, and liberation from a subsistence existence are to be achieved. Domestic science education is, in his opinion, the best way to produce the needed scientists, with strong emphasis on quality as well as quantity. Special attention must be given to retaining competent scientific manpower—"brain drain" cannot be tolerated. He asserts that scientific communication is perhaps the most important tool of science, and that the international scientific communication system is strongly biased aaginst developing countries. There are internal problems of communication as well: while many developing countries have the correct ratio of basic to applied research, connections between the two are not developed. Hence the effectiveness of each, particularly of applied research, is greatly lessened. He maintains that improvement of quality in applied research and the establishment of links between basic and applied should be the primary targets of attention. The best method of allocating funds, he says, is a mixture of individual grants based on merit and institutional grants distributed equally.

According to Moravcsik, international scientific assistance is "insufficient in quantity, not catalytic enough to have a sufficiently large multiplying power, and not close enough to the international scientific community (either at the originating or at the reeciving end) to be sufficiently effective. Much of what is being done has value, but in the face of the enormity of the problem, the response so far has been altogether inadequate." He believes that "the scientific community in the advanced countries has been ignorant, negligent, and nonchalant about active measures it could take to assist developing countries in the development of science." In his view, a much larger fraction of that community must take an active interest in science development before anything significant can be achieved.

Moravcsik does not claim to have exhausted the subject of science development. The book is intended to stimulate and provoke as well as to inform. It deals with primarily immediate problems of establishing and maintaining a scientific community in any developing country, leaving unexamined many larger questions of undisputed importance. Some of his implicit assumptions raise questions as well. There is much work yet to be done, as Moravcsik himself emphasizes. For example, an important aspect of science development is the economics of science. What is the relationship between cost and scale? Which expenses will be the same no matter what area of science is involved? What are the hidden costs of science development?

Moravcsik examines only problems which are common to all developing countries, and his recommendations are necessarily general. How can the specific science needs of a particular country be determined? What factors are important in determining a strategy for science development in a particular country? Can developing countries be categorized with regard to differing procedures for science development? Is it possible to discuss procedures for science development without examining separately the various specific sciences of which "science" is composed?

Are there alternative models for science development? The experiences of, say, the People's Republic of China, USSR, UK, and USA were not identical. To what extent do they provide alternative procedures from which developing countries could select?

Can science development be successfully undertaken in any country? A certain level of economic development must be attained before science development can be supported. Very small countries may have to undertake a joint effort at science development instead of separate national efforts. How can that be done?

Are there societal prerequisites for science? While scientific communities have been established in many non-Western societies, the problem of integrating the scientists with the larger society remains generally unsolved. If the science community is isolated it cannot make a significant contribution to the country's general development.

In developing countries much applied research is poorly done. However, some applied research is well done but has no effect: the linkages between the research and production sectors are so poor that research results never reach the places where they are needed. What are the institutional requisites of science? How can the linkages be established which will enable scientists to participate effectively in their country's development?

Would it be easier to obtain indirect support for science development? If building capability in biological and medical sciences were a supporting component of specific development projects in agriculture and public health, for example, without being conspicuously labeled as such, the development of those sciences might proceed more rapidly than if funding were sought in an academic context.

These questions and others of considerable interest have not been dealt with in this book. Presented here are a great deal of information on science development, a set of recommendations, and an enthusiastic call for involvement.

Hal S. Kibbey
PASITAM/MUCIA

Preface

I generally hold in low esteem books that promise to teach you to sing in 10 easy lessons while you are reading in your armchair. Singing is something one does, and most of it comes from practice, not from someone else's verbalization of his own experience. I think of science development in the same manner. It is a very new field in a recognizable form less than 20 years old which aims at creating conditions which allow the natural sciences to be established, practiced, and strengthened in less-developed countries. (Throughout this book, the word "science" will refer to the natural sciences.) It is an activity rather than a discipline, and those engaged in it work with the help of experimentation, improvisation, intuition, and deduction from the practical experience of themselves and their colleagues.

Why, then, did I decide to write a book on science development? Science development has now reached the stage when some collection, distillation, and perhaps generalization of this common body of experience will prove useful. For one thing, the literature on science development has become quite extensive, even though, to the best of my knowledge, this effort is the first book written on the subject. Present literature consists mainly of articles, reports, and talks and is widely dispersed in terms of source and location. Until recently, there was not even a bibliography of this material. In contrast, other aspects of development (including technology development which is somewhat related to that of science) have received more systematic attention in books and bibliographies.

A summary of the state of the art in science development might, therefore, be of interest to the builders of science in less-developed countries to stimulate and strengthen their thinking on these matters and to lend credibility and respectability to ideas they work for. It is peculiar how ideas can be made more influential and palatable in the eyes of local decision-makers by demonstrating (through references to books or visiting lecturers) that they are also held in some faraway corner of the world. Clearly, the well-known proverb, "Nobody is a prophet in his own country," has a corollary: "Even a fool can become a prophet if he travels far enough." Having often been such a fool, I have had the opportunity to observe that experience acquired in science policy, organization, and management in one less-developed country is seldom transmitted to other countries where similar problems exist (unless perhaps by a person who happened to visit both countries). I hope this book will help to bridge such an information gap.

I also hope the book will be of interest to those in the scientifically more advanced countries and in international organizations who are involved (or should be) in scientific assistance programs. I hope to convince them that science has been much neglected in developmental activities in favor of flashy short-range projects. At the same time, I shall suggest to them specific ideas which, if implemented, would help to remedy this neglect.

Finally, this book is also directed toward the scientific community without whose participation science development cannot achieve significant success. I have found that in spite of the basically international character of the natural sciences, awareness, knowledge, and concern about problems of building science in less-developed countries are very slight indeed among scientists in advanced countries. I have always thought this regrettable, since science development appears to be one of the most suitable activities for a scientist who wishes to apply his expertise to a broad area of immediate and strong social concern. From this point of view, I would be particularly gratified if the book were read by young scientists either within or outside the framework of a university course. The book is, however, not an academic study in the social sciences. Inasmuch as some social scientists may find it illuminating, it will probably be as an illustration of a strongly interdisciplinary problem viewed by an active practitioner of the natural sciences who has gained his expertise in the subject matter mainly through personal experience.

These are, in fact, my credentials for writing this book. My interest in science development was aroused in 1962 when I spent a year assigned to Pakistan as a temporary "expert" of the Internanational Atomic Energy Agency. Since then I have been constantly involved in one or another aspect of science development activities, though always parallel with my work as a research scientist in theoretical physics. Thus, I could always communicate with scientists in other countries as a colleague rather than as a "mere" administrator. My involvement has been through the writing of articles and through committees as well as through individual, personal projects, and contacts. Except for the IAEA assignment already mentioned, I have never worked full-time for a development organization of any sort. This has allowed me (together with whatever drawbacks it might also entail) a versatility, flexibility, independence, and freedom in choosing programs to create or to join. It has also enabled me to offer my views and services with a minimum of constraint.

That element of personal experience and involvement was important in the writing of this book. There are two types of information available about science development. One is formal and consists of written reports, "factual" articles, proceedings of solemn and conspicuous conferences, and similar respectable documents. The other consists of personal accounts, informal opinions, results of visits, conversations with fellow scientists and science organizers around the world, etc. The relationship between the two is similar to information about Oregon's beautiful Cascade Mountains through maps and Forest Service Pamphlets on the one hand and photographs and memories of personal hiking trips on the other. Without maps and descriptions one would get lost in the woods and would not have an overall picture of the Cascades. Yet without the aid of personal and necessarily more anecdotal information, one's knowledge of the Cascades would lack vitality. The map does not tell whether a forest consists of scrubby broken trees or beautiful pines or whether a rocky formation is just another piece of lava or a fascinating view.

Similarly, much of the formal documented information on science development lacks those elements which enable one to feel whether a certain program, institution, or group represents a dead paper-entity of a dynamic, productive force. Numbers and purely factual descriptions cannot reveal this difference. What is needed is direct personal evaluation by uncommitted, institutionally (and ideologically) free, but expert individuals, and such an evaluation is available primarily through informal, personal channels of communication. It was my intention, therefore, to include in this book, in contrast to some books dealing with other aspects of development, the crucial element of personal evaluation (together with the necessary elements of factuality and balance), even though the former will likely make the book less "objective" and more controversial.

On the other hand, this book is not an exposé. It has become fashionable to write tracts denouncing this or that as obviously evil, mismanaged, and conspiratorial. I have not joined that movement. I have always believed that problems in the world remain unsolved mainly because our know-how at any time is slightly less than that demanded, and there are always more unsolved problems than people to work on them. This book is simply an amalgamation of facts, other people's views and suggestions, and my own ideas, proposals, and critiques. I have tried to differentiate among these three classes so that facts, consensus views, and personal opinions do not become confused. Though this is a "first" book, it is certainly not written with even the slightest intention of being the last in the field. The greater the number of people who are induced, stimulated, or enraged enough by this book to write their own, the better I will consider my aim accomplished. In fact, the main aim of this book is to increase both the collective expertise and the number of interested people who, with whatever ideas of their own, will continue to work in science development.

Michael J. Moravcsik

A Word on Format

The format of this book is somewhat unusual. Since it is my hope that the book will be perused by both those wanting a brief introduction to the subject and those with a deeper involvement and more extensive background in science development, the book has a double structure. Each chapter consists of two parts: the main text and a section entitled "Background and Comments." The first is intended to serve as introductory, qualitative reading without references and small details, and can be read in sequence (omitting the second parts). The second parts contain references, documentation, statistical information, and additional details and comments. Persons with a serious interest in the subject should read both parts of each chapter. The second parts can also be used separately as an encyclopedia of science development, though I am far from claiming encyclopedic comprehensiveness here.

Each of the chapter headings deserves a book by itself. I apologize, therefore, for omissions of certain facts, programs, and details. The omissions were judged necessary in order to keep the book to a manageable length. The same can be said for the references. Although there are some 500 of them, no claim is made that everything has been included, and my apologies are extended to wronged authors. But even 500 references are too many for certain purposes, so I have included a list of about 60 references which I found particularly interesting or pertinent. For additional listings and bibliographies containing source material on science development, see the following references given in the bibliography: AID 1972b, CFA 1970, MORAVCSIK 1973b, RETTIG 1964, and RPP 1966.

A few words about terminology are necessary. The names of countries are given in the form used by the countries themselves at the time referred to. Thus, the island off India might appear as Ceylon and Sri Lanka. The mainland area of East-Southeast Asia is referred to as the People's Republic of China and the island of Formosa as the Republic of China. These rules are not necessarily followed in the notation of the bibliography where brevity is needed.

It is unfortunate that the science development literature is scattered in so many journals, reports, brochures, and other publications of limited circulation. Many are difficult to locate. Since I have a copy of all references listed in this book, I would be glad to help any reader with information about where they might be available. I will try to answer any inquiry addressed to me at the Institute of Theoretical Science, University of Oregon, Eugene, Oregon 97403, USA.

Abbreviations and Acronyms

AAPT American Association of Physics Teachers.

AC More advanced country. Not a rigorously defined term, it designates countries with a per capita GNP of more than about $900 a year. With regard to science, a country is an AC if it is capable of generating and utilizing significant amounts of new scientific knowledge in a broad spectrum of areas. Less than a quarter of the countries of the world can thus be defined as ACs. The adjective "advanced" is *not* being used to make any value judgments about the cultures, traditions, moral systems, or social structures of the countries thus labeled.

ACAST Advisory Committee on the Application of Science and Technology to Development, an advisory committee of the UN.

AEC Atomic Energy Commission.

AID Agency for International Development, a US governmental agency in charge of international assistance.

AIT Asian Institute of Technology, a regionally-supported "center of excellence" and educational institution in the applied sciences and engineering located in Bangkok, Thailand.

ASAIHL Association of Southeast Asian Institutions of Higher Learning, a regional organization of universities with headquarters in Bangkok, Thailand.

BFS Board of Foreign Scholarships, a body in charge of US governmental educational and scientific ex-
school biology program developed in the US.

BSCS   Biological Sciences Curriculum Study, a secondary school biology program developed in the US.

CASTASIA   Conference on the Application of Science and Technology to the Development of Asia, a UNESCO-sponsored regional ministerial conference held in New Delhi in August 1968.

CENTO   Central Treaty Organization, a grouping of mainly Middle Eastern countries.

CERN   Centre European pour la Recherche Nucleaire, a regional laboratory operated by European countries for the support of research in nuclear and particle physics and related science, located in Geneva, Switzerland.

CIEP   Committee on International Education in Physics, a committee of AAPT.

CIMT   Committee on the International Migration of Talent, a privately supported study group in the US temporarily established to report on the brain drain.

CLAF   Centro Latino Americano de Fisica, a regional association of Latin American countries for the support of scientific activities in physics.

CNP   Conselho Nacional de Pesquisas, the national research council of Brazil.

CONACYT   Consejo Nacional de Ciencia y Tecnologia, the National Research Council of Mexico.

CONICYT   Commission Nacional de Investigacion Cientifica y Tecnologica, the National Research Council of Chile.

COST   Committee on Science and Technology, an Indian governmental science policy-making body, superseded in November 1971 by NCST.

COSTED   Committee on Science and Technology for Development, a committee of the UN.

CSIR   Council of Scientific and Industrial Research, an Indian governmental agency in charge of a large assortment of scientific and technological research activities.

CST   See COST.

FAO	Food and Agriculture Organization, a special agency of the UN.
FORGE	Fund for Overseas Research Grants and Education, a private agency in the US providing small research grants to individual scientists in LDCs.
GNP	Gross national product, the total amount of goods and services produced by a country in a given year.
IAEA	International Atomic Energy Agency, a special agency of the UN.
IBRD	International Bank for Reconstruction and Development, an independent international agency supporting development project in LDCs. It is commonly referred to as the "World Bank."
ICIPE	International Centre for Insect Physiology and Ecology, a research center in Nairobi, Kenya.
ICSU	International Council of Scientific Unions.
ICTP	International Centre for Theoretical Physics, a research center in Trieste, Italy.
IDI	International Development Institute, a US governmental agency proposed in the Peterson report, not yet established.
IDRC	International Development Research Centre, a Canadian governmental agency concerned with research projects in the area of development of LDCs.
IIE	Institute of International Education.
ILO	International Labour Organization, a special agency of the UN.
IRRI	International Rice Research Institute, a research center in Manila, the Philippines.
ISF	International Science Foundation.
IVIC	Instituto Venezolano de Investigaciones Científicas, a government-supported research institute in Venezuela.
KAIS	Korea Advanced Institute of Science.
KIST	Korea Institute of Science and Technology.

LDC   Less developed country. Not a rigorously defined term, it generally includes countries with a per capita GNP below about $600 a year. In terms of scientific infrastructure, a country is an LDC if it is unable to engage in significant independent research in a broad spectrum of scientific problems. Well over half of the world are LDCs. The adverb "less" is *not* being used to make any value judgments about the cultures, traditions, moral systems, or social structures of the countries thus labeled.

LIPI   Lembaga Ilmu Pegetahuan Indonesia, the overall science coordinating body of Indonesia.

MOST   Ministry of Science and Technology, a ministry in the Republic of Korea in charge of scientific and technological matters.

NAS   National Academy of Sciences, a US semi-governmental body.

NBS   National Bureau of Standards, a US governmental research laboratory.

NCST   a) Nigerian Council for Science and Technology, a science policy-making body of the Nigerian government;

              b) National Committee on Science and Technology, a science policy-making body of the Indian government, established in November 1971.

NSF   National Science Foundation, a US governmental agency in charge of supporting research.

OAS   Organization of American States, a regional consortium of governments from the Americas.

ODC   Overseas Development Council, a private US organization concerned with development problems in LDCs.

OECD   Organization for Economic Co-operation and Development, a regional consortium of primarily European countries.

OST   Office of Science and Technology.
              a) an agency within UN headquarters;

b) a now defunct agency of the executive branch of the US government;

c) a section of AID.

PAEC	Pakistan Atomic Energy Commission.
PCSIR	Pakistan Council of Scientific and Industrial Research, a Pakistani governmental agency in charge of a broad variety of research in science and technology.
PINSTECH	Pakistan Institute of Nuclear Science and Technology, a research center of the PAEC in Rawalpindi, Pakistan.
PSAC	President's Science Advisory Committee, a now defunct advisory body to the President of the US.
R&D	Research and development.
S&T	Science and technology.
SEED	Scientists and Engineers in Economic Development, an AID-funded, NSF-managed program of travel and subsistence grants.
SIDA	Swedish International Development Authority, a Swedish governmental agency in charge of international assistance.
TUBITAK	Turkiye Bilimsel Ve Teknik Arastirma Kurumu, the Scientific and Technical Research Council of Turkey.
UAR	United Arab Republic.
UGC	University Grants Commission, an Indian governmental organization in charge of university education and research.
UK	United Kingdom.
UN	United Nations.
UNCTAD	United Nations Conference on Trade and Development, a UN agency.
UNDP	United Nations Development Programme, a UN agency.
UNESCO	United Nations Educational, Scientific, and Cultural Organization, a special agency of the UN.

UNIDO   United Nations Industrial Development Organiza-
            tion, a UN agency.

US   United States of America.

USAEC   United States Atomic Energy Commission.

USSR   Union of Soviet Socialist Republics.

VITA   Volunteers for International Technical Assistance,
            Inc., a private US organization active in technical
            aid to LDCs.

WHO   World Health Organization, a special agency of the
            UN.

Acknowledgments

Every book is a collective undertaking by the author and numerous others who contribute to turning a set of ideas into an actual means of communication with potential readers. In this case, the "numerous others" played an especially significant role. In particular, I want to single out William Siffin, the director of the International Development Research Center at Indiana University, whose interest in this book resulted in crucial support by the Center for its publication. I am very grateful also to Hal Kibbey of the International Development Research Center for his patient and skillful help in improving the book's clarity of presentation. The Office of Scientific and Scholarly Research of the Graduate School of the University of Oregon provided a small grant at an early stage of the work when a preliminary bibliography was assembled.

Finally, I must express my gratitude to colleagues around the world who have helped with material for this book. The list is obviously too long to be included here, but I can say that while without their help *some* book would still have been written, it would have been considerably impaired in balance and scope.

The most frustrating experience an author can have is to publish a book which brings no reaction whatever. I want to ask, therefore, that all the readers of this book communicate to me whatever comments they may have about it. I promise to answer all letters that reach me, and to take under advisement all opinions, favorable or not, for a possible future edition.

One

Why Science in LDCs?

That the building of science in LDCs is an important and timely problem is not an unchallenged statement. The statement does tend to draw more uniform support in LDCs than in ACs. The nature of often-heard objections can be illustrated by a few typical, though stylized, "quotes":

> A country with a 70% illiteracy rate and hardly enough food for everybody to eat should work on more simple and immediate problems than the building of science.

> A country so far behind on the evolutionary scale cannot compete favorably with the great scientific countries of the world anyway, and it is a waste for it to try.

> We must not destroy the indigenous culture of a country by allowing it to replace that culture with science.

> We must prevent yet untechnologized countries from taking the same disastrous road which led the Western countries to a scientific and technological world of war, crime, and pollution.

> The building of science in LDCs must be allowed only if the LDC has a social structure and government that we approve of because ideological considerations must be paramount over science and technology.

I consider the above statements fundamentally without substance. Yet, I do not propose to consider them now. It is my expectation that by the end of this book, the reader will have acquired sufficient information on the building of science in LDCs to compose his own conclusions. But the objections do point to the necessity of presenting at the outset a group of positive and compelling reasons for the urgency of building science in LDCs.

It is easy to argue that in the long run each country must have an indigenous scientific community. There are many reasons for

1

this. Science and technology are indispensable for a high standard of living, and the elimination of the gross disparities in present standards of living around the world is almost universally agreed on as being absolutely necessary. Science and technology are keys to an independent economy, and the absence of even the semblance of economic domination by some countries over others is another generally favored goal. Science and technology are indispensable to political and military power, and the concentration of such power in the hands of a few countries is generally considered undesirable. Science and technology have so far proven to be the only tools whereby humanity can free itself from a preoccupation with food and shelter, thus liberating a large fraction of the human population for "higher," more worthwhile tasks, whatever those tasks are judged to be by the different value systems of the various communities. Finally, science and technology are themselves one form of such higher activity, and limiting such a pursuit to only a few is intolerable in the long run.

The building of science in LDCs can also be justified in terms of many shorter-range considerations; the most important is education. Some knowledge and understanding of science is such an indispensable element in so many fields (engineering, agriculture, medicine, and economic planning) that the importance of good science education in any country should be evident. Even those who do not acknowledge the necessity of having an indigenous scientific community in each country readily concede that access to to technology is a matter of survival for all countries; they advocate technology transfer without indigenous science. However, it is well-established that those who participate in this transfer process must have a thorough scientific training.

Relevant and functional science education must be accomplished by people with continuing personal involvement in scientific activities. At a time when science makes rapid progress, when esoteric and "irrelevant" areas of science become within a decade or less rich sources of applications over broad realms of human activity, continuing education of the teacher is crucial. This can be accomplished only by allowing him to be continually and personally involved with science. Many LDCs today are cursed with a large body of science teachers who have lost contact with science and settled down to a routine recitation of scientific facts instead of teaching students that science is a method of inquiry and problem-solving. This attitude is amplified through the students and produces a whole cadre of technological, medical, and administrative personnel unable to participate in the dynamic activity of development. In sum, science cannot be taught to professionals unless there is a functioning scientific community to do the teaching.

Development of science in LDCs may be further justified in terms of immediate benefits which could result from the application of science and technology even at the early stages of a country's development. There are two aspects of this. First, some results of science and technology already developed in the more advanced parts of the world will be directly applicable to the country's problems. Even in rather rudimentary agricultural activities, medical programs, or engineering functions, the use of modern methods of science and technology could considerably enhance the product. In addition, there will be problems which cannot be solved by direct adaptation of something already developed by more advanced countries. Special climatic or agricultural conditions might produce novel problems, and special social circumstances might dictate novel solutions. For example, in the early 1960s West Pakistan found itself in serious trouble because of increasing salination on its agricultural land. The problem had originated in part with the extensive canal system built a half-century before which had transformed the area from a desert into a fertile agricultural center. Unfortunately, the canals were not lines, and over the decades the seepage of water and subsequent evaporation had slowly deposited a concentration of salt which finally became prohibitive for useful plant life. The situation was substantially ameliorated when, by chance, a team of scientists and engineers from an advanced country was activated to attack the problem. (To be sure, seepage from canals was not the only cause of the salination, and thus the problem has by no means been completely solved. However, significant improvement has been made, and some lost land has been reclaimed.) In countless other examples, problems undoubtedly still persist because no scientist or technologist from an advanced country pays any attention to them, and the country where the problem exists has no adequately trained scientific manpower to deal with it.

As will be discussed later, an LDC cannot necessarily have a cadre of specialists ready to deal with any problem that may arise. It can, however, have a group of scientists above critical size in continuing contact with the active areas of science who could be consulted in finding solutions. If necessary, they could contact the international scientific and technological community for further help, and they could help to assess the areas of modern science which might be relevant to the solution of such problems. With the ever-decreasing time interval between scientific discovery and subsequent technological application, such a direct connection between scientists and technological problems is highly desirable.

In most LDCs private capital plays a relatively minor role in development; the central government is the formal motive force of development. Such governments often approach development in terms of long- and medium-range development plans. Even if there is no formal plan, the country follows a definite course of development. In either case, implicit decisions are being made about the scientific development of the country. In some cases, the decision may be conscious and specific, aimed at building up the country's scientific capability. In other cases, a negative decision is implicitly made by the absence of positive action. In either case, the course of national development affects the indigenous scientific community.

It follows that the planning process must, even in the very early stages, include active and knowledgeable scientists and technologists. This claim is sometimes disputed by those who see national planning as the exclusive prerogative of economists and politicians. However, there is no example of an AC where such decision making does not include members of the scientific and technological community. The role of the economist and politician is to codify and formalize elements of an overall scheme with input from specialists in each area, including science.

Since planning sometimes extends far into the future, scientists must participate from the beginning. In the Republic of Korea, planning for science and technology covers a period of more than 15 years. Its university and scientific manpower policy is predicated to cope with projected demands in the mid-1980s, even at the possible cost of scientific unemployment during a preceding period. With such an elaborate and somewhat risky plan, it is crucial that responsibility rest jointly on all segments of the educated population.

An important argument favoring development of science in an LDC is concerned with the morale of the country. The building up of an LDC is a very arduous and difficult task. The present state of the country appears backward, the difficulties are enormous, and the gap with respect to ACs seems to increase constantly as the latter continue their own development. It is, therefore, important to find areas of development in which demonstrable and significant successes can be achieved, to show that it is possible for an LDC to "catch up" with ACs in some respects. It would evidently be difficult to find such areas of competition in large-scale undertakings like steel production or computer fabrication. But it would not be at all far-fetched to find such an area in some branch of science. Its most important ingredient, intelligence, is a universal asset in contrast with raw materials, material wealth, and empirical know-how. That a Raman in India or a Houssay in Argentina could receive a Nobel prize serves as a dramatic illustration of the capability of those countries to contribute to pioneering undertakings of humanity. Knowledge of this accomplishment then serves as a morale booster for the general development of those countries, even in areas where similar outstanding success is not yet in sight.

The importance of morale cannot be overrated. The belief that development goals are achievable through the continual efforts of indigenous people is crucial to the success of any development program. It may appear that isolated successes in restricted areas of development, amid large seas of backwardness and trouble, are tokens unworthy of serious attention. But morale is a state of mind and therefore involves both rational and emotional elements. From a functional point of view, such isolated successes have an emotional impact which strengthens and heightens morale, and the emphasis is amply justified.

Another aspect of science of great significance to an LDC is its relationship to the concept of change. If asked to single out one popular attitude that represents the crucial difference between an LDC and an AC, I would choose the attitude toward change. Consider an American, no matter how conservative in his thinking. If he had not been, say, in Cleveland for a number of years, he would upon his return expect to see many changes. He might decry those changes and speak of the "good old days," but in a functional sense he would behave in accordance with those changes, and in most cases he would generate further changes. That change is the normal state of the world and changes are brought about by human activity would be implicit in his view of the world.

In contrast, the natural expectation of most people in LDCs is a state of immutability. A person in an LDC will generally assume that tomorrow is bound to be similar to today and yesterday, and this state of affairs is something fundamentally beyond human control. As a result, suggestions for change will be considered with great suspicion, incredulity, and psychological resistance. The lower the educational level of the person, the more deeply these attitudes are likely to be ingrained. A small minority of well-educated leaders might have a more dynamic view. (This situation is often incomprehensible to intellectuals in ACs who like to believe in a different model more compatible with Western political preconceptions. According to that model, LDCs consist of a large population yearning for progress, oppressed by a small reactionary "ruling clique" which resists all change and impedes the progress desired by the masses. A notable example of this "conspiracy" model of LDCs was embodied in the former best-seller, *The Ugly American*.)

A static view of the world is clearly incompatible with the basic idea of development. The existing gap between rich and poor countries has developed because LDCs have not changed significantly while ACs have changed enormously. The ACs have radically altered their sphere of activities, their practical and spiritual horizons, and their aspirations, and the rapidly increasing body of achievements has radically changed their standard of living. If greater parity among countries is to be attained, the idea that change is a natural state of human affairs must permeate all countries, and the conviction that human efforts can bring about such change must be strengthened worldwide.

Science, perhaps more than any other human undertaking, is a vehicle for the strengthening of these desired attitudes. The concept that events are functionally related to time is one of the basic elements of the natural sciences, and every scientific experiment is a demonstration that through human effort we can regulate at least a certain part of nature to bring about certain desired results. The relationship between scientific understanding and technological achievement has been thoroughly demonstrated throughout the ages further reinforcing man's feeling of control over his environment. But the general population cannot be exposed to science without a dynamic and indigenous scientific community. What needs to be propagated is not the details of scientific laws but the spirit of inquiry, the intellectual and spiritual excitement inherent in scientific activities. This can be done only by direct contact with active practitioners of science.

Turning now to a different aspect of the role of science in LDCs, we find that science can be of major importance in solving social problems. Science is the most important foundation of technology which in turn is a tool for solving many material problems.

Material and social problems are closely intertwined, however, and science can assist in solving both. For example, the key to influencing social attitudes is communication with large segments of the population. Such communication is much advanced by indigenous applied science whether through radio and television or the eradication of illiteracy. A significant social influence of science is the opportunity it provides for social mobility. Scientific merit can be determined in a fairly objective way, and students who excel in science can rise to respected positions in many LDCs regardless of social origins. It has been pointed out in various contexts that scientific and technological advances often allow us to bypass social solutions by eliminating the causes responsible for the social problem. Examples are easily found in the history of the ACs. The conflict between industrial workers and managers in the 19th century was eliminated largely by technological advances resulting in fantastic increases in individual productivity. To be sure, labor unions and other political forces played a part, but their success would have been highly improbable in the absence of concurrent technological solutions since the economic aspects of production would have been too constraining. Similar scientific-technological solutions, or at least substantial aids to solutions, can also be expected in the development of LDCs.

In a more speculative vein, we might consider the long-term consequences for science if Western civilization should begin to decline. There are indeed some signs in the ACs which indicate a loss of faith within the scientific community and within those countries as a whole with respect to the value of pursuing science. It has been pointed out that civilizations deteriorate because their people become tired and lose the dynamic purposefulness needed to continue. Should such a decline set in, we might ask whether science would also vanish with the extinction of this civilization or whether succeeding cultures would incorporate science into their value systems. In general, civilizations are not very successful in transmitting values to ensuing civilizations. Value systems are subjective, and what appeared central and substantial in one system may appear unimportant and irrelevant in another.

Yet, science may be an exception. Because of the objective nature of the natural sciences and because the scientific method provides fairly unambiguous criteria for judgment within the realm of scientific investigations, it is possible that science as a valuable activity could, in fact, be transmitted to other civilizations. Science has already managed to fuse with the cultural and social traditions of countries with histories very different from that of Western civilization. It is, therefore, plausible that such a transmission of science could occur. If this is so, those who value science should ensure that it is firmly established in all areas of the world before the decline of Western civilization makes such a transmission impossible. It is difficult to foresee where new civilizations will arise, and a worldwide dispersion of scientific activity is required. We have, then, a very long-range, transcendental motivation for sharing science with all of humanity.

A substantial list of reasons has been given why science should be pursued in LDCs. Some are theoretical, others more practical. All could possibly be criticized as being externally imposed on LDCs as reasons invented by those in ACs who think they know what is good for LDCs. Though I do not believe the reasons listed above have this quality, I want to conclude by discussing an internal motivation for establishing science in LDCs which is rooted in clear political realities: LDCs demand that science be shared with them. Virtually all countries proclaim that they must actively participate in the scientific and technological revolution. Whether rightly or wrongly, science and technology are perceived as indispensable components of a country that has reached maturity and joined the world community on an equal footing. That this feeling is not only on the surface was well-illustrated by the reaction of many countries to the nonproliferation agreement on nuclear weapons. During and after the negotiations preceding the treaty, charges were made by a number of LDCs that the treaty was just a camouflaged maneuver by ACs to assure for themselves a permanent monopoly on nuclear science and technology.

Thus, the sharing of science is not an altruistic activity or a charitable gesture, but a necessary process in harmony with the aspirations of countries around the world. There are some who argue earnestly that we must prevent LDCs from acquiring science because science and technology have adversely affected Western civilization. Even if the argument has merit (which I do not believe), the suggested course of action would be completely unrealistic. It is in the interest of ACs and for the sake of their future relationship with LDCs to cooperate fully with LDCs in the sharing of science. In doing so, the ACs might have a beneficial effect by ensuring that the LDCs adopt the virtues and avoid the mistakes in the organization, management, and use of science. Failure to do so would not prevent the spread of science, but could produce tensions for some time to come.

Science must become part of the development of the LDCs, just as it must continue to be part of the development of the ACs. With this general ideal in mind, the task is to investigate the components of science development and determine the best ways to assist LDCs in their efforts to build science.

Background and Comments

Surveying the various justifications for pursuing science in LDCs, one quickly concludes that this question is inseparably connected with much broader questions about the meaning and purpose of human life—rather basic philosophical questions. The situation is further complicated by the fact that value systems are imposed by scientists, the population which supports science, and the government which in most cases manages science. Fortunately, science in LDCs, like many other issues, does not need to be justified on only one ground. Particularly in a heterogenous and democratic society, a cause can be argued with a whole spectrum of different justifications, each of which may carry different weight with different people. The summary given below should be regarded not as a set of contradictory arguments but as a collection of parallel propositions which together form a versatile and powerful rationale for building science in LDCs.

Let me begin with some of the negative views found in the literature. Nader, in NADER 1969 (p. 447ff), expresses a cautious concern that the spread of science may amount to cultural imperialism and advocates utilitarian justifications. She cites LOPES 1966, whose author believes that science has little to offer LDCs: "The thesis that science is universal is thus applicable essentially to the reduced universe of the rich and advanced nations themselves." A similar view is expounded in VARSAVSKY 1967, which argues that the LDCs doing science simply provide free research results for ACs to use for their own purposes. A peculiarly timid view of science in LDCs is expressed in LEWIS 1961. In all these views, there are implicitly the following two suggestions: (a) there is a science for LDCs and a science for ACs, and the two are drastically different; (b) scientific activity in LDCs should be postponed until the socio-political system is "right" (as judged, of course, by the value systems of the authors). The main fault of this viewpoint is its negativism and tendency to procrastinate. The time is already late, and we must begin to act now. Furthermore, the different "science for LDCs" is never described in detail, and the arguments are always on a fuzzy ideological plane. Particularly good examples of this are BAZIN 1972a, 1972b, and 1973. I suspect that if it were analyzed carefully and dispassionately, the "different science" would actually contain a large component of the standard international science. It is, in fact, one of the strengths of science that it has such a large body of universally accepted objective elements.

Positions such as those above are now definitely in the minority. This was not so 15 years ago when talk about science in LDCs was somewhat rare (DEDIJER 1959). After the mid-1960s, however, the situation changed rapidly. ROCHE 1966 remarks, "this whole process (i.e., the use of scientific research in the LDCs) accelerated during the past 10 years, so that now at least lip service is paid generally to science, and although there is still a widespread feeling that it is a superfluous activity at our stage of development, very few dare voice this opinion." BHABHA 1966b quotes Nehru: "It is an inherent obligation of a great country like India, with its traditions of scholarship and original thinking and its great cultural heritage, to participate fully in the march of science, which is probably mankind's greatest enterprise today." It is interesting that Nehru's justification is by no means in terms of utilitarian arguments, though of course Nehru understood the great pragmatic influence of science on human life.

Several argue that indigenous science is necessary even in the context of improving technology, as in JONES 1971 (p. 7). One of the most successful leaders of Indian technological research, Nayudamma, remarks: "But one thing must be made clear at the very beginning, namely that no country can prosper simply by the importation of research results. Every country . . . must form and maintain its own scientific personnel and it must develop its own scientific community" (NAYUDAMMA 1967).

The complex relationship between science and technology has been extensively discussed, for example, in the eloquent articles of

Derek de Solla Price. PRICE 1965a analyzes the similarities and differences between science and technology and explains how technology is dependent on what was the forefront of scientific research only a few years before.

DE HEMPTINNE 1963 cites the UNESCO Regional Conference in Cairo in 1960 as "insisting on 'scientific autonomy as an essential prerequisite to national independence.' " In the same article, de Hemptinne (a leading figure in UNESCO's science policy program) points out that to require a choice between concentrating on technical development on one hand and undertaking research at all levels on the other is to create an artificial dichotomy since in practice the former cannot be done in the complete absence of the latter. The same view is asserted in OECD 1968a (p. 8): "An adequate domestic scientific 'infrastructure' [is] necessary if the country [is] to make proper use of imported technologics." In a report of a conference on the role of science and technology in Peruvian economic development, we find that

> the unanimous opinion of the conference is that scientists constitute an indispensable element in the development of an emerging country for diverse and powerful reasons, among them: (1) their essential function in the field of scientific research directed toward better utilization of natural resources; (2) their indispensable role in training new scientists and technicians capable of planning, organizing, and implementing development programs. (NAS 1966, p. 7)

Other discussions of the need for indigenous science and technology may be found in GANDHI 1969 (p. 11), ZAHEER 1968, PERU 1970, UN 1970b (p. 10), UN 1969 (pp. 10-12), and RAHNEMA 1969 (p. 55). As mentioned earlier, technology can sometimes solve social problems. Hence, science has through its influence on technology a special contribution to make to the overall development of a country. This point is discussed in some detail by Weinberg in NAS 1967 (pp. 415-34).

Further discussions of the role of science in terms of its utilitarian, economic effects are presented in OAS 1972 (p. 3 quotes from the Punta del Este declaration), OECD 1969 (pp. 11-16), TASK 1970 (pp. 2-7), ALLENDE 1972, and OECD 1971c.

Let us turn now to more general arguments in the context of development. For example, OECD 1968a stresses the importance of indigenous science in the overall complex of development (pp. 223-33). JONES 1971 (p. 27) likewise emphasizes the importance of science to the general development process, as does UN 1970b (pp. 8, 10). Dedijer, one of the earliest contributors to the literature on science in LDCs, makes the same point in DEDIJER 1959 and 1963. In the latter, he remarks that "practically every decision in any field of national endeavor, whether it is the improvement of the trade balance or community development, requires not only know-how but also scientific knowledge produced by research performed in the local environment." The UN, in its World Plan of Action (UN 1971a, pp. 31, 45, 46), specifically emphasizes the importance of indigenous scientific research. Garcia agrees, though his statements are perhaps ambivalent. In GARCIA 1966 he stresses the utilitarian motivation for pursuit of science in LDCs while in GRUBER 1961 (p. 71), he makes an eloquent argument on much broader grounds. In both cases, it is evident that Garcia (a high-ranking academic leader in Argentina) feels that universities belong in the forefront of scientific development.

De Solla Price has demonstrated (see PRICE 1969c and most of his other published writings during the last five years) that the "scientific size" of a country (measured by the number of scientific authors) is significantly correlated with its GNP. That is, the more productive a country is in the sciences, the larger its GNP tends to be. This relationship is shown dramatically in PRICE 1969a (p. 109). One can see that while the economic size (GNP) of countries can vary almost by a factor of 10,000 and "scientific size" by a factor of 100,000, there is a straight-line correlation between the logarithms of the two quantities. The correlation holds for the overwhelming majority of the countries to within a factor of 10 or so in the quantities themselves. Obviously, a correlation is not necessarily a causation, and even if it is, one cannot be sure which is the cause and which is the effect. Nevertheless, the strong dominance of this correlation should strengthen the argument in favor of science in LDCs.

A number of other effects of science are discussed in the literature. JONES 1971 (p. 51) points out that the prestige of science is a positive element in development. NAS 1966 (p. 75) stresses the cultural values. Prothro, in NADER 1969 (p. xviii), makes a concise case for science as an enemy of stagnant traditionalism, inert stability, and a clinging to the absence of change, all of which are retardants to general development. This role of science as a creator of an atmosphere of inquiry is also stressed in DART 1971b, BURKHARD 1966, and GANDHI 1969 (p. 8). A different, perhaps dubious claim is made by Clarke in his exposition of the UN

World Plan of Action (CLARKE 1971, p. 49) where he suggests that "science promotes honesty."

I mentioned above that it might be politically unrealistic to try to prevent LDCs from acquiring science, and I cited the nuclear nonproliferation treaty as an example. Discussion of this point can be found in ZOPPO 1971 and, in a somewhat broader context, MORAVCSIK 1972c.

Let us now examine even broader justifications involving personal values and philosophies for undertaking science in LDCs. As will be evident, there are other than purely utilitarian arguments in support of science in LDCs, or for that matter of science as a human undertaking. Those who ignore these nonutilitarian arguments seem to fall into two categories. They may deny altogether that other considerations exist; that is, they hold as a personal philosophy that the purpose and meaning of human life is to feed and house human beings. Alternatively, they may admit that higher motives exist but claim that LDCs must wait until they have achieved economic prosperity before they can afford to indulge in nonutilitarian considerations. Once made explicit, these assertions appear dubious; nevertheless, they permeate discussions about science in LDCs in the literature and in conversation.

Specific responses have come from three scientists from the LDCs. Marcel Roche, one of the primary creators of Venezuelan science and an internationally respected figure, states in ROCHE 1966:

> One often hears the opinion expressed that only research which is immediately useful should be publicly supported. This is understandable but unfortunate. Latin America will start to contribute significantly to humanity's scientific progress—and to its own material well-being at the same time—when it loses its complex about the need for practical results, and simply develops a passion for knowledge rather than a simple desire for material progress. The day our community, and our scientists, discover the sense of purpose in science—whether pure or applied—we shall be able to utilize to the full, without social distortions, our real scientific potential, whatever it may be, in both the pure and the applied areas.

A different aspect is illuminated by physicist Igor Saavedra, a persistent, skillful, knowledgeable, and long-active builder of science in Chile. In SAAVEDRA 1973, he stresses the long-term relevance of building science and makes the incisive point that it is often more effective to concentrate on adequately educating a new generation than to waste time fighting with the old guard.

The long-range nature of science development is also stressed in USMANI 1964 (p. 4) and OAS 1972 (p. 5). A convincing documentation of the Japanese case can be found in PRICE 1963 (pp. 98-103).

A third example from the writings of scientists in LDCs is found in CSA 1971a (pp. 35-49). Abdus Salam, a Pakistani-born physicist and a prominent activist in building science in LDCs, presents a beautiful argument in a historical context. He points out, for example, the absurdity of the claim that Pakistan had too many mathematicians at a time when its population was 120 million and its mathematics manpower consisted of 12 PhDs. (CSA 1971a indicates two PhDs, a misprint according to Salam.) Similar arguments have been put forward by scientists from ACs. My own writings, for example, reflect this broad justification (MORAVCSIK 1964a, b, c, 1972a, and 1973c). For the desirability of transmission of a scientific civilization as an argument in favor of propagating science in LDCs, see MORAVCSIK 1973d.

A concise summary of various broad arguments in favor of science in LDCs can be found in SKOLNIKOFF 1967 (pp. 195-203). A quite different piece is Holton's in INDIA 1970, part of a 1970 conference on physics education and research in India. Holton offers a comprehensive motivation for science in his usual erudite and compelling style.

C.P. Snow, in his famous *Two Cultures* (SNOW 1964), deals with science development. Much of what he says about science in general pertains to our discussion. For example, his emphasis on science and technology as being mainly responsible for the high standard of living of industrial workers in Western societies can be broadened and applied to LDCs. On a different level, Snow's analysis of individual loneliness and pessimism versus collective optimism also applies to our discussion. In this respect, the natural sciences have a special feature largely unique among human undertakings—their definite direction of progress. Most other endeavors are either cyclic or at least noncumulative in a structural sense. (A discussion of this point can be found in MORAVCSIK 1974a.) Thus, the pursuit of science opens up a new psychological horizon which has a substantial effect on the world outlook. That this broadening effect should be restricted to a small segment of the world's population, ACs, is a thought most unbecoming of our age of egalitarianism and universalism.

Some relevant thoughts are expressed in WEINBERG 1967 (for example, pp. 36-37) about the role played by science in relieving exclusive concern for physical survival and fulfilling the human desire for purpose and meaning in life once the threats of hunger, disease, and exposure have been averted. Broad discussions of science in this context are found in CIBA 1972 and ZIMAN 1969 (pp. 350-53).

A different but equally interesting aspect of the question is the historical one discussed, for example, in BASALLA 1967. Basalla traces the spread of Western science to LDCs. Perhaps a certain historical inevitability plays a part in this process just as other revolutionary ideas have swept the world. In that sense, sharing science with LDCs may be necessary not only from a political but from a historical point of view.

A rather remarkable book on attitudes toward science in LDCs has been written by a politician. A deputy in the National Congress of Venezuela, Rodolfo Jose Cardenas drew on his extensive experience of interaction with the fledgling Venezuelan scientific community (CARDENAS 1970). It should be taken as a model for contact with science by politicians in every country.

The preceding discussion has illuminated various attitudes, mainly those of scientists, other intellectuals, and governmental personnel. It is evident that the subject is controversial, and many opinions exist. This is generally true even within a particular country. For example, India has a very active and continuing debate on matters of science policy, including the justification of science itself. Speeches, conferences, and articles serve as vehicles, and a special journal, *Science and Culture*, has served for many years as an outlet for such discussions. The same is true, perhaps to a lesser extent, in most other countries. There is, however, a notable exception. In the People's Republic of China, the rationale for science is determined solely by the political leaders in terms of political ideology. The aims were expressed, for example, by Chou En-lai shortly before 1960:

> Only by mastering the most advanced sciences can we ensure ourselves of an impregnable national defense, a powerful and up-to-date economy, and adequate means to join the Soviet Union and the other people's democracies in defeating the imperialist powers, either in peaceful competition or in any aggressive war which the enemy may unleash. (WU 1970, p. 46)

More explicitly, the justification of science is summarized as follows:

> (1) Attainment of great-power status; (2) accelerated economic development, which is identified with rapid industrialization; (3) the maintenance

of the Communist Party as supreme political power. The first two goals call also for an intensive pursuit of military R&D, with the aim of establishing a techno-scientific organization to meet the defense needs of a great power, including the creation of an independent nuclear deterrent and the development of ballistic missiles and delivery systems. (WU 1970, p. 46)

The contrast between this set of aims and those of other LDCs is not in the absence of other than utilitarian arguments. In other LDCs, governmental pronouncements are sometimes also strongly utilitarian in tone, but in China they are couched in a very explicit language emphasizing the military advantages of science. This attitude has a long-standing tradition in Chinese history (WU 1970, pp. 12-18). It is undoubtedly true that other LDCs have aspirations toward military strength through science. But even in politically explosive areas, such as the Middle East or the Indian subcontinent, those aspirations seldom play an openly significant role. Only time will tell to what extent Chinese scientists share this particular justification for undertaking science.

Two

Education and Science

Education in any country has a dual function. It must impart general knowledge and a broad-minded attitude to the population as a whole, and it must produce creative specialists in various areas of human activity. Science education in LDCs shares this function. Successful development can hardly be visualized unless the spirit of inquiry and the attitude of experimentation permeate the population on a wide scale, characteristics best established through a broad science education. At the same time, in order to cope with the specific technical problems of scientific and technological development, a sufficiently large cadre of appropriately trained scientists and technologists must be produced.

A comprehensive discussion of the various problems pertaining to science education at all levels in LDCs would be a thick volume in itself. I will, therefore, describe only the general framework in which science education takes place and then discuss in greater detail the specific problems of the education of specialists in science.

Science education in any country is carried out in the context of the prevailing cultural environment. When a country has substantial scientific and technological activity, and most of its people have substantial daily experience with science-based technological products, science becomes part of the general cultural milieu making it easier to build more science. But in countries where science exists at best for a tiny group of highly educated people with specialized interests, and science-based technological products are not regularly used by the majority of the population, the traditional cultural context may differ considerably from the "scientific" outlook. The characterisitics of such a traditional nonscientific background vary considerably from one geographical region to

17

another. Some examples will illustrate the difficulties frequently encountered by science education in LDCs.

In Nepal, the traditional outlook on nature and the knowledge we can acquire about nature demonstrate three important features. First, popular Western scientific explanations of natural phenomena exist side-by-side in the mind of each person with traditional mythological explanations. There are no indications that the two sets of explanations are seen in conflict with each other. Thus, earthquakes are simultaneously regarded by the same person as caused by a fire inside the earth and by a slight change in position of the turtle on whose back the earth rests. That phenomena have a unique explanation (a basic tenet of the scientific method) is, therefore, not part of the traditional thinking.

Second, regarding the method of learning about natural phenomena, the virtually exclusive opinion in Nepal is that all new things about nature can be learned by looking them up in a book or by asking an old man. Thus, the most fundamental principle of scientific thinking, that new information can be gained by experimentation, is not part of the traditional view of the nature of knowledge.

Third, and perhaps most important, when asked how one would learn about natural phenomena not described in books or known by old men, the people answer that there are no such phenomena. According to the local view, knowledge is closed and has already been exhausted; anything there is to know is a matter of record. Thus, the central belief of science, that we have just begun to learn about the world and by expanding our knowledge and utilizing it we can create novel conditions for ourselves, is not shared by the traditional view. Inasmuch as this belief in the power of an experimental approach to expand the frontiers of knowledge is the basis of any significant development process, the discrepancy between it and the traditional view is crucial.

Another example of traditional views of scientific knowledge is found in Papua New Guinea, where such knowledge is viewed as the personal magic powers of the scientist or teacher who expounds or utilizes it. The acquisition of scientific knowledge is considered an imitative process achieved by association with the masters who have such magic powers. The idea of experimentation, the absence of authoritarianism, and the feeling of human control over knowledge are not part of the local view.

As mentioned, traditional views vary from one region to another, and it is difficult to abstract the general effects that such views might have on the implementation of science education in LDCs. But it is likely that they contribute to one of the greatest impediments, rote learning or memorization.

Mentioned above are some elements of scientific thinking that will boost a country's ability to generate meaningful development: events constantly change as a function of time, events can be influenced by human efforts, and continued experimentation and learning is the road to acquisition of knowledge and control of nature. But the characteristics of science influence us on an even broader scale. For example, many human efforts and attitudes are oscillatory in time. The attitudes of humanity as a whole or of particular societies toward social problems (community welfare versus individual welfare, individual responsibility for actions versus societal responsibility for the actions of its members, man as a rational and nonreligious being versus man as a child of God) have been changing throughout the ages, not by moving in a definite direction but by swinging back and forth between two extreme positions. From a long-range point of view, these oscillations in human attitudes appear somewhat pointless, consuming much energy in situations where the absolute benefits of one position or another can hardly be established.

In contrast, science is one of the few human activities that has a definite overall direction defined by relatively objective standards. This long-term purposefulness generates a spirit of optimism seldom encountered elsewhere. Developments in science occur not because people happen to have gotten tired of the way things were done yesterday, but because the whole process of scientific exploration has a cohesive structure which virtually determines the nature of future developments. I believe that this perception of an overall direction is particularly important in the awakening of creative powers in an LDC.

Science reinforces optimism in another important way. It is assumed that every scientific problem has a solution. In the onerous task of developing an LDC, when many of the greatest problems appear to be insolvable, it is heartening to have contact with at least one realm of human activity where solutions are always attained when sufficient effort is exerted.

Finally, science is an antidote to provincialism and promotes global contact and understanding. As the most international activity, science tends to broaden horizons and promote cooperation and the exchange of ideas, thus cutting across cultural and political barriers. In an age of intensifying nationalism, when the number of countries in the world steadily increases, such denationalizing tendencies are important for the future.

I have mentioned some general features of scientific activity which will have a strong effect on local cultural patterns, and I have pointed out examples in which local patterns appear to be on a collision course with scientific influences. This poses the question of whether scientific and technological development entails the extermination of traditional cultural and societal patterns. Science in the non-Western world is a sufficiently recent phenomenon that the question cannot be answered with certainty. However, two considerations strongly indicate that science and traditional cultural values can be blended.

First, they already coexist in the ACs. Not even the most single-minded scientist would claim that Western civilization in the 20th century is determined *solely* by science. Not only is it influenced by many extrascientific cultural factors, such as religion, national and communal beliefs and traditions, and personal and collective value judgments, but these influences can vigorously coexist with the elements of science and technology. Indeed, popular attitudes in ACs are frequently no more "rational" than those described in Nepal: people in ACs also accept several simultaneous explanations of a problem even if they appear to conflict with each other. As examples one could cite current environmental debates, discussions surrounding the "energy crisis," beliefs about the origin of life, or the upsurge of astrology. Thus, preeminence of science need not mean the death of other cultural factors. Science as such does not impose a complete set of values nor is it an entire culture. It is simply an ingredient that can combine with a variety of other elements.

The other strong indication that development of science does not imply cultural conformity is the experience of the only markedly non-Western country that has become a leader in science—Japan. Has Japan, as a result of preeminence in science and technology, lost its cultural traditions and values? Has it changed its social patterns to those of the European tradition? I asked these questions during my stay in Japan in 1972 when I discussed various problems of science policy with Japanese physicists. The overwhelming consensus was that considerable superficial resemblance has indeed been created between Japan and other ACs through Japan's evolution in science and technology: subways in Tokyo resemble subways elsewhere, white-shirted commuters flood Tokyo in the morning and return home late in the afternoon, and so forth. But on a deeper level, the feeling was that development has not substantially affected the Japanese cultural, historical, and philosophical tradition, and Japan continues to be fundamentally different from Europe or America. In view of these considerations, it seems likely that science does not destroy traditional culture but can be harmoniously incorporated into a variety of traditions and philosophies.

Let us now examine some specific problems of science education in LDCs. Perhaps the most important point to emphasize is that the most effective and appropriate science education must be indigenous to the country. For reasons discussed below, education abroad is in the long-run inferior to education at home. Thus, a primary effort in LDCs must be directed toward the building up of a high-quality, substantial system of science education well-matched to local conditions as well as to the worldwide scientific community.

In some LDCs, the construction of such a system is just beginning, while in others, such as India, there is already a huge network of educational institutions. To aid the creation of future institutions and to bring about reform of existing ones, it would be best to concentrate on the two most serious shortcomings of advanced science education in LDCs.

First, there is a predilection for rote learning and memorization. Not altogether unknown in ACs, this habit is deeply ingrained in many LDCs. Examinations requiring exact recitation of material are the rule. The situation is perpetuated by the system of external examiners originally instituted to establish uniform standards. The advantages of the original intention are by now almost completely outweighed by the disadvantages found in the lack of flexibility in examinations. An effective antidote would be the widespread introduction of open-book examinations for which memorization and rote learning are of little use. The switch to open-book examinations is easier to advocate than to execute, however, since it would involve a drastic change in attitude toward science in general. It would also require a teaching staff more knowledgeable and flexible than that which is often available. Teachers educated in an atmosphere of memorization and rote learning are often unable to adapt themselves to a situation in which science becomes a method of inquiry rather than a set of dead facts.

The second major shortcoming is premature specialization. After exposure to science at what is considered the undergraduate level in the US, students plunge into "research" which necessarily amounts to the work of a glorified laboratory assistant. Resulting scientists have extremely narrow interests and an inadequate understanding of the fundamentals even in their special fields. I have often observed this phenomenon, especially during the interviews conducted by the Physics Interviewing Project in 1969.

A peculiar argument is often made that a broad education is unnecessary because the student is being prepared for applied work and can afford to specialize early. This argument is based on a complete misconception of the nature of work in the applied sciences. On the contrary, being productive in the applied sciences requires a much broader education than being active in the basic sciences. This is partly because the basic scientist is more able to choose research problems within the bounds of a single discipline than the applied scientist who is generally confronted with a ready-made problem seldom falling within the traditional disciplinary lines. This point has been emphasized in a number of studies on the nature of applied science and has been confirmed by the experience of innumerable research institutions.

These two detrimental features in science education can produce serious problems in science development. Scientists with a non-functional understanding of science and an extremely narrow area of competence are virtually useless from the standpoint of scientific productivity and its connections with technological development. Thus, a body of scientific deadwood accumulates, clogging the system of science development and education and constituting a serious obstacle to innovation, development, and reform. Perhaps the most serious example of this situation is in India, but there are many smaller countries plagued by the problem.

There are two other problems of a more general nature. One is the common prejudice against experimental work in favor of theoretical pursuits, probably originating with the prevalent feeling that work not involving one's hands is more prestigious than manual labor. This attitude is one of the reasons for the serious lack of technicians. They are usually in very short supply in LDCs, even relative to the small number of scientists. A further consequence is that scientific communities develop great distortions in the ratio between theorists and experimentalists, which is bad not only for the relation of science to technical application but also for science itself, since theory separated from experiment tends to become ingrown and baroque.

The second deficiency is the almost complete lack of concern in the curricula for the history, philosophy, and methodology of science and their implications for science policy and management. Admittedly there is not much discussion of these topics in the scientific communities of ACs either, but the need there is less. In a large scientific community with its institutions already well-established, only a few of the older members are involved in such matters. In an LDC, however, where the scientific community is very small, and the infrastructure is still being formed, a substantial fraction of scientists must be concerned at the beginning of their careers with activities in which these subjects are relevant. There is a much greater need for education in these areas.

It is not difficult to conclude that the listed shortcomings greatly hinder the effective infusion of indigenous science into applied developmental activities. The result is often a lack of contact between the two or a feeling of hostility which in turn decreases the value of science in the eyes of those making local decisions in development. Science is consequently neglected, a situation decried by all and caused by all.

Many LDCs do not yet have an indigenous system of higher science education and must send their students abroad. The situation may be unavoidable, but it also raises hosts of problems. There is the matter of cost. Foreign education tends to be expensive and requires foreign currency. A few countries, such as Venezuela, Iran, and Malaysia, export sufficient amounts of raw materials to produce reserves of hard currency for such education; most LDCs do not. It becomes important for students to obtain financial assistance from the universities they attend rather than from their home countries.

The situation in the US illustrates other problems. The US is selected for illustration because of the large number of foreign students in its universities, and statistical information is readily available. A similar situation exists in many other ACs, such as the United Kingdom, France, and Germany. There are some 150,000 foreign students at colleges and universities in the US, about 110,000 of whom are from LDCs. Though this is a large number, it represents less than 10% of the total college student population in the US. It is understandable, therefore, that such students do not receive much special attention, except perhaps in language training and general cultural orientation. Yet, the needs of these students are different and more extensive than the needs of most of their American counterparts. In particular, students in the sciences have a number of special problems.

The first pertains to their selection. Science departments in most American universities are ill-prepared to evaluate applications to their graduate schools from students in LDCs. Lists of courses, transcripts, and letters of recommendation mean little in the abstract. Mistakes in admissions are often made. Consequently, either the safe action of refusal is taken, or students are favored from a few somewhat developed countries where the department has personal contacts through alumni, expatriate faculty members, or acquaintances from scientific conferences.

A partial remedy for this situation has been the Physics Interviewing Project operated by CIEP. The project sends physicists to LDCs to interview students interested in graduate education in physics in the US. The interviewers prepare a brief report of the interview which is made available to any university in which the student is interested or to any university interested in the student. The program has been supported by small contributions from a number of physics departments, though this method of financing has proved unstable, time-consuming, and inequitable.

Another problem is the unavailability of appropriate information about educational institutions in ACs to students in LDCs. This results in many misconceptions and a general inability of students to select institutions, to manage the application procedures, and to prepare themselves for the transition once they have been accepted.

Skipping the problem of travel costs, let us turn to problems encountered in the US. American students are likely, after the completion of their education, to engage in scientific research or teaching in an established institution managed by older scientists. In contrast, students from LDCs, even in their first jobs, will almost certainly have to work both on science and on the creation of institutions and opportunities to do science. Thus, students from LDCs, in addition to absorbing the usual science curriculum designed for American students, should also have an opportunity to learn how science is organized and managed. To do so, they must be exposed to the problems of science shops and libraries, purchasing and repairing instruments, science policy and organization, university and laboratory administration, science-technology links, etc. Such things are not taught in US graduate schools. A special interest on the part of knowledgeable faculty is necessary to carry out such a program. Perhaps summer seminars could be organized for science students from LDCs who are already being trained at US graduate schools. A prototype of such a seminar is being organized by CIEP.

It is most important that students in their beginning years in graduate school lay a solid foundation of knowledge and competence in order to appropriately develop later. Such caution and thoroughness will probably be contrary to their own feelings which will urge them to finish quickly, not repeating subjects they have already "learned" in their home country. It is the duty of advisors to prevail on them to proceed circumspectly. In this respect and others, the importance of a faculty advisor cannot be overrated.

Advisors assigned to foreign students should, if possible, have had personal experience in LDCs so they are able to comprehend the problems likely to arise. Advisors should also feel a responsibility for the students *after* they have received their degrees and left for home since the students are likely to need further advice and assistance in their first jobs in their home country (in contrast to students in ACs who are likely to be placed under somebody else's wing after completing their doctorates).

Some scientists, confronted with students from disadvantaged backgrounds, are willing to make allowances for that and develop them into second-class professionals. I must strongly oppose this philosophy: it is likely to result in further discrimination against the students during their professional careers. What LDCs can least afford is second-class scientists. In ACs, run-of-the-mill scientists can find some spot where their mediocre contributions can be utilized. In LDCs, where every person counts, such niches for the mediocre are much less tolerable. Thus, emphasis on quality is of utmost importance. In some LDCs, quality has already been compromised and the manpower pool polluted giving the impression of a manpower surplus. Such waste must be avoided.

A problem causing considerable vexation is the question of language. In many LDCs, debates rage as to whether the local language or the international language of science (English) should be used for advanced education in the sciences. There are serious arguments on both sides. Local languages often do not have the terminology for science. Some argue that scientific concepts are influenced by the language of those who invented them, and science would actually be more difficult to comprehand in a non-European language. In some cases (like India) where there is no single predominant local language, the universal science language might as well be English. It is also argued that since every scientist has to learn some English in order to function in the international scientific arena, learning the language early in the educational process would be beneficial.

On the other hand, science education must also reach the masses; hence, an indigenous terminology for science must be developed. Science education in primary and secondary schools must be done in the local languages, and, it is claimed, switching to English at a later stage would disrupt the learning process. Furthermore, learning science only in English could prevent some students from accepting it as really their own in a cultural sense, giving the impression that science is specifically associated with ACs. Some even suggest that the discouraging predilection for rote learning might be due to students' having to absorb science in a foreign language, though this claim is arguable.

A practical and reasonable solution to the problem is to require bilingualism at the university level. Learning a second language is sufficiently simple for someone capable of being a scientist, and its advantages are sufficiently numerous that the requirement of proficiency in two languages by the age of 20 seems a very reasonable one.

Background and Comments

Alfred North Whitehead once observed that while modern science was born in Europe, its home is the whole world. His remark points up the basic predicament of science education in LDCs: with origins external to the country, science must nevertheless grow strong indigenous roots.

The history of the spread of modern science from Europe to other countries is perceptively analyzed in BASALLA 1967. He notes three stages in this development: (a) initial contact and work by foreigners; (b) "colonial science" (local efforts strongly influenced by the dominant countries); and (c) independent or national science when the country is a full-fledged member of the international scientific community. "Colonial science" might or might not overlap with political colonialism. For example, US science was "colonial" under the influence of Germany at the beginning of the century.

A history of science in India from this point of view can be found in LARWOOD 1961. Another description of Indian science, more from the point of view of dominant personalities, is in RANGANATHAN 1959. A vivid portrait of S. Bose, one such person, is given in BLANPIED 1972. Discussing the same geographical area from the viewpoint of what is now Pakistan, SALAM 1964b and 1965c provide a historical background in terms of the Moslem world. For an account of scientific activity in India prior to contact with the British, see DHARAMPAL 1971.

These accounts indicate that the science of the British colonies in the 19th century was basically the same as that found in Britain. To be sure, it did not take as well in the colonies as in Britain, but the real divergence between the scientific development of the ACs and the LDCs occurred in the second quarter of the 20th century when science "exploded" in the ACs but failed to do so in the LDCs.

A historical account of science in Egypt is given by Ibrahim I. Ibrahim in NADER 1969 (p. 541). A brief description of the situation in the Philippines can be found in SALCEDO 1972 (p. 176). In these historical accounts, cultural elements play a prominent role. Among the general discussions of the subject, CIBA 1972 contains a broad collection of views. A thoughtful essay with particular reference to LDCs is in DART 1963.

There appear to be conflicting views in the literature as to whether indigenous culture and science are incompatible from the point of view of the educational process. LARWOOD 1961 (p. 95) gives this cultural conflict as one of the main reasons why science did not take so well in India. In a concise resumé of social factors in science, DESSAU 1969 (p. 18) emphasizes that fixed traditions are inimical to science. This is also stressed in DART 1967 and 1972. UNESCO 1970a (an outstanding, well-organized volume generated by a conference on science and technology in Asian development) mentions traditions as an obstacle to free inquiry (p. 40). In an interesting analysis, ODHIAMBO 1967 (pp. 878-79) explains in some detail why African traditional culture is not easily compatible with the philosophy of modern science.

Taking a longer view, however, while conceding that these elements are indeed obstacles, the overall situation does not appear to involve a true conflict. In MOREHOUSE 1967 (p. 371), Milton Singer argues that traditional value systems and cultural elements will become perfectly compatible with the results and ideals of modern science. A more detailed account of his view can be found in MOREHOUSE 1968. A similar argument is advanced by DART 1966, who suggests that people do not have a single "culture," and science will be acceptable to many as a second culture. More specifically, two scientists from LDCs assert that religious values and modern science are quite reconcilable (SINHA 1967 and BHATHAL 1971c). ZIMAN 1969 (pp. 354-55) believes that the cultural barriers in the path of acquiring modern science are not exceedingly large. APTER 1961 goes even further and claims that, because of their different cultural history, the Western "two-culture" syndrome (discussed in SNOW 1964) will not develop in LDCs, and in some ways the cultural absorption of science will be even smoother.

Aside from inherent cultural conflicts, there are what might be called the environmental effects of technical development. For example, BHABHA 1966a (p. 334), 1966b, and JONES 1971 (p. 137) point out that in ACs, acquaintance with modern science and technology starts with the toys of the young child and continues to develop from then on. The importance of early educational experience is also stressed by ZIMAN 1969 (p. 356).

Specific studies of cultural factors in various countries can be found in DART 1967, 1972, and 1973b with respect to Nepal; in PRINCE 1968, MACKAY 1973, DART 1973a, and 1973b concerning New Guinea; in OLDHAM 1966 and WU 1970 (p. 15) regarding China; and in RANGANATHAN 1959 on India. An interesting point is made by Mosse in ADAMS 1968 (p. 157). He contends that the distinct cultural identity of France has played a major role in maintaining a low rate of brain drain from France to the US.

I have emphasized that science education must be indigenous, an assertion with ample backing in the literature. RAO 1967 justifies it in terms of the high cost of foreign education. (See, however, a comment by a Japanese in OECD 1968a, p. 55, who argues otherwise.) In NAS 1965b (p. 9) and RIAZUDDIN 1970, the argument is presented in terms of the local relevance of indigenous education. For other general statements, see NAS 1965b (p. 2), Pihl in GRUBER 1961 (pp. 244-47), and MORAVCSIK 1970b. The nature of the regenerative cycle of local education is pointed out in RAO 1967 and MORAVCSIK 1964a, b, and c. MORAVCSIK

1972a (p. 205) states there is not enough room for all LDC students in AC institutions. In the same paper (p. 206), indigenous education is linked with a reduction of the brain drain.

A somewhat sensitive matter is the staffing of local educational institutions with foreign teachers, especially in the former colonial countries (see, for example, NAS 1965b, p. 2). However, the problem of expatriates is short term; they eventually retire and are replaced by the first indigenous generation. Therefore, the question should not be of high priority in the overall picture.

With indigenous education, the question of the language of instruction leaps to the foreground. For the situation in India, see KARVE 1965a, b and 1967 as well as BOSE 1965, RAY 1967a, CHATTERJI 1968, and RAHMAN 1973 (p. 171). For Pakistan, see USMANI 1971 (p. 17). The same problem is discussed in the Arab context in ZAHLAN 1970 (p. 11) and with respect to the People's Republic of China in OLDHAM 1966. For some general comments, see MORAVCSIK 1970b (p. 12). The broad consensus here is that English has been established for the present as the international scientific language, but local languages must be developed to serve as a medium for mass education and elementary levels of science education.

The importance of mass science education is overwhelmingly proclaimed in the literature. One of the few dissenting voices is that of LEWIS 1961 who asserts that "we have made a fetish of universal elementary education" (p. 44), and "the sciences upon which the various branches of engineering depend may prove to be a menace rather than a help to the new states" (p. 43). Most other opinions are in sharp contrast. RAM 1968 (p. 5) quotes Nehru: "My interest largely consists in trying to make the Indian people and even the Government of India conscious of scientific work and and the necessity for it." PIRIE 1967 (p. 64) emphasizes the importance of training future political leaders in the rudiments of science. There are many references dealing with specific countries or regions: see, for example, PERU 1970 (p. 38) and OAS 1972 (pp. 42-46) for Latin America. The situation in the People's Republic of China is described in NATURE 1968, OLDHAM 1966, and WU 1970 (p. 81). Particularly strong efforts have been made there to achieve universal education in the sciences. The effort is also significant in Iran (RAHNEMA 1969, p. 55 and AID 1972a, pp. 77-78). The work of UNESCO in this area began almost at the agency's birth (BOK 1948, p. 346) and was reemphasized in 1963 by the

Secretary General (MAHEU 1963). Since then, UNESCO conferences have repeatedly dealt with the importance of mass education in the sciences (see UNESCO 1964c, pp. 9, 17, for details of the Lagos conference dealing with Africa and UNESCO 1970a, p. 34, for a description of the New Delhi conference pertaining to Asia). For UNESCO's role in East African education, see ODHIAMBO 1967 (pp. 878-79).

If science education must be universal, then no student should be denied it on grounds irrelevant to science. Thus, DESSAU 1969 (p. 15) advocates equal opportunity for all social classes. Discrimination on political grounds is discussed in HAMBRAEUS 1972 (p. 152) and OLDHAM 1966 (p. 44). A specific program in Singapore to design science education for nonscientists in LDCs is detailed in BHATHAL 1970.

Those who plan science education in LDCs must keep in mind that knowledge grows so rapidly that the *factual* basis of science education soon becomes obsolete. An educational system which produces scientists who are obsolete at the time of their graduation is a dubious investment indeed. This difficulty is discussed in MORAVCSIK 1972a (p. 209). In ADISESHIAH 1969, the problem of rapid obsolescense appears in an analysis of unemployment among Indian engineers. The need for quick adaptability is also emphasized in JONES 1971 (p. 140).

With regard to specific shortcomings of present science education in many LDCs, rote learning is often mentioned in the literature. An incomplete collection of such citations is found in MORAVCSIK 1972a (p. 211), UNESCO 1970a (p. 40), with respect to Asia; LARWOOD 1961 (p. 92), indicating that by 1840 this was already a significant problem in India; MAHEU 1963 (p. 27); UNESCO 1964d, with respect to Africa; ROCHE 1966 (p. 60), in the context of Latin America; and ZAHLAN 1972d, concerning the Arab world.

The problem of premature specialization is analyzed in MORAVCSIK 1972a (pp. 208-209) and 1973f. The importance of broad competence in scientific work, particularly in applied areas, is stressed by Teller in NAS 1967 (p. 375). An interesting case of premature specialization is the "red and expert" scheme initiated in the People's Republic of China in 1958. The plan was to rapidly educate millions to bolster the scientific manpower. The scheme had failed by 1963 and was abandoned only to be reinstituted in a slightly different form during the cultural revolution. It was withdrawn again after that period. (See WU 1970, pp. 83, 96, 101, 103, 105, 400; HAMBRAEUS 1972, p. 152; and RANGARAO 1966, p. 343.)

Examinations are another obstacle to improvement of the educational system in many countries. Often the student is evaluated only on the basis of a single final examination (KARVE 1963, p. 269). Examinations are so important that cheating is quite common, and measures to end it can cause student riots (WILSON 1972). Sometimes examinations are graded on unrealistically fine scales (KARVE 1963, p. 270). The general problem is grave enough to be singled out in the UN World Plan (UN 1971a, pp. 95, 107). For an argument advocating open-book examinations, see AID 1970 (p. 28).

A special problem concerning student evaluation is the external examination system originally instituted to assure uniform standards throughout a large educational system. It resulted not only in a uniformly low standard but in the stultification of the educational system and the obstruction of educational experimentation. For criticisms of this practice, see KARVE 1963 (p. 267), BLANPIED 1970, INDIA 1970 (p. 1), and INDIA 1969 (p. 63).

A conspicuous manifestation of the formalistic view of education is the intense preoccupation with the syllabus, with *what* one teaches rather than with *how* one teaches. In JONES 1971 (p. 139), Elstgeest comments that education in such countries is "rusted in syllabusitis." My personal experience with the problem is related in MORAVCSIK 1966c (p. 381). The conference proceedings in INDIA 1969 and 1970 are rife with such concerns over the syllabus.

Science teaching without experimental activity is hollow, and yet lack of laboratory training in LDCs is a common shortcoming. MAHEU 1963 lists this as a major problem. It is acute in India (RAM 1968, p. 7) and is prominently placed among the recommendations in INDIA 1970 (p. 1). It is also given conspicuous mention in the UN World Plan (UN 1971a, p. 106). The problem seems to be much less severe in the People's Republic of China (OLDHAM 1966).

Science teaching can be improved by encouraging interaction between teachers and outstanding local scientists. An experiment to promote such interaction is reported in NORTHROP 1965, the Science Lise Project sponsored by the Ford Foundation with a grant of 1.5 million dollars. The report does not contain an evaluation of the experiment.

The training of technicians is a neglected area. ZAHLAN 1967 (p. 9) gives some striking illustrations. The UN World Plan considers this a serious shortcoming (CLARKE 1971, p. 38). In the Asian context, the same point is made in UNESCO 1970a (pp. 59-61).

Science education in LDCs has little concern for the background of science, for the history, philosophy, and methodology of science, and for science policy and administration. Besides my own criticism, MORAVCSIK 1972a (p. 219), it is mentioned in RAY 1967b regarding India and ZAHLAN 1970 (p. 10) concerning Arab universities.

Textbooks are another weak point. ZAHLAN 1972d describes present Arab science textbooks as "beyond salvation" and urges translating programs. UN 1971a (p. 110) calls for low-cost textbooks, particularly for Latin America. The Franklin Book Program (discussed in chapter 4) is a step in the right direction.

Complaints are sometimes made that, for practical purposes, there are no "institutions" in some countries. ZAHLAN 1972c, for example, speaking of the Arab Middle East, states that "not one single state in the region has so far equipped itself with the institution that could identify and analyze problems of science and technology." And there are a fair number of nominal institutions in that region. Hans A. Bethe remarks in SALAM 1970b that if Indian universities started normal graduate schools on the US pattern, every Indian scholar at present in the US—their number exceeds five thousand—could be absorbed into the new educational system with incalculable benefits to the quality of Indian education. Further discussion of graduate education for research can be found in ZIMAN 1969 (pp. 358-59).

Many educational systems in LDCs offer few opportunities for younger, more energetic scientists. While lack of experience and other considerations bar young scientists from assuming exclusive control of the educational system, their participation on a meaningful level in decision-making as well as in daily duties should be strongly encouraged (MORAVCSIK 1972a, p. 213).

Because of these shortcomings, science education in LDCs often fails to be functional. This is seen in DESSAU 1969 (p. 16) and NAS 1971e (discussing mathematics education in Colombia). This brings us to the question of the role of applied sciences in education.

Some claim that the inapplicability of science in LDCs has resulted from a conscious effort by ACs to retard technological development. Such a view was voiced, for example, in ALLENDE 1972 (p. 32) with regard to Chilean copper technology. However, the record seems to indicate exactly the opposite. Countless scientists from ACs have urged their colleagues in LDCs to make strenuous efforts to bridge the gap between science and its applications. But if science education is nonfunctional, such a bridge cannot be built.

The goals to be achieved are eloquently described in NAS 1967: "A good applied scientist should first of all be a good scientist by standards similar to those applied to basic scientists" (p. 7); "To an increasing degree the advance of technology requires contributions from a variety of scientific and technical fields" (p. 14); "The highest-quality applied work is often done in an environment in which a substantial pool of people with original training in the basic sciences can be drawn upon for applied research and development activities, especially as these people broaden and mature in experience" (p. 17); "A fundamental problem in the education of the modern applied scientist is how to train him to bring a basic research viewpoint and approach to science without creating in him a disdain for, or impatience with, applied problems" (p. 40).

These problems have been discussed in a number of writings. The need for breadth in applied science education is emphasized in MORAVCSIK 1972a (p. 207) and in engineering and agricultural education in UNESCO 1970a (pp. 54-63, 68). BHABHA 1966a (p. 340) and 1966b stress the need for special training in certain key areas not provided by the universities. Such special training was undertaken, for example, in metallurgy in Argentina (SABATO 1963). Often there is a lack of understanding of the nature of applied scientific work, and an overly narrow view is taken in assessing the educational requirements for it (pointed out in ZAHLAN 1967, p. 9).

Should universities then undertake applied research activities in order to enhance the coupling between education and applied science? That basic research activities must be part of the university is generally agreed on (and is emphasized particularly in GARCIA 1966, p. 13; OECD 1968a, pp. 93, 123; and ZAHLAN 1972c). The balance between teaching and research at universities is indeed a matter of concern in the People's Republic of China (WU 1970, p. 62). But whether and how *applied* research should be undertaken at universities is less settled. JONES 1971 (p. 147) maintains that when students are exposed only to basic research, they become biased and prone to "elitism." GARCIA 1966 is also in favor of applied research. He believes that Latin American universities could provide badly needed leadership in the development and application of science. More contact between universities and applied research activity is also urged in CST 1970 (p. 95). Brooks, in NAS 1967 (p. 36), is more cautious speaking about the US. He proposes criteria to be met by a university-run applied science project: it should be readily generalizable, involve student participation, produce broadly publishable results, have roots in basic research, benefit the public sector, and have a leader drawn from the university's science faculty. At any rate, applied research in the universities would invariably strengthen contacts between university scientists and industry (MORAVCSIK 1972a, p. 222, and INDIA 1969 and 1970).

So far, I have dwelled on the shortcomings of science education in LDCs, but the picture is not altogether bleak. Much is being done to remedy the situation. General affirmation of the importance of universities is found in all parts of the world, and thoughtful studies exist which analyze the shortcomings. See Garcia in GRUBER 1961 (pp. 203-206) on Latin America and Shils in SHAH 1967 (pp. 475-500) on India. For a narrative account, see WILSON 1972. Asaihl has a long list of publications dealing with problems of science education in Southeast Asia; see, for example, ASAIHL 1964, 1967, and 1969. Further information can be found in RODERICK 1962, ODHIAMBO 1967 (p. 878), and UNESCO 1970a about UNESCO's work; OAS 1970 on the programs of OAS; and CLAF 1971 (p. 6) concerning the activities of CLAF. INTERAMERICAN 1969 (p. 29) discusses the loan of 134 million dollars made by the Interamerican Development Bank to educational institutions in Latin America. Suggestions regarding a World University are offered in SALAM 1970a.

Curricular improvement is taking place everywhere. The worldwide listing of curricular developments in science and mathematics (LOCKARD 1972) shows 44 events (among 187) which are taking place in LDCs. (For East Africa, see ODHIAMBO 1967, pp. 878-79.) A less sanguine impression is created by UNESCO 1970g, a directory of educational research institutions in Asia. Among the approximately 1500 projects listed, only about 70 pertain to science. Educational reform in LDCs is urged strongly by ZIMAN 1973.

International bodies are interested in curriculum improvement; for examples, see OAS 1972 (pp. 40-44) and UN 1971a. In addition, various American science curricula have been adopted in LDCs (see ASIA 1972b for the BSCS biology program and Zacharias in GRU-BER 1961, p. 237, for a physics program). Project Physics, instituted by Gerald Holton of Harvard University, has been collaborating with LDCs. The process must not be a mere transfer of the original American curriculum but rather an imaginative adaptation of its basic principles to local circumstances.

A rather extensive program to improve Indian education has been the US National Science Foundation's Science Education Improvement Project designed to retrain and reorient teachers through summer seminars and to develop institutions through curricular and material improvement. NSF 1973 gives a detailed account of the project as well as a frank evaluation of its successes and failures. Concerning the latter, there may be differences of opinion, as seen in HAFNER 1967 which deals with a predecessor of the NSF project.

When the problem involves a quantitatively large but qualitatively questionable educational system, a possible solution is to single out a few promising institutions and develop them into centers of high caliber. This concept of "center of excellence" has been used in both international and domestic contexts, including the US. An energetic exponent has been Carl Djerassi, a chemist who first organized such a program to build up steroid chemistry in Mexico some 20 years ago (DJERASSI 1968 and TELLEZ 1968). The program proved to be generally beneficial to chemistry in Mexico, although limiting the centers of excellence to a particular applied area (whose importance might fade with time) is perhaps unwise. (For comments on this project, see UNESCO 1970b, p. 123, and ROMO 1973.) Recently, Djerassi has been primarily responsible for the NAS-Brazil chemistry project, discussed in more detail in chapter 7.

The Rockefeller Foundation favors the concept of centers of excellence. Over an extended period of time, it has channeled substantial funds into 10 universities in various LDCs for the development of such centers. Beginning in 1961, the first eight years saw a total expenditure of 40 million dollars. For an account, see THOMPSON 1972 and ROCKEFELLER 1971. Apart from international efforts, LDCs have utilized the idea. For examples in India, see KARVE 1965a (pp. 165-66) and Maheshwari in SHAH 1967 (pp. 402ff). A few Indian universities have become centers of excellence, some through purely indigenous efforts, and some through international cooperation. The People's Republic of China has occasionally attempted to establish such centers such as the University of Science and Technology in Peking (WU 1970, pp. 102, 417).

The center of excellence is one manifestation of the eternal problems of quality versus quantity which looms particularly large in the case of science in LDCs. The temptation is almost always to concentrate on quantity, and yet a mediocre scientific cadre is virtually useless regardless of its size. Thus, admonitions to emphasize quality over quantity appear profusely in the literature (ZIMAN 1969, pp. 360-61). For India, see Shils in SHAH 1967 and KARVE 1965a. The situation in Greece is mentioned in OECD 1968a (p. 62). The "red and expert" scheme in the People's Republic of China was a manifestation of excessive emphasis on quantity (WU 1970, pp. 99, 103, and OLDHAM 1966, pp. 42, 45). Regarding the Arab world, the problem is discussed in ZAHLAN 1967 (p. 7), 1972c, and 1972d. Eric Ashby makes a distinction between quality and standards: the former must be high, but the latter should be limited to what is realistically attainable (JONES 1971, p. 1414). Ashby has in general been a perceptive commentator on university matters in LDCs (see SHAH 1967, p. 3, for a brief appraisal of his work).

Although LDCs encounter difficult problems in sending students abroad, every country in its initial development stages must utilize other countries for the education of its scientific personnel (illustrated for Japan in PRICE 1963; for China in WU 1970, pp. 20, 95, and HARARI 1968, p. 81). For a general discussion of the problems of education abroad, see MORAVCSIK 1966c (p. 384-85), MITCHIE 1968 (pp. 25-27), and ENG. ED. 1970 which describes a symposium devoted to the education of foreign engineering students in the US. Problems of the cost of such education are detailed in RAO 1967 (p. 3) and BURKHARDT 1966. It is indeed fortunate that in some countries financial help is available for students on a postgraduate level in the form of teaching or research assistantships. For example, some 12,000 students from Iran are studying science and technology abroad. Development is so rapid that local institutions cannot keep pace with the demand for manpower (UNESCO 1970a, p. 19, and AID 1972a, pp. 77-78).

Selecting students for education abroad is a primary problem. For criteria, see Maheshwari in SHAH 1967 (p. 404) and MITCHIE 1968 (pp. 25-26). Some actual projects designed to facilitate selection are described in DART 1971a. This booklet, written for foreign students who wish to undertake advanced study in physics at an American university, contains elementary but hard-to-find information about the American educational system. The Physics Interviewing Project is described in MORAVCSIK 1966c and 1972e.

The main obstacle encountered by students from LDCs when they return after education abroad is the difficulty of creating opportunities and a favorable environment for the pursuit of science (see MORAVCSIK 1973c and ZAHLAN 1970, p. 10).

The idea of a summer seminar for foreign students is elaborated in MORAVCSIK 1970b, 1971a, 1972a, and 1973c. The first attempt to organize during the summer of 1973 failed for lack of funds. Foundations said they had no slots for such new projects, and US AID characteristically said that they preferred to support engineering students. A gratifying partial contribution was obtained from the IBM Corporation.

It is desirable that students who study abroad be channeled into fields of science compatible with existing and potential scientific activities in their home countries. MORAVCSIK 1972a (p. 215) stresses that a subtle approach must be used lest one increase the brain drain. The best method is to send students to institutions where the desired field plays a prominent role in the hope that students will naturally drift into it. For an account of the personal problems of students studying abroad, see Kindleberger in ADAMS 1968 (pp. 135ff).

In view of the difficulties of education abroad, commentators generally urge that students go abroad as late in the educational process as possible. For views on this, see Patinkin in ADAMS 1968 (pp. 92-108) and LEWIS 1962 (pp. 317-18). A view almost completely opposed to foreign education is presented by Bandekar in ADAMS 1968 (pp. 203-32).

An examination of quantitative, statistical details pertaining to science education in LDCs indicates that financial outlays for education are of prime importance. UN 1970b (p. 25) provides quantitative targets for the total educational outlay of LDCs in 1980 as percentages of GNP: 6-7% for Africa, 4-5% for Asia, and 6% for Latin America. (For comparison, the present figure for the US is 3%.) A table of needs is given in CLARKE 1971 (p. 37) where funds needed for *science* education are broken down into categories and possible sources. The total for the decade for all LDCs is about 17 billion dollars, half of which would come from LDCs, three-eighths from bilateral agencies, and one-eighth from the UN. Those are the targets.

Statistics are available in various areas. In RANGARAO 1966 (p. 344) we read, for example, that in 1951 the educational budgets in the People's Republic of China for all education, higher education, and science education were (in million yuans) 813, 114, and 8, respectively, while in 1957 the figures were 2906, 637, and 327. (For more financial data on this country, see WU 1970.) In India, the total educational expenditure (in million rupees) rose from 1,144 in 1950-51 to 4,000 in 1965-66 (INDIA 1970, p. 314). Yet, considered per capita, these expenditures are very small compared to those in ACs. In the US, for example, spending per capita on education is about 100 times higher than in India (WILSON 1972, p. 353). Statistics on university expenditures in Pakistan indicate that in 1964-65 the amount was 123 million rupees, of which about 20% was spent on science (PAKISTAN 1968, p. 15). In the Philippines, according to UNESCO 1970e (p. 57), the total public expenditure on education in 1966 was about 197 million US dollars, 4.2% of the national income (not GNP). Of this, about one-eighth was spent on scientific and technical research. Obviously, a problem exists in comparing statistics because of the lack of uniformity in categories of data.

CERNUSCHI 1971 deals with numerous aspects of the interaction of science, education, technology, and development. It indicates the total national expenditure per capita on education versus the GNP per capita for various Latin American countries (p. 94). As one would expect, the relationship is illustrated by a straight line.

A great deal of information is available concerning numbers of students. Overall world statistics can be found in UN 1970b (p. 29). Excluding the US, USSR, and People's Republic of China, the total number of third-level students enrolled in the natural sciences in 1967 was about 1.2 million, or about 13% of all third-level students enrolled in those countries. Of those 1.2 million, about 520 thousand lived in Europe, North America, and Oceania; 14 thousand in Africa; 55 thousand in Latin America; 22 thousand in the Arab states; 180 thousand in India; and 390 thousand in the rest of Asia. Figures for students of science and technology per million population are 180 for Africa, 445 for Asia, 550 for Latin America, and 1,170 for Western Europe (UN 1971a, p. 100). CLARKE 1971 (p. 36) reports that the proportion of university students enrolled in science and technology in 1963 was about 20% in Africa, 16% in Asia, 27% in Latin America, and 33% in Western Europe. These figures illustrate the large discrepancies in various parts of the world. CERNUSCHI 1971 (p. 95) plots GNP per capita versus the number of university students per capita in the sciences and in technology for various Latin American countries. The scatter here is much larger than on Cernuschi's financial plot.

Statistics on students in various other countries are available in profusion. For the People's Republic of China, see OLDHAM 1966, WU 1970 (pp. 86, 88, 92, 94), and RANGARAO 1966. For Iran, figures are given in RAHNEMA 1969 (p. 56) and AID 1972a (pp. 77-78); for Pakistan, see PAKISTAN 1968 (p. 14); for India, see INDIA 1970 (pp. 310-20), CST 1970 (pp. 116, 118), and RAHMAN 1973 (pp. 28-30); for the Republic of Korea, see KOREA 1972a (pp. 84, 88, 89); for the Philippines, a country with an unusually low percentage of science students, see UNESCO 1970e (pp. 57-68) and MURIEL 1970 (p. 38); for Cuba, a country which drastically increased its percentage of science students, see RAO 1970 (p. 2); for Arab countries, see QUBAIN 1966; and for Africa, see OTIENO 1967 (p. 34). ZAHLAN 1968 gives data for foreign students attending the American university in Beirut. CIMT 1970b is a treasure-house of data on student populations, covering Thailand, Korea, Malaysia, Singapore, Lebanon, Turkey, East Africa, and Latin America.

Concerning foreign student populations in ACs, see IIE 1972 for the total number of foreign students in the US; see STATE 1971 and BFS 1971 for those on some kind of exchange. SCHROEDER 1973 (p. 20) discloses the startling fact that about 41% of the graduate students in Canadian universities are not from Canada.

That the number of foreign students in ACs has increased dramatically in recent decades is illustrated by statistics in BALDWIN 1970. In the US, the number of foreign students in 1938 was 6,000; in 1968, 110,000; and in 1972, about 150,000. Of these, in 1938, 3,200 came from LDCs; in 1968, 70,000; and in 1972, about 110,000. During the same period in Great Britain, the number of foreign students rose from 600 to 73,000, of which about 75% came from LDCs. In Germany, the number of foreign students increased in 15 years by a factor of 310, and in France by a factor of about 50. Australia, prior to 1950, had practically no foreign students, but by 1966, it had 12,000 from Asia alone.

For the number of students graduating, world data are given in
UN 1970b (p. 31) and JONES 1971 (p. 143). The number of science degrees per 100,000 population is given in UN 1970b (p. 33)
as 0.2 for Africa, 3 for the Arab states, 2 for Asia (including Japan), 13 for Europe, 37 for North America, and 1.4 for Latin
America. Indian statistics on numbers of graduates can be found in
INDIA 1970 (pp. 310-20), CST 1970 (p. 118), and RAHMAN
1973 (p. 29).

The following are sources of additional information about science education in specific countries: Africa, BURKHARDT 1966,
OTIENO 1967, VIOLINO 1973, and CRAWFORD 1966; Arab
states, ZAHLAN 1969a, 1970, 1972d, 1973, SHIBER 1973, and
QUBAIN 1966; Pakistan, KHAN 1969 and PAKISTAN 1968 (p.
29); Latin America, GREENE 1971, RAO 1970, and ALONSO
1969; Colombia, NAS 1968a (describes the institutions of higher
education, research, and planning) and NAS 1971f; India, JOSHI
1967; Thailand, GLYDE 1973; China, OLDHAM 1966 and WU
1970; and Greece, OECD 1968a (p. 41).

There are two sources covering several countries. MORAVCSIK
1973g deals with the Republic of Korea, Nigeria, Brazil, Turkey,
and Indonesia. SHAH 1967 contains information on Southeast
Asia, Africa, India, Ceylon (now Sri Lanka), and Pakistan.

Three

Manpower

It is generally believed that the main obstacle to the development of poor countries is lack of money. Whether this is correct with respect to general development is open to question. In science development, however, it is almost invariably incorrect. Science in most LDCs is primarily limited not by money but by manpower. It is natural that the bottleneck should be manpower rather than money. Prominence, power, and wealth in the international community have been generated by different factors at different times. In ancient times, agriculture was the key. Later, mercantilism became the main source of wealth and power. With the rise of the industrial era, possession of raw materials became the primary factor, superseded still later by large-scale industrial infrastructure. Presently, all these factors have faded into the background compared with the importance of brainpower. Britain was thus able to maintain its prominent position after its colonies had achieved independence; Japan rose to major international status though void of raw materials and only marginal in agriculture. For example, a piece of computer memory core, containing $3 worth of raw material, might have a value of $10,000. The difference of $9,997 was supplied by those who arranged the $3 worth of material in a highly specific way in order to perform a highly sophisticated task. Under such conditions, it is understandable that a country trying to modernize rapidly would find itself, above all, short of manpower to carry out the task.

Shortage of manpower constitutes a bottleneck in development simply because manpower development is a long-range proposition. A major problem in science development is the desire of LDCs to perform quickly in order to enjoy the fruits of development as soon as possible—fruits all too evident in the ACs. What took a century or more for ACs is expected to take a few decades in LDCs.

41

Some development activities can, in fact, be accelerated. It is possible to give a country large sums of money in a short time. It is possible, within a few years, to build an extensive network of power stations, to construct houses, to build factories, or to install a transportation system. But it is impossible to develop in a few years a substantial pool of sophisticated manpower no matter how much money is spent. Such a task requires several decades representing several generations of manpower.

A number of historical examples illustrate this; the best documented is found in Japan. The first generation of Japanese scientists, near the turn of the century, was mainly educated abroad. That small group then returned to produce the next indigenous and significantly larger generation. They in turn formed the nuclei of important research centers in Japan, which, through subsequent generations of scientists, developed into one of the most important scientific communities in the world. All this took about 50 years.

Manpower development in LDCs is a crucial and long-term project. Consequently, it must be started immediately, even if other short-term problems appear to dictate different priorities. Efforts must also be made to plan for scientific manpower far in advance. This may involve estimates of manpower supplies and needs as far as two decades ahead requiring a long-term general science policy. Such long-range planning has thus far proved unreliable, except perhaps when strict centralized controls are employed which are otherwise detrimental to science. It follows that problems of oversupply, shortage, and dislocation in scientific manpower are likely to be fairly common in most LDCs.

It is not sufficient simply to fulfill numerical quotas of scientists. Appropriately trained, functional scientific manpower is needed. Measures of scientific quality are hard to come by; thus, considerations of quality are generally absent from development plans, evaluations of past scientific performance, and other formal documents. Yet quality is of crucial importance. An LDC with a quite modest pool of scientific manpower may have acute unemployment of its scientists at a time when pragmatic analysis of the country's state of development would call for the employment of considerably more scientists. In some cases, the disparity may have resulted from incompetent management of the country's economy or its science policy in particular (for the latter, indigenous scientists may be partly responsible). But in other cases, the cause is the inappropriate and nonfunctional training of scientists. Overly narrow specialization, reliance on memory rather than on problem-solving techniques, disdain for experimental and applied work, and lack of background in ways to create opportunities for doing science can all contribute to misdirected learning.

One of the most pernicious traits of poor quality is self-perpetuation. Bad teachers and research supervisors breed bad successors; mismanaged institutions repel the creative and the dynamic as they accumulate the mediocre and the timid. Those with questionable standing in the sciences are loath to have around or under them people with more promise or accomplishments. Thus, the system of mediocrity propagates itself while giving the appearance of existing scientific manpower by consuming the funds laid aside for science.

Some argue that at the outset of scientific development one should compromise on quality in order to create the beginnings of scientific community, a dangerous argument. Quality is difficult to achieve even under the best circumstances, when one is fully intent on it. Compromising from the start can result in clogging the scientific manpower system with unemployables who are unable to contribute to the scientific development of the country.

Development of scientific manpower involves more, however, than an adequate production of new scientists. A more serious problem is often the retention of such manpower in a meaningful and satisfactory scientific atmosphere. In this respect, science development is particularly frustrating for the country trying to develop its manpower because science is extremely international in scope, perhaps more so than any other profession, trade, or skill. The content of science is to a great extent independent of geography, cultural background, political ideology, or language; and scientists from extremely different environments can quickly establish communication with each other as long as their interaction is restricted to scientific matters. For the same reason, scientists can usually find employment anywhere in the world (provided positions are available). A scientist is a readily marketable commodity on the international market.

Science is also a collective undertaking demanding a well-developed network of communication both written and personal among scientists. It is impossible, therefore, to retain indigenous scientific manpower by restricting their communication with the worldwide scientific community. The retention of scientific manpower must be achieved by methods more subtle than coercion.

Why might a scientist in an LDC want to leave his country and join a scientific community elsewhere? It is often believed that the overriding motivation for emigration is financial, and higher salaries in some ACs create an irresistible pull for most scientists. However, interaction with scientists from LDCs indicates that this is not so. First, scientists are relatively well-paid the world around and tend not to be money-minded anyway. Second, most people are concerned with their standard of living compared to the population of the country in which they live. Many scientists in LDCs are considerably better off than their counterparts in ACs. Third and perhaps most important, scientists have other concerns which to them have much higher priority.

Scientists require an adequate physical environment in which to carry on research, including adequate equipment for experiments, sufficient channels of communication with other scientists, and appropriate auxiliary personnel such as technicians, librarians, and computing personnel. These facilities need not equal the best in the world. They must, however, exceed a certain minimum level to permit productive research. Another requirement is an adequate human environment for scientific activity. For example, it is important to have a certain "critical mass" of scientists in close geographical proximity with considerable overlapping of interests promoting daily interaction. There is no blanket rule as to how many people constitute a critical mass, since it depends on the individuals, the area of science, and other factors. However, the number is certainly not larger than five, well within the capabilities of a budding institution.

The environment also includes interaction with administrators, policy-making officials, and other intermediaries between the scientists and the rest of society. This is a particularly sensitive area in the context of retaining scientific personnel. An endless battle with formalistic and uncomprehending adversaries is a frequent and effective way of exhausting the scientist's energy and morale. In this connection, I must mention the frequent occurrence in LDCs of rather vicious infighting within the scientific community. Such problems also arise in ACs, but the size of the scientific community tends to soften personal animosities by giving opponents a chance to avoid each other. In a small group, however, when the scientific development of a country is still nascent, conflicts tend to persist to the detriment of the building of science. A particularly severe instance concerns the dispute with political overtones occurring in countries where everything is politicized. Ideological tools can be used to undermine fellow scientists because of sheer professional jealousy. To defend against such attacks wastes time and energy.

Indeed, politics can contribute to a detrimental atmosphere in which to do research. Scientists are rather independent-minded and resent being involved in politics by external coercion. In countries with totalitarian ideologies and the attitude that "if you are not with us you are against us," science development may run into considerable difficulties.

The environment also involves the relationship between scientists and the public. The image of science in the eyes of the citizens affects their attitude toward the practitioners of science. This attitude can either discourage or comfort a scientist faced with other difficulties in building science. In LDCs the influential public, for all practical purposes, includes only the small educated part of the population. Their attitude can be crucial in creating a receptive atmosphere for science.

In addition to the objective elements discussed above, LDCs have some subjective methods of retaining scientific personnel. Though science is international, scientists as human beings are not. Most are at least somewhat inclined toward the society, geographical environment, and cultural traditions in which they have been raised. Other things being equal, most Indians prefer to live in India or most Chileans in Chile. In addition, there may be a feeling of loyalty and indebtedness to the home country which could tip the balance in favor of remaining there.

Remaining in the home country may actually have specific advantages. A scientist in an AC is usually one of many of similar capability and accomplishment. In contrast, a scientist in an LDC may very well be unique and thus have more stature and room for creativity. This is particularly true if the scientist is interested in the structuring of science. A Bhabha in India or a Roche in Venezuela clearly had a much greater opportunity to exert talents than if they had worked, say, in the US. Personal satisfaction derived from unique and crucial contributions cannot easily be acquired in a country with a huge scientific community where very few people can fancy themselves as indispensable.

I have described the general conditions which affect the retention of scientists in their home countries. It is evident, I believe, that none of the factors contributing to a desirable atmosphere is beyond the realm of possibility for an LDC. Yet, from time to time and in one country or another, some of these conditions are not fulfilled, and an emigration of scientists results. The phenomenon called the brain drain has received considerable attention from various quarters. The extent of the brain drain varies tremendously from country to country. Students educated abroad are the most frequent participants—about one-quarter of the students from LDCs studying abroad do not return to their home countries. The younger they leave, the more likely it is that students will not return. This fact further emphasizes the importance of indigenous education.

There is considerable controversy as to whether the brain drain is a blessing, a tragedy, or a neutral fact of life. Those not dismayed by the brain drain argue that the migration of scientists permits LDCs to "deposit" their trained manpower abroad until it can be fully utilized at home. Since manpower development and the capability of institutions to receive such manpower do not necessarily go hand-in-hand, the argument runs, the type of storage offered by migration is a useful aid in development, particularly because the scientists receive further training at no cost while "in storage." This argument is implicit in the development plans of some countries. For example, the Republic of Korea has officially planned a huge excess in production of scientists through much of the 1970s to meet an equally huge demand anticipated in the 1980s. Though not stated explicitly, the excess would, in the intervening time, be stored abroad.

A different argument favoring the brain drain views it as a particularly advantageous export business. Since LDCs can produce valuable brain power virtually as well as ACs, they should enter the business of training scientists for export. The return, claimed to be very high, comes when the scientists, after emigration, regularly send back foreign currency to support their relatives.

It is also claimed that the very fact of a significant brain drain puts pressure on the governments of LDCs to create conducive conditions for the pursuance of science to lessen the drain. Still others claim that since science is international and scientific discoveries are not proprietary, it makes little difference where a certain scientist works—the fruits of his labor will be available everywhere. According to a somewhat different version of the same argument, the maximal development of the talents of any scientist is to the moral and practical advantage of the whole world, and scientists should therefore be allowed to go wherever they think they can best accomplish that goal. Some complacently remark that in most countries the actual percentage of scientific manpower lost to the drain is rather small, and one should simply accept this loss as a minor blemish on the overall efficiency of manpower development.

However, there are convincing arguments that the brain drain does considerable harm. For example, it is pointed out that temporarily depositing scientific personnel abroad will actually result in a permanent loss of most of that personnel. Statistics are not easily available, but it certainly appears that the repatriation of a scientist who has established a substantial career abroad over a number of years is a difficult proposition. Viewing the brain drain as an export business, it is conceded that producing highly trained people might be advantageous even as these people emigrate. Yet the gain is much larger if they do not, since they contribute directly to the scientific development of the country (without which, in the long run, the development effort cannot succeed). Experience also seems to indicate that governments which are not eager to prevent the brain drain will not be spurred to action by its occurrence. A more realistic pressure would probably be generated by the presence of many dissatisfied scientists at home.

The argument that science is international and not proprietary is negated by the necessity of having indigenous science in every country. Though the results of science are in principle free and publicly available, the transfer and utilization of scientific knowledge can be successfully accomplished only be indigenous scientific manpower.

One of the most powerful arguments supporting the detrimental effects of the brain drain is concerned with the loss of exceptional people. Even if the percentage of scientists permanently emigrating is small, among them are most of the exceptionally talented and dynamic individuals the LDC has produced. They feel the inadequacies most keenly and find it the easiest to resettle in other scientific communities. It is further argued that the impact of such people is far beyond their numbers, causing their departure to be a major blow. Some even assert that virtually every significant advance is engineered by such people, and a country deprivied of them faces virtual paralysis. It is certainly evident that some who returned to their home countries have had a major impact on those countries, and the countries would have been much worse off had they not returned.

In balance, I believe the brain drain is a considerable detriment to the scientific development of an LDC, and steps should be taken to lessen it. What can be done? I have already described the general atmosphere required in an LDC if the brain drain is to be resisted. The achievement of those conditions is primarily a task for the LDC itself. However, two other factors are considerably more difficult to compensate.

The general feeling of isolation common to scientists in LDCs can be relieved only by the joint efforts of both the LDC in question and the rest of the scientific world. Scientists in LDCs must be made full members of the worldwide scientific community in terms of access to international communication and other benefits of membership. Geographical location, lack of funds, or lack of longstanding reputation must not be obstacles. (Problems of scientific communication are examined in chapter 4.)

The other factor, much less tangible, is morale. Brain drain is frequently caused by the various circumstances already discussed, but the deciding element is often identified as loss of morale. Scientists simply cease to believe that science can be done in their country, that a productive scientific development of that country is possible within a reasonable period of time, and that they can promote such development through their own efforts. This state of mind is not just a sum of reactions to adverse circumstances (see chapter 8). It is a much deeper force which has had a powerful influence on civilizations throughout history. The secret of high morale is not among the tools to which science managers or policy-makers have access, though they can certainly try to promote it by following the "rational" procedures for creating a conducive atmosphere.

A specialized but crucial area greatly neglected in manpower development is the creation of policy-makers, organizers, and managers of science (see chapter 6). First-class scientists may be in short supply in many LDCs, but an even rarer phenomenon is a first-class formulator of science policy. Many science policy and managerial positions are occupied by aging scientists with lessened interest and skill in research and no other opportunities. Their ability to perform the required tasks and to communicate effectively with their governments is often weak with the result that scientists have no effective spokesmen. If scientists were systematically introduced to the growing discipline of science policy, they could be gradually educated and would be prepared when the time came for them to assume leading roles.

Background and Comments

The problems associated with scientific manpower in LDCs are numerous and controversial. It is, therefore, especially useful here to survey the various positions and establish a springboard for further research. The literature has emphasized that LDCs have a shortage of trained manpower. For a general comment, see Pihl in GRUBER 1961 (p. 244). In the context of Latin America, see GREENE 1971 (p. 3). For other countries, see: Thailand, GLYDE 1973; Pakistan, SHAH 1967 (p. 365); Mexico, ECHEVERRIA 1972 (p. 48). The importance of the issue is stressed repeatedly with respect to the People's Republic of China in WU 1970: "Most serious problem" (p. 49); "The retrenchment in the scope of the R&D projects was dictated largely by the shortage of trained personnel" (p. 74); "Trained manpower is probably one of the scarcest resources" (p. 78); "Yet manpower planning during this stage was no more successful than previously" (p. 105); "The actual barrier, . . . has not been finance but scientists" (p. 410). See also OLDHAM 1966 (pp. 44, 47, 50). The same statement can be found in virtually any national development plan pertaining to an LDC. UN 1968 (p. 16) states: "A recent ILO draft report on the brain drain shows that unemployment of high level personnel is exceptional . . . shortages of high level personnel, especially engineers, natural scientists, and medical . . . exist in most development countries."

In view of these remarks, it is surprising to find the following statement in BALDWIN 1970 (p. 362): "For every LDC with an overall shortage of professional manpower today there are probably two with surpluses, present or impending." Baldwin's statement is somewhat reinforced by Robert Clark in CIMT 1970b (p. 197), who differentiates four stages in the development of an LDC: (1) no indigenous personnel; (2) foreign personnel replaced by indigenous; (3) indigenous personnel in equilibrium with local demand; and (4) surplus of indigenous personnel.

Two remarks are relevant here. First, there is a distinction between the real need of a country for manpower and its momentary capability to absorb a certain number of trained people. Most claimed surpluses are associated with the second category, but clearly manpower planning, which by its nature must be long range, should be done in terms of the first category with concurrent attempts to reconcile capability with real needs. Second, any actual surpluses are generally small (less than a quarter of the current stock of manpower which, in turn, grows very rapidly). It is evident that in a rapidly changing manpower structure, a perfect coordination of supply with demand is not easy to achieve, and small discrepancies are to be expected. A general argument expressed, for example in WU 1970 (p. 77), stresses that since strict planning of science is impossible, the aim should be to endow science with a structure flexible enough to respond to discrepancies between plans and reality.

At any rate, there is general agreement that most LDCs lack *senior* scientific manpower simply because rapid growth has not allowed time for the production of enough seasoned leaders. For this reason, senior foreign visitors are often beneficial for the scientific development of an LDC (MORAVCSIK 1964a). The need for scientific leaders is mentioned with respect to the People's Republic of China by WU 1970 (p. 429) and OLDHAM 1966 (p. 47) and with respect to the Arab world by ZAHLAN 1967 (p. 6). The scarcity of scientific leaders might be related to the contention that the number of exceptional people in science is proportional to the *square* of the population of the scientific community (PRICE 1965c, p. 9).

The lack of scientific manpower is perhaps the most important bottleneck of the development of science in LDCs and has been mentioned frequently in the literature. Clifton Wharton believes that "the manpower trained in the Rockefeller Foundation's Mexican [agricultural] program has always been a greater contribution than the new varieties," though the Nobel Price was awarded for the latter (CIMT 1970b, p. 186). CIMT 1970b (p. 681) states that the "strategy of modernization is, by its nature, talent oriented." Further references can be found in UNESCO 1964a (p. 41), UN 1970a (p. 47), MORAVCSIK 1964c (p. 173), MORAVCSIK 1973e and 1972b, and UN 1968 (p. 2). In NAS 1969c (p. 3) dealing with Argentine science, the first recommendation is for a manpower survey. SIDDIQI (p. 37) argues with reference to Pakistani science that "developing human resources should have the highest priority." BLACKETT 1967 (p. 306) speaks of "QSE's" (qualified scientists and engineers) as the key element. PIRIE 1967 (p. 65) asserts that "the main difference between scientifically productive and unproductive countries does not depend on the incidence of genius in them but on the extent to which they are successful in combing their populations for talent."

Apart from considerations of quantity, however, the crucial characteristic of manpower is quality. Here, as in the context of education, there is a long series of warnings to emphasize the point. CIMT 1970b (pp. 687, 689) observes that "in some nations shortages of highly qualified people exist simultaneously with a glut of those with mediocre training." ZAHLAN 1967 (p. 8) declares that 60% of the PhDs from the Arab world are incompetent. LEWIS 1962 (p. 314) points out that inferior standards eventually have a negative psychological effect on the whole indigenous scientific community because of its resulting inability to compete at the international level. DESSAU 1969 underlines the importance of both quality and flexibility to adapt to existing problems. The latter point is also made in UNESCO 1964a (p. 41). SABATO 1970, an unusually perceptive and meaty article, discusses the quality of manpower in the context of the civil service system that prevails in many countries (see chapter 6). Poor quality in manpower also creates and perpetuates "scientific featherbedding," described in MORAVCSIK 1964c (p. 166).

Since qualified manpower is so precious, countries must make a strenuous effort to retain what they have (JONES 1971, p. 149). This is difficult because of the international character of science and is argued in CIMT 1970b (p. 394). It is also difficult because ACs sometimes have a great need for qualified manpower, as pointed out in WATANABE 1969 (p. 420).

The problem cannot be solved by cutting off scientific communication with other countries. CIMT 1970b (p. 395) argues, for example, that while too much migration is harmful, some migration is actually beneficial. The necessity of this sort of communication is emphasized in BALDWIN 1970 (pp. 370-71). BOWDEN 1964 makes some historical remarks on the subject, while UN 1968 (p. 4) quotes the Universal Declaration of Human Rights, Article 13, Paragraph 2: "Everyone has the right to leave any country, including his own, and to return to his country." LINDBECK 1969 traces the changes in policy of the People's Republic of China with respect to worldwide scientific communication. LOW 1967 maintains that the lack of domestic and international mobility of scientists in the USSR and in the People's Republic of China has not impaired science in those countries. PRICE 1969d (p. 103), however, thinks otherwise, at least with respect to mobility within the USSR.

Yet, a significant number of scientists from LDCs leave their countries. To supplement the discussion of the problem, the following list enumerates some prominent causes of the migration with pertinent references.

(1) Financial incentives: UNESCO 1964a (pp. 45, 46); UNESCO 1970a (p. 46), see Castasia targets (p. 183); CIMT 1970b (pp. 449, 464, 469, 693); SHAH 1967 (p. 408) for India; ADAMS 1968 (p. 6); ZAHLAN 1972b (p. 9); WATANABE 1969 (p. 420); GRUBEL 1968c (p. 548); PRICE 1965c (p. 16); and UN 1968 (p. 12). For opposing views, see MORAVCSIK 1966c (p. 385), where salaries are relative, and BALDWIN 1970 (p. 365) which gives examples of Indians returning home at much lower salaries.

(2) Physical environment: CIMT 1970b (pp. 469, 693); ZAHLAN 1969a (p. 9); ADAMS 1968 (p. 6); MORAVCSIK 1966c (p. 389); WATANABE 1969 (p. 42); and UN 1968 (p. 12).

(3) Human environment: CIMT 1970b (p. 693); MORAVCSIK 1966c (p. 385); WATANABE 1969 (p. 420); UN 1968 (p. 12); COPISAROW 1970; and ZAHLAN 1969 (p. 9).

(4) Influence of foreign education: PIRIE 1967 (p. 67); and ADAMS 1968 (p. 6).

(5) Conflict with bureaucrats: UNESCO 1970a (p. 41); CIMT 1970b (pp. 449, 693); and SHAH 1967 (p. 413) for India.

(6) Lack of university reform: CIMT 1970b (pp. 452, 693).

(7) Infighting: CIMT 1970b (pp. 469, 693); and SAAVEDRA 1973.

(8) Political pressure: CIMT 1970b (pp. 449, 462, 269); ADAMS 1968 (p. 6); WATANABE 1969 (p. 422); and TELLEZ 1966 (p. 34), an account of a large group of Argentine scientists who left Argentina for political reasons, with a sizable fraction settling in Chile. After the Tellez article was written, the same group was collectively expelled form Chile, partly for political reasons. On the other hand, ZAHLAN 1972b (p. 10) points out that for some scientists ideological identification with a particular government might represent a positive incentive.

(9) Inadequate positions and opportunities for promotion: UNESCO 1964a (p. 46); UNESCO 1970a (p. 41); and DESSAU 1969 (p. 16), stating that about 10% of India's scientists and

technologists are unemployed (pp. 17-18). Some commentators, such as CIMT 1970b (p.693), WATANABE 1969 (p. 422), and ROCHE 1966 (p. 53) particularly decry the lack of creative opportunities for young scientists. ZAHLAN 1972b (p. 5) argues that "there is no relationship between manpower surplus and high-level manpower migration. For example, there is a surplus of lawyers in Lebanon, Syria, Egypt, and Iraq—but very few lawyers emigrate. There is a shortage of physicians, engineers, and technicians, but these do emigrate'" One should note, however, that international mobility in the legal profession is intrinsically much lower than in science, medicine, or engineering.

(10) Relationship to the general population: UNESCO 1970a (p. 46) and ADAMS 1968 (p. 6).

Emigration is hindered by the fact that, other things being equal, most people have a certain attachment to their original environment. Bernard Houssay, the Argentinian Nobel laureate, observed: "Science does not have a homeland, but the scientist does—the land where he was born and educated; the land that nurtured him, gave him his schooling, and gave him his place in his profession; the home of his friends and family" (CIMT 1970b, p. 450). BALDWIN 1970 (p. 364) cites the virtual lack of brain drain from Japan (and, incidentally, *to* Japan) as evidence that this cultural and linguistic element plays a substantial role in international migration.

A conspicuous and sometimes emotional issue, the brain drain has a huge literature. A bibliography of 415 items on the migration of scientists, engineers, doctors, and students is given in RPP 1967. As an introduction to the problem, I recommend CIMT 1970a, UN 1968, and WATANABE 1969 followed by two more extensive volumes, ADAMS 1968 and CIMT 1970b. Other general discussions can be found in MORAVCSIK 1970b (p. 7), GRUBEL 1968c, THOMAS 1967, and UNESCO 1970a (pp. 43-46).

Turning to the debate concerning the effects of the brain drain, note the condensed discussions of the beneficial aspects listed below.

(1) The brain drain is a profitable business of exporting brainpower on the part of LDCs (NADER 1969, p. xix; WATANABE 1969, p. 406; GRUBEL 1966, p. 273; SHURCLIFF 1967; JOHNSON 1965).

(2) The brain drain is only an overflow of unneeded manpower (BALDWIN 1970, p. 364, with respect to Asia).

(3) The brain drain does not affect economic growth (BALDWIN 1970: "But there is little evidence that these losses have had any significant effect on economic growth," p. 364, with respect to the Republic of Korea and the Republic of China; "There is practically no one, in India or outside, who feels that India's economic growth is being held back because the country has lost educated manpower," p. 365).

(4) The brain drain will remedy itself (BALDWIN 1970, p. 367).

(5) The brain drain allows individuals to optimize their own personal opportunities (WATANABE 1969, p. 406).

(6) The brain drain results in maximization of the total scientific output of the world (WATANABE 1969, p. 406, and GRUBEL 1966, p. 274).

(7) The people who emigrate do not have the right kind of education, and it is beneficial to remove them (Myint in ADAMS 1968, p. 233).

The detrimental aspects of the brain drain are dealt with in the following. The idea of a profitable export business in brainpower is challenged in AITKEN 1968 in a specific reply to GRUBEL 1966. Both papers argue in economic terms while ignoring the more subtle aspects of the problem. Grubel replies to Aitken's argument in GRUBEL 1968a without yielding the point. Yet GRUBEL 1968c indicates a somewhat broader point of view, perhaps stimulated by the previous debate.

A significant detriment is the cost of educating the person and other direct financial losses incurred when emigration occurs. WATANABE 1969 (p. 407) gives a table of such losses for India. UN 1968 (p. 14) also presents some figures. GRUBEL 1968c points out, however, that such bookkeeping is somewhat ambiguous.

The major difficulty, however, concerns the loss of exceptional people. Even those not otherwise concerned about the drain drain concede this to be a serious problem (BALDWIN 1970, p. 363), perhaps the *only* serious problem (CIMT 1970b, p. 394). Charles Kidd (CIMT 1970b, p. 450) claims that *all* scientists should be considered exceptional individuals. The Committee on the International Migration of Talent (CIMT 1970b, pp. 689-93) concludes that the loss of exceptional individuals is damaging. ZAHLAN 1967 (p. 8) claims that a large percentage of Arab migrants are in the category of superior brainpower. WATANABE 1969 (p. 411) describes the migrants as "talent-intensive." SALAM 1966 speaks of "the supply of towering individuals" as "first and foremost among the factors" affecting scientific development. In the Indian context, RAM 1968 writes of "the shortage of able people." In a particularly striking example, MIRABOGLU 1972 concludes that the productivity of the migrants in Turkey is much higher than that of those who remain. (However, inherent ability and environmental factors could not be separated in this study, and its conclusions are not watertight.)

Recent advances in the sociology of scientific communities have produced "theoretical" reasons why we could expect a marked effect from the presence or absence of exceptional scientists. PRICE 1965c (p. 9) suggests that the number of exceptional people is proportional to the *square* of the population of a scientific community. Thus, LDCs with a small scientific manpower can expect fewer exceptional scientists. For the definition of an exceptional scientist, we have the abstract of PRICE 1972b: "Statistical studies indicate that most authors of scientific papers have never been heard of again, and will never be heard of again, and, at the other end of the productivity scale is a small and dominating group whose names occur almost every year." In these studies, scientists are classified on the basis of publication or citation counts. While such counts are by no means immune to doubts of reliability, they do serve as qualitative indicators of the structure of the scientific community.

The catalyzing effect of such exceptional people is demonstrated by studies such as GRIFFITH 1972: they become the leaders of so-called invisible colleges which in turn are the centers of new scientific innovations, breakthroughs, and ideas which have an immense effect on the rest of the scientific community. This stimulating role of exceptional people is stressed in CLARKE 1971 (p. 45).

Any discussion of the brain drain must eventually confront the inadequacy of available statistical information. (See WATANABE 1969, p. 402; CIMT 1970b, pp. 393, 448, 671; WILSON 1972, p. 360; BALDWIN 1970, p. 359; THOMAS 1967, pp. 504-506; and UN 1968, a list which includes some of the most thorough studies of the subject.) Some countries do not keep a record; others do not categorize meaningfully. The return flow is often not recorded, thus exaggerating the drain. The reader must, therefore, cautiously interpret the data presented below.

It is useful to distinguish between figures pertaining to students educated abroad and figures pertaining to the migration of "full-fledged" scientists, though the distinction is not always a sharp one. Of the students, 20-25% do not return home after education

abroad. CIMT 1970b (p. 574) states that about 75% of those educated in Britain return home. A breakdown by country of origin
and field of study is given showing some scatter in the percentages
(pp. 575-76). ZAHLAN 1967 (p. 8) asserts that 20% of Arab students do not return from Europe and the US after their studies.
BALDWIN 1970 (p. 361) describes the situation in Australia where
about 20% of the 12,000 Asian students do not return home after
graduation. In a study of Tanzania reported in CIMT 1970b (p. 425),
a census of students from that country studying abroad revealed that
60% returned, 10% were still studying, 20% were of unknown status,
and 10% had definitely settled abroad. According to UN 1968 (p. 11),
15-25% of foreign students in the US do not return home at the end
of their education (30% for Asia). Of the new PhDs, 51% wished
to remain in the US explicitly for a post-doctoral appointment, an
almost obligatory extension of education in the natural sciences.
Many may have returned to their home countries after their post-
doctoral experiences. In CIMT 1970b (p. 21), it is noted that 46%
of the scientific immigrants to the US from LDCs entered permanently by changing from student status. For scientists from the Republic of China, the figure is 86%.

Apparently, the rate of brain drain can be dramatically reduced
when study abroad is financed by governmental support from the
home country. CIMT 1970b (p. 500) reveals that of those studying in the US on such support, only 1% remain in the US after
completion of studies. CHINA 1972 (p. 7) claims that 97% of governmental fellowship-holders from the Republic of China studying
abroad return to their homeland.

Information concerning the total brain drain (including non-
student professionals) is scattered among many sources. Early data
found in DEDIJER 1964b has been superseded, however, by more
extensive statistics. For a graphic view of migration, see the maps
in CIMT 1970b (pp. 674-77) reproduced in CIMT 1970a (pp. 23-27).
The total highly skilled manpower flowing yearly from LDCs to
ACs numbers 50,000 according to CIMT 1970b (p. 671). CIMT
then reduces this number to about 25,000 by eliminating refugees
(which might not be justified) and incompetents. Of the resulting
25,000 about 3,000 are considered exceptionally able. A figure of
40,000 per year is given in CLARKE 1971 (p. 47) as the total migration of scientists from LDCs to ACs, a probable overestimate.

For figures on migration *to* specific countries, the best-
documented case occurs in the US. UN 1968 (p. 20) gives statistics

for migration of natural scientists to the US for 1962-67 by country of origin. The 1967 figures are given separately (p. 22) showing the accelerating trend. The total from all LDCs for the six years was about 4,000. The figures for 1962-66 are reproduced in WA-TANABE 1969 (p. 405) which also gives the aggregate worldwide totals for individual years showing the trend toward an increase. The percentage of natural scientists in the immigrant population stayed constant, however, at about 0.7%. UN 1968 (p. 25) also provides the aggregate numbers up to and including 1967. ADAMS 1968 (p. 38) lists combined figures for migration of scientists and engineers from 1962 through 1964 by large geographical areas and some average figures for 1956-61 (p. 56).

Of the approximately 10,000 professional immigrants to the US from LDCs in 1967, about 14% were natural scientists (see UN 1968, p. 16). ZAHLAN 1968 (Table 3) shows that the ratio of the number of immigrants to new graduates in US institutions is 0.02 for natural scientists and 0.08 for engineers (ratios are constant with time). The absolute numbers of immigrants have increased sharply, however, particularly in the 1963-67 period when US im-migration laws changed to redistribute unused immigration quotas. CIMT 1970b (p. 672) reports that the number of highly trained immigrants from LDCs to the US doubled between 1964 and 1969. BALDWIN 1970 (p. 360) demonstrates that the number of scientists and engineers immigrating from all other countries also doubled between 1963 and 1967. If one considers only Asian countries, the increase is even more striking: a factor of 10 be-tween 1965 and 1967 (BALDWIN 1970, p. 361). CIMT 1970b (pp. 479, 494, 496) provides figures and graphs for the influx of Latin American professionals by country and field over time. The figures are rather small if we subtract refugee scientists from Cuba who constitute about 80% of the total Latin American influx of scientists between 1965 and 1968. UN 1968 (p. 13) reveals that the total number of professional immigrants from Latin America to the US during 1962-67 constituted 1.7% of Latin America's stock of professionals in 1965.

Significant data are also available on other ACs, though not as well-documented as in the US. UN 1968 (p. 25) supplies world ag-gregate figures for yearly migration of natural scientists to Canada between 1962 and 1967. They increase more rapidly with time than the US figures, and in 1967 they reach about two-thirds of of the US figure (though Canada's total population is only about

10% of that of the US). Figures by country of origin for natural scientists moving to Canada can be found for 1962-66 in WATANABE 1969 (p. 404); for 1962-67 and 1964-67 in UN 1968 (p. 24) with India and the Philippines supplying over half of the influx. As WATANABE 1969 (p. 405) demonstrates, the percentage of scientists in the total immigration population is about the same for Canada as for the US—about 0.6%.

Immigration to France is documented in UN 1968 (p. 25) by country of origin; the same figures appear in WATANABE 1969 (p. 404). The total number of scientists immigrating to France is about half that entering Canada. Interestingly, the distribution of immigrants among countries of origin is, in some cases, drastically different for the US, Canada, and France, thus showing the effects of affinity (cultural or other) between certain countries.

An overall figure for Britain is given in BALDWIN 1970 (p. 359), illustrating yet another complexity of statistics on the brain drain and involving the inclusion of flow in both directions. During 1961-66, Britain lost 28,000 scientists and engineers through emigration but gained 19,000 through immigration. See THOMAS 1967 for additional data.

WATANABE 1969 (p. 415) calculates the annual ratio of scientist emigrants (to certain countries) to science graduates by country or origin. These "certain countries" are grouped in two categories: France and the US; and France, the US, and Canada. The figures are fragmentary, and some appear to be in violent contradiction with overall assessments (see p. 59) of the size of the brain drain from various countries. For example, the figure given for Venezuela is 40-50% while BALDWIN 1970 (p. 367) claims that the brain drain from Venezuela is very small. Some indication of the migration to Australia can be found in CIMT 1970b (pp. 647-55) which gives the birthplaces of Australian professionals. Extensive tables show that about 5% of Australian scientists (about 450 people) were born in LDCs.

Statistics pertaining to "donor" countries or regions are available. That Africa in general has no problem is affirmed in BALDWIN 1970 (p. 364) and CIMT 1970b (p. 405). BALDWIN 1970 (p. 367) also claims that Latin America in general has no great problem with about 600 scientists, engineers, and doctors lost per year. In contrast, the situation in the Arab world as described by ZAHLAN 1972d (Table I), 1968 (Table IV), and 1972c (Table I) is catastrophic. Between one-half and two-thirds of all Arab PhD scientists and two-thirds of engineers live outside the Arab world. Detailed figures for immigration of Arab scientists to the US by country of origin are available in ZAHLAN 1968. In fact, according to Table I in ZAHLAN 1972c, of Arab PhD scientists engaged in research of any kind, only about 6% are now in an Arab country. For more information in a broader context, see ZAHLAN 1969b.

There is a scatter of statistics for individual countries, some of them contradictory.

Argentina: CIMT 1970b (p. 672), major loss; BALDWIN 1970 (p. 367), very little loss.

Brazil: BALDWIN 1970 (p. 367), very little loss.

Chile: BALDWIN 1970 (p. 367), very little loss.

Colombia: CIMT 1970b (p. 672), major loss; UN 1968 (p. 13) indicates that the number of professional emigrants per year is 15-20% of the number of students graduating per year.

Dominican Republic: BALDWIN 1970 (p. 367), heavy loss.

Ecuador: BALDWIN 1970 (p. 367), heavy loss.

Greece: CIMT 1970b (p. 672), major loss; ADAMS 1968 (p. 170) demonstrates that 27% of science graduates in 1961-65 emigrated permanently.

Guatemala: BALDWIN 1970 (p. 367), very little loss.

Haiti: BALDWIN 1970 (p. 367), heavy loss.

India: CIMT 1970b (p. 691) and BALDWIN 1970 (p. 365) state that 1% of all Indians with college degrees are abroad, but 10-20% of all Indians with graduate degrees are abroad. BALDWIN 1970 (p. 365) indicates that 5-10% of high-level manpower is temporarily or permanently abroad, 15% of the annual production of high-level manpower goes abroad, and about 40% of those do not return. INDIA 1970 (p. 159) shows that 17% of the scientists and engineers are abroad. CIMT 1970b (p. 672), major loss.

Iran: CIMT 1970b (p. 672), major loss.

Republic of Korea: CIMT 1970b (p. 672), major loss. BALDWIN 1970 (p. 364) states that emigration was on the rise during the past decade. MORAVCSIK 1973g (pp. 77, 78) and CIMT 1970b (pp. 137, 140) in which a table of scientists and engineers emigrating to the US by year from 1962 to 1967 shows an increase by a factor of six, but even in 1966 the number emigrating was only 3% of the rapidly increasing stock of scientists in 1967.

Lebanon: ZAHLAN 1972a gives estimates for scientists on the BS and PhD levels. Ninety percent of all Lebanese PhD scientists live abroad, and the total Lebanese emigration in 1971 was four times the number of students in the educational pipeline. Additional relevant data are given in Table 9.

Malaysia: BALDWIN 1970 (p. 364), no problem yet.

Mexico: TELLEZ 1968 (p. 48), not serious; BALDWIN 1970 (p. 367), very little loss.

Pakistan: CIMT 1970b (p. 672), major loss.

Peru: BALDWIN 1970 (p. 367), heavy loss.

Philippines; CIMT 1970b (p. 672), major loss. BALDWIN 1970 (p. 364) states that emigration was on the rise during the last decade. UNESCO 1970e (p. 54) indicates that in 1952-66 some 5,500 educated Filipino professionals emigrated to the US. Heaviest losses were MScs and PhDs in the natural sciences.

Singapore: BALDWIN 1970 (p. 364), no problem yet.

Republic of China: CIMT 1970b (p. 672), major loss. BALDWIN 1970 (p. 364) demonstrates that emigration was on the rise during the last decade.

Thailand: BALDWIN 1970 (p. 364), no problem yet.

Turkey: MIRAGOBLU 1972 shows that the number of PhDs in the natural sciences who have emigrated is seven times the annual production of PhDs in the natural sciences. CIMT 1970b (p. 672), major loss. MORAVCSIK 1973g (p. 101) states that 5.6% of Turkish engineers work abroad.

Venezuela: BALDWIN 1970 (p. 367), very little loss. Compare with WATANABE 1969 (p. 415).

Measures designed to alleviate the brain drain have been discussed above. The following is a summary of other such discussions in the literature. For an overall survey I recommend CIMT 1970b (pp. 699-723). See also INDIA 1970 (p. 161).

(1) Relieve isolation: UNESCO 1970a (p. 46), fellowships for temporary visits abroad; CIMT 1970b (pp. 693, 707), improved communication; INDIA 1970 (p. 166), bilateral programs; SCHROEDER 1973 (p. 19), involvement of Canadian international scientific assistance programs; MORAVCSIK 1966c (p. 388), improved communication; BRODA 1964, more meetings.

(2) Provide functional education and training (see chapter 2); INDIA 1970 (p. 321); UN 1971a (p. 86); WATANABE 1969 (p. 421); DE HEMPTINNE 1963 (p. 240); ZAHLAN 1969a (p. 10).

(3) Create new and attractive jobs: UNESCO 1970a (p. 46); CIMT 1970b (pp. 685, 686, 707), manpower should be used after it is produced; NADAR 1969 (p. xix), difference between real need

for manpower and momentary capability to absorb; UN 1971a (p. 87), career opportunities; DJERASSI 1968, centers of excellence; GRUBEL 1968c, opportunity gap; WATANABE 1969 (p. 427), new jobs through universities and private compaines; NAS 1971b (p. 17), creation of new institutions in the Republic of China.

(4) Maintain contact with students being educated abroad: CIMT 1970b (p. 424), registries kept by Kenya and Tanzania of students being educated abroad; SAAVEDRA 1973, contact maintained both officially and privately; (p. 459). INDIA 1970 (p. 163). I know personally of physicists in Peru who carry on frequent and extensive correspondence with their students who are working toward advanced degrees abroad.

(5) Avoid coercive methods: MORAVCSIK 1966c (p. 386), the bond system as an attempt to force students to return.

(6) Try to reattract lost personnel: CIMT 1970b (p. 395), a complex process involving more than salaries. This study emphasizes the importance of a good mechanism and cites Pahlavi University in Iran as a successful case. CIMT 1970b (pp. 246, 257); SHAH 1967 (p. 405); MOREHOUSE 1967 (p. 369); RAHMAN 1973 (pp. 161, 162); WATANABE 1969 (p. 431). These studies discuss the Indian scientists' pool in which the government temporarily pays scientists just returned from emigration until they find permanent domestic employment. The authors differ on whether the scheme was a success. Morehouse thinks it was, stating that in a given four-year period, of the 2,000 people brought back under the program only 2% left India again. See also S. Husain Zaheer in MOREHOUSE 1968. Rahman considers the pool to have been successful. On the other hand, Watanabe claims that 16,000 persons were registered in the list of "Indians abroad" in 1965, about 3,200 were invited to join the pool, but only 1,300 did. He adds that only half of those subsequently obtained suitable employment in the country. Reattraction of emigrated personnel played an important role in the early development of the People's Republic of China (WU 1970, pp. 428, 53, 82). The effort there is termed a moderate success. Between 1955 and 1962 some 200 PhD or ScD scientists returned to the country from the US, Western Europe, or Japan. A different type of incentive program to persuade emigrants to return home is described in WATANABE 1969 (p. 432) in the context of Greece. Other discussions of the problem of reattraction in India are found in RAM 1968, NATURE 1964b, and INDIA 1970 (p. 164). BALDWIN 1970 (pp. 365, 366) considers

the Indian program a partial success and the programs in Iran and Turkey complete successes. The need for aggressive initiation of contacts with personnel abroad is stressed in UN 1971a (p. 87).

(7) Obtain the cooperation of ACs: In Chapter 2, I discussed the necessity for supplementing the education of students from LDCs with know-how which will be valuable in their home countries. The importance of understanding faculty advisors is discussed in INDIA 1970 (pp. 165, 167). The cooperation of research leaders in ACs is urged in CIMT 1970b (p. 459). With regard to modifications in immigration policies of ACs, see CIMT 1970b (p. 717); INDIA 1970 (p. 165); WATANABE 1969 (p. 422); and UN 1968 (p. 7).

(8) Obtain financial compensation from ACs: BALDWIN 1970 (p. 370); WATANABE 1969 (p. 432); LONSDALE 1969 (p. 28).

(9) Undertake group repatriation: MORAVCSIK 1971a (p. 59); SAAVEDRA 1973; lessen isolation by educating abroad small groups of students in the same field and returning them to the same institution as a group.

(10) Encourage dual appointments: MORAVCSIK 1971a (p. 61), a prominent scientist originally from an LDC divides his time, for example, in two-year segments, between an institution in an AC and one in his own country.

(11) Avoid political measures: ZAHLAN 1972b (pp. 10-11), examples of unsuccessful efforts.

(12) Learn from the experience of the Mexican steroid chemistry program: Initiated by Carl Djerassi, the program took advantage of an existing Mexican plant for artificial synthesis of cortisone to establish a flourishing system of educational fellowships and commercial production. Within 10 years of the first artificial synthesis, Mexico had a research institute with internationally recruited manpower to work on these problems and produced 50% of the world's steroid hormones. The benefits affected related disciplines in Mexico, and the economic contributions of the Syntex company were of decisive importance in further scientific development. After another 10 years, however, the picture faded. A single, rather limited scientific subject cannot long serve as a basis for a research community. Yet, some beneficial effects of the once-flourishing atmosphere live on (see DJERASSI 1968, TELLEZ 1968, and ROMO 1973).

(13) Learn from the experience of the Brazilian chemistry program: A cooperative venture by the US, NAS, and the Brazilian

CNPq, the program was designed to upgrade Brazilian chemistry by means of a massive exchange program between US and Brazilian chemists and students. Begun in 1969, the program is now terminating its five-year tenure. As of September 1973, 10 projects in research laboratories have been initiated, 15 NAS Research Fellows have worked in Rio and Sao Paulo for two to three years, and many senior American chemists have made numerous visits. The program has produced 10 MS and 2 PhD degrees, with another 17 PhDs in the pipeline. Some 23 papers have been published, and progress has been made on inducing administrative changes to promote research in Brazil. Four students trained in the program have been appointed faculty members in Sao Paulo, evidence of the long-range benefits of the program. Yet it is too early to judge whether this expensive program will leave sufficient imprint on Brazilian science after the US participants have been withdrawn (see CEN 1970, NAS 1970a and 1973b, and chapter 7).

The lack of manpower to formulate science policy is a problem even more acute than the shortage of manpower in the technical aspects of science. Comments can be found in JONES 1971 (p. 151), RAY 1967b, and MORAVSCIK 1972a (p. 219). While 91% of all scientists are in ACs (LONSDALE 1969, p. 27), 97% of all historians of science are in ACs (PRICE 1969b, pp. 53-54). Inasmuch as the history of science is an important ingredient in the making of science policy, this exemplifies a particularly acute shortage in LDCs.

Various special education and training processes to produce specialized manpower are described in SABATO 1963 and 1968 in connection with Argentinian metallurgy, in NAS 1971b (p. 2) in connection with the Brazilian chemistry project, and in CLAF 1971.

The shortage of technicians is documented in JONES 1971 (p. 135), UNESCO 1964a (p. 42), and 1970a (p. 39). In MORAVCSIK 1973g (pp. 69, 70), the supply of and demand for technicians in the Republic of Korea are analyzed. UNESCO 1970e (p. 70) reports on the number of technicians in the Philippines.

The problems of distribution of scientific manpower within a country are sometimes referred to as internal brain drain, as in CIMT 1970b (p. 395). The manpower potential of a country is sometimes characterized in terms of the Harbison-Myers (HM) index (see HARBISON 1965 and WATANABE 1969, pp. 412-13). The index is the arithmetic sum of the enrollment in second-level education as a percentage of the age group 15-19 adjusted for length of schooling, and five times the enrollment in third-level education as a percentage of the age group. Tables for various countries are given in WATANABE and in UN 1968 (p. 26).

A serious problem in ACs and LDCs is the fate of the "aging" scientist. On the average, research productivity in the natural sciences peaks at an early age (20s or 30s). Older scientists must, therefore, have the flexibility to become creative in scientific activities other than research. SALAM 1970b (p. 8) calls this "a terrible problem." MORAVCSIK 1970a also discusses it in some detail in the context of national laboratories in the US.

There is some concern in the literature about the supply of "experts" from ACs who can assist LDCs with science development (see chapter 7). Commentators calling for the increase of such manpower are OECD 1968a (p. 218), MORAVCSIK 1964b (p. 10), and ALLISON 1960a. In contrast Piganiol (OECD 1968a, p. 242) thinks there are enough such experts. For example, 240 experts were provided by IAEA in 1972 (IAEA 1973b, p. 22).

A number of manpower projects are being conducted by international agencies. Besides the work of IAEA (for further references see IAEA 1973a, pp. 14, 63, and 1973b, p. 32), there is work by OAS (OAS 1972, pp. 5, 6), UNESCO (KOVDA 1968, p. 16, and RODERICK 1962), and various organizations jointly in the form of the ICTP (see, for example, SALAM 1965).

Before an examination of manpower statistics for LDCs, it should be noted (PRICE 1969c, p. 2) that 90% of all scientists who have ever lived are alive today. In a sense, then, the LDCs, dormant so long, have not missed much: the drama of science has just begun and most of it is still ahead of us.

Manpower statistics in LDCs are poor, partly because the nomenclature is not uniform despite international efforts to make it so, and partly because some countries simply do not have the means to collect such statistics. An illustration of the current state of affairs is, for instance, found in UNESCO 1970a, the proceedings of a conference at which many Asian countries were to report on the state of their science. These reports are in most cases sketchy with respect to hard facts about manpower (pp. 11-32). For other fragmentary collections of manpower statistics, see SPAEY 1969 (p. 70) and UNESCO 1961 and 1970c (pp. 16-41).

To place the following figures in perspective, first note (UNESCO 1970b, pp. 107, 118) that in 1965 the total number of engineers and scientists in the US engaged in research or development was about 500,000, with about 70% in private industry, 13% each in the Federal government and education, and the remaining 4% in nonprofit institutions (see also PRICE 1972a, p. 16).

The Republic of Korea has extensive statistics as well as comprehensive forecasts for manpower supplies and needs. From KOREA 1972a (p. 8), we learn that in 1971 there were some 5,300 researchers and another 3,100 research assistants representing an increase by a factor of two since 1965. (More detailed information is given on pp. 9, 28, 34, 40, 70 of that publication as well as in KOREA 1971b; 1972c, p. 50; WON 1972; and MORAVCSIK 1973g, Tables 14-24).

Data about the People's Republic of China cannot be found directly in governmental publications, but a sizable amount of data have been collected in WU 1970 (pp. 36-39, 429, 431-33, 539). For example, between 1952 and 1964 the research and technical manpower (not counting auxiliary personnel) increased by a factor of 10, reaching about 100,000 in 1964. A similar factor of 10 was registered in the increase in the number of senior research workers of the Academy between 1949 and 1964 (see also MENDELSOHN 1960).

Statistics about India are plentiful. INDIA 1970 (p. 320) reports that, in 1961, the total educated manpower was 190,000. By 1966, however, the stock of *postgraduate scientific* manpower alone was 115,000, an increase over 1950 by a factor of over seven. For more details, see UNESCO 1970b (pp. 201, 202). From SESHACHAR 1972 (p. 138) we learn that the research and development personnel in 1969-70 numbered about 80,000, of which only about 4% were in private industry. The increase in such personnel has been extremely rapid: CST 1969 (p. 63) shows that between 1958-59 and 1968-69 this increase was more than three-fold. For more figures on India, see CST 1970 (pp. 94, 114, 116, 118, 122) and RAHMAN 1973 (pp. 40-44, 155). The workings of Indian science are unusually well-documented. Indian society is for the most part an open one, and a variety of opinions expressed both by Indians and by foreign visitors is therefore available. As one of the most populous countries in the world, India is particularly conspicuous and interesting. It is also exposed to much criticism. I consider this a strength rather than a weakness: it should ultimately benefit the country by helping the development of a creative scientific structure.

Information on Turkey is supplied in OECD 1969 (pp. 199, 200) and MORAVCSIK 1973g (Tables 47, 48, 50, 51). In 1969, research scientists in Turkey numbered 4,500, of which about 1,500 were in research institutes. The situation in the Arab world is documented in ZAHLAN 1972d (p. 14) and 1972c (Table 1). The total for the region is 5,000 scientists at the PhD level. Manpower statistics for other countries may be found in MORAVCSIK 1973g (Tables 3, 4, 40, 41) for Indonesia, Nigeria, and Brazil; UNESCO 1970e (pp. 53, 69, 70) for the Philippines; QUBAIN 1966 (p. 291) for Iraq; CIBA 1972 (p. 149) for various countries in Latin America; ODHIMABO 1967 (p. 878) for East Africa; and MEXICO 1970 (pp. 345ff) and ECHEVERRIA 1972 (p. 48) for Mexico.

Perhaps a more instructive figure is the number of researchers per million population. The figure for the US is about 2,500 (CIBA 1972, p. 149). For other countries the numbers are as follows: Argentina, 194 (CIBA 1972, p. 149); Brazil, 70 (ibid.); Cuba, 150 (ibid.); Chile, 246 (ibid.); Mexico, 57 (ibid.); Venezuela, 179 (ibid.); Republic of Korea, 230 (KOREA 1972a, p. 8); Africa, 20 (UNESCO 1964a, p. 42, sets the long-term target for 1980 at 200); Nigeria, 20 (NAS 1965b, p. 64). Figures for both India and the People's Republic of China can be estimated at about 200. DE HEMPTINNE 1963 (p. 240) gives the figure for ACs between 500 and 2,000. This is confirmed in KOREA 1972a (p. 8) which lists 1,000 for the UK and France, 1,100 for West Germany, 900 for Canada, and 1,400 for Japan. ZAHLAN 1972c (p. 14b) suggests that a self-sustaining, fuctional research infrastructure requires at least 1,000 research-active persons in science and 3,000 research-active persons in technology per million population. For other figures, see SPAEY 1969 (p. 70), KOREA 1972a (p. 50), and UNESCO 1970c (pp. 51-54).

Unemployment figures are not easy to find. INDIA 1970 (p. 159) states that about 17% of the scientists and technologists in India are unemployed, but mainly on the lower level. The same figure for engineers at the "degree" level is only 7%. UN 1968 (p. 12) gives 10.4% as the fraction of scientific and technical personnel unemployed in India in 1961. India is often cited as an example of a country where unemployment of skilled manpower is extreme; these figures provide a perspective for such claims. The waste is regrettable, but compared with the rapidly growing overall manpower figures, it can be considered a relatively small discrepancy between supply and demand in a system in dynamic disequilibrium.

Foreign manpower in LDCs is not often mentioned. Some data are given in GRUBEL 1968b and ROCHE 1966 (p. 54) for Venezuela. A table of overall professional and technical manpower by countries together with the Harbison-Myers indices can be found in UN 1968 (p. 26).

None of the above figures include any information on the *quality* of manpower. To the extent that publications can be used as an index of scientific quality, PRICE 1969a (pp. 106, 109) provides figures by country for the number of scientific authors listed in the International Directory of Research and Development Scientists, 1967. An interesting figure may be derived by dividing a specific country's percentage of the world's scientific authors by that country's percentage of the world's population. Some representative figures are the following: US, 7.0; USSR, 1.1; UK, 5.0; France, 3.9; Japan, 1.4; Italy, 1.5; Canada, 5.4; Switzerland, 7.0; Israel, 11.1; India, 0.16; remainder of Near East, 0.16; and Latin America, 0.13. Price asserts that one can determine that the distribution of the number of authors among various scientific disciplines is independent of the country. Thus, the ratio of authors in chemistry to authors in physics is about the same in any country of the world (PRICE 1969c, p. 4). This has some interesting implications for science policy (see chapter 6).

Four

Scientific Communication

Scientific communication is perhaps the most important tangible tool for doing science. Through default, ignorance, and lack of concern, the worldwide scientific communication system has evolved in such a way that it maximally benefits those countries and communities which are already highly developed in science and handicaps those which are less developed and need it most.

There are good reasons for the prominent role of communication in scientific activities. Research in the natural sciences is, in contrast to most other human endeavors, a highly collective undertaking. Scientists learn from the work of others and build on it. The cumulative structure of scientific knowledge is made possible by considerable objectivity in the process of resolving scientific disputes and by the apparent structure of scientific laws compatible with such a cumulation.

Another factor is the ease with which scientists can communicate. As long as the discussion pertains to scientific matters, national, racial, political, or cultural differences vanish, and a dialogue can be established almost immediately. This circumstance is fully utilized in conferences, summer seminars, lectures by visiting scientists, and many other modes of personal interaction in addition to the journals and preprints used worldwide.

The importance of scientific communication is, in fact, so paramount that recent trends in sociological analysis of the scientific community or attempts to establish measures of scientific output are formulated in terms of scientific communication. Apart from technological applications several steps removed from the underlying scientific research, the visible manifestation of scientific research is mainly the communication of research results. The

69

"product" of scientific activity is a new discovery or idea which, if it is to be utilized, must be communicated. This feature of science is sometimes singled out as the main distinction between science and technology. The latter is not much concerned with communication per se but instead aims at patents or actual prototypes of industrial products.

Recent sociological studies indicate that communication shapes the manpower structure of science. It is now known that one of the crucial modules of scientific research is the "invisible college," a group of scientists (geographically spread over the world) with common interests who collaborate extensively and have a vital influence on the direction of research in a given area. These "invisible colleges" are not organized by governments or science administrators; they spring up spontaneously, usually influenced by a few exceptional people who form the nucleus of the group. If the scientific manpower of a given country is completely outside such "invisible colleges," the country is likely to be forced to resign itself to mediocrity.

Various aspects of scientific communication are used as measures of scientific activity. Numbers of articles, authors, or citations have been used to measure scientific activity for an individual, a group, or country to describe the temporal development of such entities. The concept of cocitation (i.e., two papers citing the same previous paper) has been used to map out the connections between scientific fields and to draw further conclusions about the operation of "invisible colleges." Some investigations are subject to criticism (basically because they both define and measure science in terms of the same quantity, products of communication), but the interesting insights produced by this approach demonstrate its relevance.

It follows that isolation is perhaps the most detrimental factor in the building of science in an LDC. Scientists cut off from communication are like birds with trimmed wings. They struggle for a while but then give up and quit research, settling down to some routine, semiscientific activity often of doubtful value. This is a common occurrence in LDCs and in small isolated institutions in ACs. It represents a waste of manpower and resources, especially since providing communication for scientists requires small expense compared with the cost of primary maintenance.

There are situations in which lack of communication impels scientists to do research in an obscure area where worldwide activity is low and individual resources appear sufficient to continue the output. The output nominally continues, to be sure, but the product of such work is likely to be of little interest or utility.

Let us now examine the assertion that the worldwide scientific communication system is heavily slanted against LDCs. It must be emphasized that this is *not* the result of a conspiracy on the part of the scientifically developed countries to prevent others from attaining scientific knowledge. It is the natural consequence of short-range considerations (in space and time) on the part of those scientists who have made primary contributions to scientific discovery. Their almost exclusive preoccupation is with assuring the fastest possible progress in science. It will require a much broader view on the part of the scientific community to make the structure of communication more equitable.

Scientific communication involves both internal communications, interaction of scientists within an LDC, and international communications between LDCs or between an LDC and an AC. Since communication can occur either in writing or in person, let us turn first to problems of written internal communication in LDCs.

There is disagreement about whether an LDC should publish its own scientific journals. Some argue that there are already enough scientific journals in the world (some 50,000), and the formation of more will make information retrieval more difficult. Others point out that journals with a small circulation are expensive, and a journal with a small authorship tends to have lower standards of quality. Indeed, one could cite journals in LDCs which illustrate these drawbacks. On the other hand, the organization and management of a journal is in itself an educational task for the local community. The existence of such a journal promotes internal communication, it raises national scientific morale, and it provides an inexpensive channel of communication independent of the expenditure of foreign exchange. These arguments are fairly convincing to an extent that might justify occasional double publishing, publishing the same article in both a local and a large international journal. Double publishing is a valid anathema to most journal editors. Yet, if judiciously used, it combines the attractions of local and international journals.

There is much to be said for producing locally written and published science textbooks as they can be adjusted to special cultural and geographical demands. Furthermore, LDCs could compete with ACs in the production of scientific texts in general. The technology of producing books is not overly sophisticated, and it is sufficiently labor-intensive to be favorable for LDCs. It could also serve as a source of foreign exchange for LDCs.

An especially important aspect of publishing is the matter of translations. Scientists can use the worldwide scientific language (English at present), but books for students and laymen often must be in the local language. To exploit this channel of communication properly, the mechanism of scientific recognition within a country should provide an incentive for such translations; they must be done by someone with at least some scientific training.

Discussion of books brings up the problem of libraries. That a library is not only a pile of books was illustrated vividly when I noticed, in the library of the physics department of a university in an LDC, books arranged alphabetically according to title, thus negating much of the collection's value. Library science is not well-advanced in LDCs, and a competent staff to handle books is often thought a luxury. The system for interlibrary utilization of books available in a country is extremely rudimentary; coordination of the acquisition policies of neighboring libraries is rare.

In this era when every year produces two or three million new scientific articles, accurate and fast retrieval and dissemination of existing information becomes a major task. This is increasingly recognized, at least nominally, by LDCs as they establish national centers of documentation of information. But the handling of information can easily be misdirected into purely formalistic activities. Organizations in some LDCs are especially prone to this with the result that the information center assumes an existence of its own and fails to meet the needs of the scientific community.

The use of computers in handling, retrieving, and disseminating scientific information should be strongly encouraged. The existence of computers in an LDC is not at all incompatible with the existence of camel carts and outhouses (just as jet planes are a vital necessity for internal transportation). There are examples of LDCs making good use of computer techniques; the technology of small computers is within many countries' capacity in phases of repair and assembly, if not of manufacture. To be sure, many LDCs are dependent on labor-intensive methods of operation in order to provide full employment. But it is often impossible to run a complex service with strongly interrelated components using semi-skilled labor for individual tasks. The inevitable individual failure somewhere in the system will cause the operation to collapse.

While written forms of communication are useful in science, the heart of scientific interaction is personal contact among scientists. In this area, LDCs are probably lacking more than in written communications. Yet this deplorable situation could be remedied rather easily. First, for a scientist to remain productive in his research work, he must be part of a group of scientists (the "critical mass") who have similar interests and who participate in regular (i.e., daily) interaction. The size of the critical mass depends on the individuals and the field of research, but it averages about four active people on the post-PhD level. When hiring university personnel or when establishing research laboratories, LDCs should keep in mind the necessity of the critical size and not spread their resources over too many fields. An appropriate method is to hire entire groups of people (discussed in chapter 3).

A critical mass alone is insufficient; scientists of a given country should also have ample opportunity to interact among themselves. Professional societies can often be an effective tool to accomplish this. In some countries, such societies have a purely ceremonial function with meetings often consisting of little more than back-slapping and celebration. The element of scientific communication is missing. Societies must be set up in such a way that membership is a challenge as well as an honor. If rewards for accomplishments are to be given, they should be closely geared to achievement in functional scientific tasks. Professional societies are certainly not a novelty in LDCs. A country with a very small scientific community may have a scientific society with a long history. Since the "science explosion" of the 1940s, however, such societies have multiplied and expanded evolving from small, somewhat elitist clubs into mass organizations. Professional societies can be effective representatives of the scientific community in dealings with, for example, the government. Yet there is a serious danger of science becoming politicized. The line between being an effective spokesman for the profession and a political machinator is thin and delicate. Even societies in ACs with longstanding traditions have problems resisting the temptation.

Interaction among scientists need not be limited to meetings of professional societies. More informal channels of communication should also be emphasized. For example, in research groups of many ACs it is common practice to have frequent visiting speakers from other, geographically accessible research groups. Almost any science department at an American university will have at least one such speaker a week. In sharp contrast, interaction of this sort is virtually unknown in LDCs. Even institutions located in the same city, where problems of transportation cannot be blamed, fail to make good use of the proximity of colleagues. Where distances are somewhat larger, the usually state-subsidized means of transportation make it quite possible to engage in domestic travel. It is indeed regrettable when contact with foreign colleagues 10,000 miles away is stronger or more sought after than interaction with compatriots. To set up a scientific infrastructure with no incentives for local interaction is an example of being penny-wise and pound-foolish.

In supplementing personal contact with colleagues, the telephone plays an increasingly important role in ACs. Indeed, it is often less expensive in time, effort, and resources to telephone somebody 3,000 miles away who knows the answer than to spend an hour in the library trying to locate it. In many LDCs, however, the telephone system is so substandard as to be practically useless. Every attempt should be made, therefore, to equip scientists with whatever telephone facilities there are to make their work more efficient. As communication satellites become increasingly common and efficient, international telephone rates may drop sufficiently to make that channel a more realistic means of international scientific communication. Perhaps a special satellite system will eventually be established for international scientific communication.

Certain special kinds of interaction are often weak in LDCs. One is the relationship between scientists in universities and those doing applied research in institutes and laboratories. The time-honored method of communication between these institutions, namely, the use of part-time consultants, should be encouraged. Communication should also be improved between scientists and the public. Modernization of societies necessarily involves general exposure of the population to science, and this task is the responsibility of the indigenous scientific community. But for social or organizational reasons, the task is frequently neglected.

A vital link often missing is communication between scientists and government. Scientists must participate at a high level in the formulation of science policy lest the task be done by people not knowledgeable in, perhaps not even sympathetic to, scientific matters. Individuals such as Bhabha in India, Roche in Venezuela, and Salan in Pakistan illustrate what can be accomplished by an eminent scientist in close contact with the highest levels of government in an LDC. In addition, however, more systematic contact between a larger group of scientists and a wider segment of government must be maintained.

A few LDCs are plagued by the problem of secrecy in scientific research. While there are legitimate reasons for classifying certain types of scientific research, preserving national "prestige" and concealing weaknesses in plans for science development are not among them. A country should present a detailed, public description of its efforts to develop science so appropriate steps can be taken toward further improvement.

In sum, the improvement of *internal* communication can and must be done primarily by the indigenous scientific community itself, in cooperation with the local government. It requires a coordinated national policy as well as individual action. In contrast, problems in *international* communication, to which we shall now turn, are primarily the responsibility of the international scientific community, of which over 90% reside in ACs.

The major scientific journals of the world are aimed at scientists in ACs, and it is difficult for those in LDCs to gain access to and publish in those journals. Some journals have publication charges to be paid in fairly large amounts of hard currency. Though the charges are not always obligatory, nonpayment is sometimes rewarded by a delay in publication. Subscriptions to journals also require hard currency, and unless expensive air-mail delivery is chosen, the journal may be delayed many months in its arrival. A possible remedy is the local production of satellite editions of the primary journals, perhaps on a regional basis. This, however, is adamantly rejected by journal editors who fear the reimportation of such satellite copies and the consequent undercutting of regular subscriptions. The problem does not appear to be insurmountable, and with a modicum of interest on the part of the professional society sponsoring the journal, some arrangements could surely be worked out. This, however, has not been done.

Much more important are the reports and preprints which constitute the main channel of communication at the front line of research, especially within "invisible colleges" or among specialists in the same field. Journals now tend to assume a purely archival role. In order to be creative in research, a scientist must have access to the preprints in his field. These preprints are produced by the authors and distributed in a rather haphazard fashion which favors the Nobel laureates at large institutions and neglects the unknown young scientist in a small group. Colleagues in L D C s are particularly neglected, if only because the postage to them is more than to the grand old man only 300 miles away.

Attempts have been made from time to time, at least in one area of physics, to centralize the duplication and distribution of preprints making the process more economical and equitable. Again, opposition has come from journal editors who claim that "institutionalizing" perprints would interfere with the regular distribution of journals and would undercut subscriptions. It now appears that a system could be worked out in subnuclear physics for a centralized handling of preprints with assurances of equity to research groups in L D C s. The proposed system would use microfiche, an example of the new technological tools which are making channels of communication more efficient and less expensive. Microfiche costs notably less than other methods of reproduction; it is light and can be shipped by air; it saves stoarge space; and the reading device needed to utilize it costs less than $100. The reading device is an extremely simple machine, well-suited for manufacture and sale in L D C s.

Other microfilm processes should also be considered. In establishing communication between libraries, for example, telex is increasingly used. For information retrieval and classification, taped versions of titles, abstracts, and articles are being tried. The latter are extremely expensive at this time, but improvements will presumably be made in the future. These techniques open up new vistas for international communication in which bulk and weight are crucial factors. There are great advantages in sending information in the form of electromagnetic waves rather than pieces of matter. There is really no reason to continue favoring a system of communication which, by its use of outmoded technology, discriminates against a large fraction of the world's scientists.

Material dealing with science policy is particularly hard to find in L D C s. While some 92% of scientific researchers are in A C s, an even higher percentage of those knowledgeable about science policy are in A C s. And yet, increasing expertise in science policy and management is perhaps the most urgent need in L D C s. Whatever written material is available on this subject must therefore be distributed to those who need it. Sometimes the material is available in a library, but neither the staff nor those who seek the information know about its existence or location.

Scientific books are published mainly in A C s and are increasingly expensive. They must be paid for in hard currency or, in many countries, at a black-market rate in soft currency. Some publishers have authorized satellite editions in LDCs, a practice to be encouraged. There are programs in ACs which distribute scientific books to LDCs without charge; but while the number of books thus distributed is not small, compared to the need it is a drop in the bucket. Because the market for scientific books is primarily in ACs, publishers' policies are oriented in that direction; material of particular interest to LDCs has a much lower priority in publication. Here, also, realistic ways must be found to make access to books more equitable.

International communication at the personal level presents different problems. For example, visitors from ACs to LDCs have much to contribute. They can provide new scientific information, criticize local scientific research, establish a rapport between a group in an AC and a counterpart group in an LDC, provide impartial opinions on matters of local science policy, and boost local morale by reasserting the local group's ties with the international community. Since scientists from ACs frequently travel abroad, visits to LDCs could be arranged if information on impending trips and interested hosts could be coordinated. A registry of such information is now available to physicists and should be extended to other fields as well. Another registry in physics serves those from ACs who wish to go to LDCs for a more extended period.

When scientists from LDCs travel abroad, the primary problem is the scarcity of hard currency which must be paid even if they travel on the national airline. For an extended visit, such as a one-year leave, the problem expands with the need to provide long-term support. A generous policy of leaves for scientific personnel is most important. A stay abroad for a year or two after four to five years of domestic service should not be considered a paid holiday but an opportunity to acquire new ideas and increased competence. Positions for visiting scientists from LDCs can sometimes be created by ACs through existing research grants or university departments, but these sources are closing up as science positions become scarcer in the ACs. Since 92% of all scientists are in ACs, and a scientist in an LDC would need a visiting position only about 20% of the time, the problem could be solved by increasing the number of scientific positions in all ACs by 1.5% (1 in 70) and offering the new positions to visiting scientists from LDCs. Providing such opportunities for scientists in LDCs is a task of the highest priority in manpower creation. Ironically, it is much easier for a young person from an LDC to come to an AC for graduate education than for a postdoctoral stay whereas, because of the brain drain and other factors, the situation should be reversed.

Bilateral programs between groups in ACs and LDCs can be an effective way of building international scientific cooperation. Such links exist between universities, departments, or sometimes research groups. Studies have been made to determine the circumstances under which these links will flourish. Results indicate that small, informal links usually function better partly because they engender a feeling of personal responsibility. The link can include the exchange of personnel, training of students, coordination of research, assistance in the acquisition of parts for equipment, channeling of preprints and other information, etc. Initiation of such links takes only a little coordination which can be provided by people or organizations already experienced in international scientific interaction. Some of these activities require no new source of funds, only a proper utilization of existing resources; others may need external support sometimes available from governmental or other organizations, such as NSF or OAS.

The dual appointment is another channel for international cooperation. A productive scientist originally from an LDC is given a joint appointment by an institution in an AC and an institution in an LDC; he divides his time evenly between them in, say, two-year segments. The few examples of such appointments appear to be working out well. There are administrative difficulties on both sides in arranging the position (mainly because it is unusual), and funds are needed every two years for travel. But the arrangement has numerous advantages for both institutions and should be explored more extensively.

Two rather unusual institutions illustrate another aspect of interaction of scientific manpower. One is the ICTP in Trieste which reserves a sizable number of positions for visitors from LDCs. A continuing relationship is maintained which allows scientists to visit the Centre from time to time provided they spend the intervening time in their home countries. The Centre also hosts visitors from ACs and thus serves as a meeting place with considerable international stature enhanced by the personal weight of its director, Abdus Salam. It is jointly financed by the Italian government, IAEA, and UNESCO, with smaller amounts from other sources. Now about 10 years old, the Centre has made an immense

contribution to the fostering of science in LDCs. But it is specialized and relatively small; many similar institutions are needed in
other fields.

Another organization is the ICIPE in Nairobi where joint research is conducted by local scientists and scientists from ACs on
problems related to the applied science of the particular geographical area. Again, because of the stature of some scientists associated
with it and because of enthusiastic support from a variety of sources
internationally distributed, the Centre has made substantial contributions. Such bright spots are more the exception than the rule in
a generally bleak picture.

For special interactions of shorter duration, international scientific meetings are useful. However, these are also heavily weighted
in favor of ACs. They are often held in an AC with the justification that holding a meeting in an LDC would greatly increase travel
costs. The same consideration, however, does not prevent people
from holding large conferences in Japan, which is probably even
more distant from other ACs than most LDCs. Some claim that
LDCs do not have the organizational and physical resources to organize a large conference, a statement that has been proven wrong
a number of times. The result is that scientists from LDCs must
travel far on nonexistent funds. Furthermore, indigenous scientific
communities are denied the valuable educational opportunity to
host such a conference and observe its proceedings. Some international sources try to aid LDCs in the holding of conferences, but
the total impact of their programs is rather small. Some so-called
summer schools or summer seminars organized to educate experts
on the latest developments in a specialized field have been held in
LDCs. But even there, the surface has hardly been scratched.

One of the most valuable links in the chain of scientific communications is simple, personal knowledge of fellow scientists. Here
again, scientists from LDCs are greatly handicapped: they travel
and are visited much less and have fewer opportunities to develop
friendships. In some LDCs, general patterns of social interaction
are more formal and less gregarious than those in some ACs; scientists brought up in these societies will be less prone to make friends
with hundreds of colleagues. Yet, collaboration, sharing of information, opportunities for visiting positions, sources for financial
support, and many other facets of scientific activity depend heavily on personal acquaintances and contacts. Thus, the vicious circle
of handicaps disadvantages scientists in LDCs even further.

Scientists from LDCs must become more vocal about their science development needs. One of the main themes here is that the scientific community in the ACs has been ignorant, negligent, and nonchalant with regard to active measures that could be taken to assist LDCs in the development of science. Part of the remedy is to create a broader awareness of these problems within the scientific community. While books like this may have some effect, the credibility and shock value of a book, lecture, appeal, or article by a group of scientists from the LDCs would be much greater. Perhaps there should be a formal organization of scientists in LDCs for this purpose: delegates could be sent to scientific meetings in ACs to deliver talks, provide vivid illustrations, and propose specific action.

Several programs are currently being employed to alleviate problems of communication. Some are regional efforts, such as OAS and CLAF in Latin America and CENTO in the Middle East; others are of international scope, such as IAEA, UNESCO, and other UN agencies. While undoubtedly helpful, they represent only a pale response to a prominent challenge, a challenge that will remain unmet until the rank-and-file members of the international scientific community decide that it should be met.

Background and Comments

That science is a collective undertaking is such an obvious statement that it hardly needs documentation. Among other discussions are, for example, MORAVCSIK 1972a (p. 224) and 1974c. Similarly, the international nature of science has been affirmed in MORAVCSIK 1974c. Most commentators assume the truth of these two statements and emphasize the crucial role of communication in the pursuit of science. In the context of Nigerian science, NAS 1965b (pp. 8, 43) suggests that great emphasis must be placed on communication, both internal and with other African countries. MORAVCSIK 1972a (pp. 225-26) stresses that problems of communication are the primary cause of the feeling of isolation experienced by many scientists in LDCs. In MORAVCSIK 1974c, science is contrasted with the arts in terms of the role of communication. In

ROCHE 1966 (p. 59), Ramon y Cajal asserts that *enquistamiento* (encystment) is the main cause of inadequacy in Spanish science. The same theme permeates the discussion in SAAVEDRA 1973 with respect to Chilean science. DEDIJER 1963 lists adequate communications as one of the criteria for a full-fledged national scientific community. UN 1971a (p. 49) underlines the same contention and calls for renewed efforts to transfer knowledge from ACs to LDCs. CIMT 1970a constantly stresses the effect of poor communications on the brain drain. The literature is probably unanimous in contending that communication is a *sine qua non* for the development of indigenous science.

The role of communications in sociological analysis of the scientific community is also well-documented. Derek de Solla Price has been a leader in the exploitation of this relationship. In PRICE 1965c (pp. 6-8) and 1969c (p. 91), he shows that the number of scientific publications doubles every 10-15 years. He distinguishes science from technology by claiming that in science the published paper is the end product while in technology it is only an epiphenomenon. Accordingly, scientists read a lot (they are "papyrocentric") while technologists do not (they are "papyrophobic"). (See PRICE 1969d, pp. 96, 100; PRICE 1968 and 1972a; and NAS 1967, pp. 38-39). Another interesting distinction made by Price is his separation of "research front" papers and references from "archival" papers and references, relevant because of the differing patterns of dissemination of the two (PRICE 1965c, p. 10, and 1969d, p. 92). Price points out (see also MORAVCSIK 1965a) the central role of *informal* communications in science (PRICE 1965c, p. 10). He documents the unequal distribution of scientific authorships among scientists and among countries. Certain scientists numbering the square root of the total number of scientists account for about half of the scientific literature (PRICE 1969d), while six countries produce 80% of all scientific papers in physics and chemistry (PRICE 1964c, Table 4). In fact, 14 countries produce 90% of all scientific literature; only one (India) is an LDC (PRICE 1969a, p. 106; the statistics in this paper were compiled at a time when many publications in the People's Republic of China were inaccessible to the rest of the world).

More recently, Price has incorporated some weighting by quality in his investigation by turning to citations as a measure of scientific activity. For some interesting results on patterns of citations, see PRICE 1965d and 1970. Price advocates certain standards in

publication on the basis of these studies of publication and citation
(PRICE 1964b). By building on such results, the structure of "invisible colleges" and the connections between various scientific disciplines can be "mapped." Recent work in this area may be found,
for example, in GRIFFITH 1972, 1973a, 1973b, GARVEY 1972,
and SMALL 1973. In other types of sociological studies (MUL-
LINS 1973), communicative links also play a decisive role.

Consequently, isolation looms as a major threat to scientific
communities in LDCs. I have stressed this factor repeatedly (MO-
RAVCSIK 1970b, pp. 7, 12; 1972a, p. 225; and 1972b); in particular, I have pointed out that scientific work is very dependent on
the criticism of colleagues which requires suitable communications.
Much more eloquent, however, are the accounts of two scientists.
In SALAM 1966 (p. 465), the author recalls: "Looking back on
my own period in Lahore, as I said, I felt terribly isolated. If at
that time someone had said to me, we shall give you the opportunity every year to travel to an active center in Europe or the United
States for three months of your vacation to work with your peers;
would you then be happy to stay the remaining nine months at
Lahore, I would have said yes. No one made the offer." In SAA-
VEDRA 1973, the author remarks that "after a couple of years
back in Chile I felt like a squashed lemon." The same theme is also
found in SALAM 1968. According to UN 1970b (p. 19), a particularly concise and pertinent document, "there is a great doubt that
the growth of an indigenous scientific community can be affected
without active participation by the international scientific community. An active cadre of scientific personnel cannot develop or
exist in isolation." RIAZUDDIN 1970 and ZIMAN 1969 (p. 363)
make the same point. GREENE 1971 (p. 10) suggests that isolation
is particularly baneful to young scientists barely beyond their
PhDs. DEDIJER 1957 (p. 242) discusses scientific isolation imposed by local governments for political reasons and its destructive
influence on the indigenous scientific community. Similar points
are outlined in ZIMAN 1969 (p. 365).

The role of domestic scientific journals has received attention in
various contexts. BASALLA 1967 (p. 618), in a general historical
analysis of the spread of science in LDCs, singles out the establishment of local journals as an indispensable element in the creation
of a self-sustaining scientific infrastructure. Various advantages and
drawbacks are summarized in MORAVCSIK 1970b and 1972a (p.
228). The *Journal of West African Association*, for example, suffers

financially because of small circulation (UNESCO 1965b, p. 201). That many LDCs have an impressive list of journals, some decades old, is demonstrated by WU 1970 (pp. 22, 439) which discusses the history of scientific journals in China, and RAHMAN 1973 (pp. 167-69) which lists Indian journals. Smaller countries, such as the Philippines (UNESCO 1970e, p. 21) and Egypt (QUBAIN 1966, p. 182), also have a sizable number of journals. Often the problem is not the quantity of such journals but the quality of the papers published. Examples of effective regional communications are the duplicated notices and bulletins issued by CLAF (CLAF 1971, p. 7).

Publication of books can be documented for a number of LDCs. For example, in the People's Republic of China some 65,000 books were published between 1954 and 1958; about 40% were in science and technology (WU 1970, p. 439). Wu gives data on translations which are of special importance in that country. Between 1949 and 1955, some 12,000 foreign books were translated, mainly from Russian and English, of which about 25% were in the sciences (WU 1970, p. 438).

An active translation program is operated in many countries by the Franklin Book Program (see FRANKLIN). Supported primarily by local governments, US private foundations, book publishers, and US business firms (with about 3% contributed by the US government), the organization had a budget of 7 million dollars in 1970. The program translates publications into Arabic, Bengali, Indonesian, Malay, Persian, Portugese, Spanish, and Urdu; between 1952 and 1970, it produced some 2,600 translations, about 6% in the sciences.

Local libraries in LDCs are described in a number of publications. WU 1970 (pp. 438-39) shows how the People's Republic of China dynamically carried on and expanded a rich library tradition inherited from previous regimes. Foreign books play an essential role, and library policies are coordinated. OLDHAM 1966 (p. 47) also comments on the excellence of libraries in that country. UNESCO 1970e (p. 21) and PHILIPPINES 1966 describe the situation in the Philippines where a system of interlibrary loans exists, but purchasing policies are not coordinated. The National Library is concentrating particularly on scientific reports. NAS 1971f (p. 4) reports on the network of libraries in Colombian chemistry; efforts are being made to coordinate the libraries and interconnect them with a Telex-Xerox system that will supply unavailable articles.

This report emphasizes the importance in science of browsing in journals in order to maintain an overall awareness of advances in related fields.

National documentation and information centers are proliferating in LDCs. NAS 1969c (pp. 2, 23) and 1970b describe a particularly advanced system in Argentina, including computer-based in-information tapes; KIM 1969 (p. 95) reports on the Republic of Korea. An information system that is part of CONACYT is described in MEXICO 1971; USMANI 1971 (p. 7) and PAKISTAN 1968 (p. 19) describe the Pakistani situation. PERU 1970 (p. 35) describes a proposed information system for Peru. UNESCO 1970e (p. 21) and PHILIPPINES 1966 (p. 26) discuss a proposal for an information center in the Philippines. General comments recommending the establishment of such centers and stressing their importance can be found in JONES 1971 (p. 14); OECD 1971a (p. 108), urging support from ACs; UN 1970b (p. 13); and CLARKE 1971 (p. 44). However, there is practically no evidence of how well these centers operate as judged by the indigenous scientific communities.

We now turn to internal personal communications. The concept of critical mass is analyzed in MORAVCSIK 1971a (p. 59), urging the scheme of group repatriation; 1972a (p. 228); 1973f; and 1974c. Problems of professional societies and meetings are discussed in ZAHLAN 1969a (p. 10), in Arab countries; NAS 1972b (p. 8) decries the lack of informal meetings in Brazil to exchange information; WU 1970 (pp. 23-32) gives a history of societies in China with statistics and tables; NSF 1973 discusses conferences on physics and chemistry in India; NAS 1971e (p. 18) recommends professional meetings and symposia in the context of Colombian mathematics; PHILIPPINES 1966 (p. 26), Philippine Chemical Society; RAHMAN 1973 (pp. 163-65) discusses societies in India; and PAKISTAN 1968 (p. 18) summarizes the situation in Pakistan. These examples tend to reinforce my suggestion that societies and meetings be less formalistic and more devoted to scientific matters. A good overall discussion of the role of societies, with particular reference to African science development, is given in Olaniyan's article in UNESCO 1965b (p. 193). MORAVCSIK 1974c advocates an internal network of visiting speakers traveling from one institution to another. Some general comments on internal communication can be found in DESSAU 1969 (p. 21). ZAHLAN 1972d asserts that Arab social customs do not favor teamwork, and Arab scientists may therefore find it more difficult to adjust to scientific collaboration.

The importance of the telephone as a tool of communication is noted in MORAVCSIK 1972a (p. 237) and UN 1969 (p. 19). A specific instance of deficiency is documented in the context of the NAS-Brazil chemistry program in NAS 1972b (p. 8).

A generous policy with respect to leaves to go abroad is advocated in MORAVCSIK 1966c (p. 387), 1972c (p. 228), 1972a (pp. 229, 230), and 1974c. In Malaysia, such leaves are granted with pay at the ratio of six months every three years (THONG 1968, p. 368).

For comments concerning communication between basic and applied scientists, see NAS 1967 (p. 13), PHILIPPINES 1966 (p. 26), MORAVCSIK 1974c, and CST 1971 (p. 94). NAS 1967 (p. 16) urges such a liaison as necessary for a balanced science structure.

A number of commentators are dissatisfied with relations between scientific communities in LDCs and local governmental officials (DESSAU 1969, p. 21; PHILIPPINES 1966, p. 26, and MORAVCSIK 1974c are some examples). There is a similar criticism of the relationship between rank-and-file scientists and their administrative superiors. For obvious reasons such complaints are difficult to document in the literature. Some recommendations, however, are found in NAS 1967 (pp. 47ff). The question of secrecy is similarly delicate (NAS 1967, p. 16).

The general lack of scientists from LDCs at meetings of scientific communities in ACs has been largely ignored in the literature. Occasionally scientists from LDCs are invited to speak at scientific meetings, mainly about technical science. If the discussion turns to matters of science development, politeness often extinguishes any meaningful dialogue or any specific organization for action. This state of affairs is criticized in MORAVCSIK 1974c.

Examples of literature dealing with countries with national policies concerning scientific communications are: WU 1970 (p. 438), People's Republic of China; NAS 1969c (pp. 23-28, 68-75), Argentina; MORAVCSIK 1973g (p. 19), Brazil; and MORAVCSIK 1973g (p. 20), Indonesia. Most national development plans include a program to improve scientific communication.

As the literature demonstrates, problems of international communication are more frequently discussed than internal problems. The number of scientific journals and articles is estimated in several places, such as PRICE 1965c (p. 8), CLARKE 1971 (p. 43), and BULLETIN 1964 (p. 32). Estimates differ by less than a factor of two, so that the estimate given in the first section of this chapter is roughly correct. Problems of foreign currency in connection with subscriptions are mentioned in SAAVEDRA 1973. The same author stresses the importance of air mail in the delivery of communications concerning research-front activity, a point also made by NAS 1972b (p. 10) in the context of the NAS-Brazil chemistry program. Suggestions for solving the various problems associated with distribution, page charges, and similar items can be found in MORAVCSIK 1972a (p. 234), 1972b, and 1974c.

Emphasis on the importance of preprints and research reports has been a longstanding preoccupation of mine. For exhaustive details, see MORAVCSIK 1965a, 1966b, 1966c (p. 388), 1970b, 1971a (p. 58), 1972a (p. 235), and 1974c. The Publication Committee of the Division of Particles and Fields of the American Physical Society is initiating centralized distribution of preprints in particle physics (mentioned in the first section of this chapter). My campaign for this cause has, however, been amply reinforced by concurring opinions from a variety of sources. PRICE 1965c (p. 10) states: "Detailed investigations by the American Psychological Association have now clearly proved that much of the communication of research results is done long before formal publication." For other relevant work by the same author, see PRICE 1965c (p. 10) and 1969d (p. 92). SAAVEDRA 1973 presents a supporting opinion from a scientist in an LDC.

New techniques in communications are described in the literature. Microfilm techniques are advocated in NAS 1971f (p. 5) in the context of Colombian chemistry. Microfiche is described in MORAVCSIK 1974c. The potential of Telex is demonstrated in NAS 1970a, b with regard to Argentina. Computer-based information retrieval systems are mentioned in MORAVCSIK 1972b.

The contention that material on science policy is not sufficiently available in LDCs is echoed by ZAHLAN 1972c which urges the UN to distribute more information on the relationship of science, technology, and development. National and international organizations, such as UNESCO, OECD, and OAS, do produce some high quality material (see, for example, ACS 1966 and OAS 1972, p. 27). Access to it, however, is not easy. Even in the US, the documents are mainly available only at one outlet; the average scientist's awareness of the existence of such publications (let alone his acquaintance with them) is virtually zero. (This is partly a result of the general attitude of scientists toward science policy, discussed in detail in chapter 6.) Furthermore, material on science policy is widely scattered among innumerable journals, reports, and other documents (seldom catalogued under "science policy"). One purpose of this book is to improve access to this type of material.

Problems concerning books are mentioned in MORAVCSIK 1972b (p. 235). The Franklin program of book translations produces copies of translations for LDCs. NAS 1966 (p. 66) mentions other programs which provide books for LDCs. One of the largest is the Books for Asia program operated by the Asia Foundation (see ASIA 1972b and BOOKS 1973). Operating in 19 Asian countries, it distributed some 11 million books and some 1.5 million journals between 1954 and 1973. The rate of distribution is now about 750,000 books per year, of which about 20% are in the natural sciences; most of the latter are textbooks superseded and out of print. The budget of the operation is about $200,000 a year and is provided by the Asia Foundation. While the absolute size of this program is commendable, the following calculation shows that it is only a beginning. If we assume a modest 10 libraries in each country, and 10 disciplines in the natural sciences, the average donation at present is perhaps 75 science books per discipline per library per year. Since a functional library should contain at least several thousand books in each scientific discipline, this method alone would take several decades to satisfy the need (even if it could supply all types of scientific publications).

A number of other "book aid" organizations operate on a smaller scale. For example, the Darien Book Aid Plan (DARIEN 1973) has shipped 950 tons of books to 100 countries over 25 years, a significant fraction of them in the sciences. "Operation Bookshelf," "Reader's Service," and "The International Book Project" are examples of other book-sending organizations in the US. Within the scientific community, CIEP, collaborating with ICTP, has organized a project to send surplus physics journals to institutions in LDCs.

Perhaps it would be useful to mention briefly some of the problems that arose in connection with the publication of this book, since they may be characteristic of material pertaining to LDCs. It was evident in advance that the sales of a book on this subject would not pay for the time spent by the author in writing it, so I first attempted to obtain outside support. Scores of governmental

and private foundations were approached with a uniformly negative result. Most organizations were not interested in sponsoring
books, or science development was not within the range of their
activities. Finally, the problem was "solved" by my working 70
hours per week for a year. (Since the book was written after all,
perhaps the foundations and agencies were right in refusing my
request.)

The second problem was to find a publisher for the book. I decided at the outset to have the book published only under circumstances which would make it easily available to potential readers in
the LDCs. In other words, the book should be available for a low
price payable in local currency in all LDCs. Since most publishers
in the ACs are unable to meet those conditions because of the high
cost of producing a book in the ACs, and because of their inexpe-
rience in marketing outside the ACs, I again approached various
agencies and foundations to obtain a subsidy for the publication of
the book. The result of this search was similarly negative: some organizations publish only internal studies while others were not interested in the sciences or LDCs. At the same time I approached
scores of publishers, again receiving negative replies. All this took
place before the book was completed. The publishers, agencies, and
and foundations made their decision on the basis of a brief outline
of the book-to-be.

Finally, quite by chance, I came in contact with the International
Development Research Center at Indiana University, whose director, William Siffin, had a special interest in problems of science
and technology in LDCs. The result was the publication of this
book by the International Development Research Center.

Though the story has a "happy ending," it illustrates some of
the barriers which hinder effective communication with LDCs. As
mentioned before, these barriers are not intentionally built by
"saboteurs." They are simply natural hurdles that nobody has had
the energy, devotion, and vision to remove. This pattern is characteristic of most matters pertaining to the building of science in
LDCs.

Personal contacts between scientists in LDCs and colleagues in
ACs must be encouraged. The importance of such personal inter-
action is widely recognized (see, for example, UN 1969, p. 19, or
CLARKE 1971, p. 45). Discussion of invisible colleges first ap-
peared in scholarly analyses of the structure of science such as
PRICE 1965c (p. 10); it has now found its way into writings on

science development. Various other aspects of personal contacts are dealt with in MORAVCSIK 1966c (p. 388), maintaining contact with former students now returned to LDCs; MORAVCSIK 1971a (p. 62), joint research projects between scientists in ACs and and LDCs; and MORAVCSIK 1973f, benefits from development of personal friendships. The visitors' registry operated by CIEP mentioned in the first section of this chapter is described in MORAVCSIK 1970b, 1971a (p. 62), 1972a (p. 231), 1974c, and 1974d. Proposals for itinerant lecturers who would visit LDCs are presented in MORAVCSIK 1970b. The idea of brief trips by scientists from ACs to institutions in LDCs is urged in MORAVCSIK 1970b and 1971a (p. 60). This proposal was incorporated into the SEED program, financed by AID and run by NSF, which provides travel grants to US scientists who visit LDCs for one year. Very short trips (a few days in duration) by senior US chemists were part of the NAS-Brazil chemistry program (see NAS 1972b, p. 10, and 1973b, pp. 4-6). BFS 1971 and 1972 give a total count of US exchange visitors abroad; however, scientists are not distinguished from those in other fields. ZAHLAN 1970 (p. 14) reports a program of visitors arranged jointly by universities in Cairo and Beirut, a rare example of LDCs taking the initiative in this area. ZAHLAN 1972c (p. 42) comments on the frequently poor interaction between visiting "experts" and the local scientific community. His remarks are specifically oriented toward UN agencies, such as IAEA, which now send about 300 such experts per year to LDCs (see IAEA 1973a, pp. 11-13, and 1973b, pp. 22, 53, 67-69). The OAS, which works on a regional basis in Latin America (and hence might send an expert from one Latin American country to another), has a program of similar size: between 1968 and 1971 it sent out 204 experts in basic sciences, 101 experts in applied sciences, and 120 experts in technological development (OAS 1972, pp. 10-16, 19). For the opportunity to register for longer stays in LDCs, see MORAVCSIK 1971a (p. 63), 1972a (p. 232), and 1972d. An eloquent general discussion of the importance of travel, personal contacts, and exchange of personnel can be found in ZIMAN 1969 (pp. 361-66).

The most acute problem in extended foreign travel for LDC scientists is the lack of temporary positions for them. UN 1970b (p. 13) stresses the importance of mobility and urges the creation of visiting appointments. Similar appeals are made in UN 1971a (p. 50), MORAVCSIK 1974c, and PRICE 1965c (p. 15). BFS 1971 and 1972 give the number of exchange visitors *to* the US, but again it is not broken down into fields. Some international organizations award fellowships to scientists in LDCs for visits abroad. In the regional context, between 1968 and 1971 OAS awarded 352 fellowships in applied science and 257 in technology (some of these may have gone to regional centers in the recipient's own country). In 1972, IAEA awarded training fellowships to 513 candidates from 61 countries and regional organizations, each candidate averaging six months of training (IAEA 1973a, pp. 11-13, 63, and 1973b, pp. 32, 53). NAS 1971e (p. 18) urges the establishment of such opportunities for Colombian mathematicians, particularly for younger ones. To improve the efficiency of short visits to ACs by scientists from LDCs, I have advocated a registry for them which would match them with institutions interested in hosting such visitors (MORAVCSIK 1972a, p. 231).

The idea of bilateral links is certainly not new: various versions exist in the literature. (See, for example, ALLISON 1960, concerning "lend-lease" to Egypt and MORAVCSIK 1971a, p. 57; 1972a, p. 232; 1972b; and 1974c outlining the activities of CIEP in this area.) In MORAVCSIK 1973g (p. 107), a table illustrates bilateral links of Brazil, Indonesia, Republic of Korea, Nigeria, and Turkey. SCHROEDER 1973 (p. 57) mentions a link between Canada and Brazil. The most extensive survey of such links can be found in UNESCO 1969a, though by now it is somewhat out of date. There is general agreement that bilateral links are desirable: UN 1971a (p. 50) praises the concept while TASK 1970 (p. 20) singles it out as a worthwhile objective (citing the Executive Corps as an example).

Perhaps the most interesting work on bilateral links is GLYDE 1972 which reports an in-depth study of such links between 16 pairs of groups, one set in Britain and one in Thailand. Though working with a small sample, this unusually careful and intelligent study was able to reach some tentative conclusions concerning conditions which promote the success of such links: (1) links should be initiated by direct contact between individuals in the two groups, not through an intermediary; (2) objectives should be set by the LDC; (3) personnel from the AC should visit repeatedly for short periods of time rather than for one long stretch (the importance of recurrent visits is also stressed in MORAVCSIK 1972a, p. 232); (4) funding for links should be given directly to the institutions in question rather than being administered from outside on an item-by-item basis; and (5) small links tend to be more successful than large ones (GLYDE 1972, pp. 1, 2). Glyde also remarks, however, that no single factor is absolutely dominant in guaranteeing success. For some background on dual appointments, see MORAVCSIK 1971a (p. 61) and 1972b. (For a further examination, see chapter 7.)

Detailed information on ICTP can be found in SALAM 1965a, 1966, and 1968 and, to a lesser extent, in UN 1971a (p. 50), MORAVCSIK 1970b, 1972a (p. 230), 1974c, and JONES 1971 (p. 150). When the creation of ICTP was discussed in the early 1960s, some (including myself) suggested that it be located in an LDC. The decision to locate it in Italy was influenced primarily by a very generous offer of financial support from the Italian government; no LDC considered could possibly have matched that commitment. A similar institution, ICIPE, is described in BULLETIN 1972 and is mentioned in JONES 1971 (pp. 92, 190).

MORAVCSIK 1972b and 1974c urge the location of some international scientific meetings in LDCs. JONES 1971 (p. 150) mentions the problem of meetings, and ZAHLAN 1969a (p. 10) urges that Arab scientists be given the opportunities to attend such meetings. Some international organizations arrange their own meetings. For example, IAEA held 14 such meetings in 1972-73, with about 2,500 participants from 65 countries. UNESCO supports large international organizations of scientists (like the ICSU) which stimulate many meetings; UNESCO pays half the "organizational" costs of such meetings (RODERICK 1962, p. 217). UNESCO has arranged several regional meetings to discuss science development in certain groups of countries, such as the Lagos conference in Africa (see, for example, UNESCO 1965b). These have almost always been held in an LDC.

Summer schools are established channels for catching up on the latest developments; ZAHLAN 1969a (p. 10) urges that Arab scientists be sent to such seminars. CLAF has played an important role in Latin America by organizing a series of seminars and meetings among the physicists of the region. Another creation of the scientific community is the group of Latin American Schools of Physics.

Where adjacent countries have a common tradition and political antagonisms do not play a major role, regional science development can be very effective. Possibilities are regional seminars (MORAVCSIK 1970b) or regional research centers (MORAVCSIK 1966c,

p. 387, and 1972a, p. 230). OAS, which works primarily on a regional basis, is arranging such seminars in Latin America (OAS 1972, pp. 6, 11, 12, 17, 30, 27). NAS 1971e (p. 18) urges regional collaboration in mathematics between Colombia and neighboring countries. Collaboration is also recommended for African countries (see, for example, NAS 1965b, p. 53). Foreign visitors or representatives of the worldwide scientific community can often contribute to the formation of such regional groups since they are not involved in the petty rivalries that may exist even in areas where severe animosity is not present (MORAVCSIK 1973f and 1971a, p. 64). Scientists' organizations have had little impact on science development mainly because they are usually satisfied with oratory. (For a discussion of the Pugwash meetings, for example, see GLASS 1968.) Some of the UN special agencies are active in certain areas, as mentioned above; for example, UNESCO supports meetings, provides documentation services, publishes dictionaries, tries to standardize publications, and donates coupons to LDCs which can be used to buy books (see BOK 1948; BULLETIN 1964, p. 32; and RODE-RICK 1962, p. 216). IAEA, in addition to sponsoring experts and fellowships, operates the International Nuclear Information System and issues a large number of scientific reports (IAEA 1972, 1973a, and 1973b). Further discussion of UNESCO and IAEA can be found in chapter 7. Similar activities are pursued in other UN special agencies to the extent that they deal with science. Yet the UN agencies are not only specialized within science, but also quite isolated from the day-to-day research work of individual scientists in LDCs. Their efforts, therefore, make only a small dent in the overall problem of scientific communication.

Five

Scientific Research

Research is the essence of science. Other scientific activities—
teaching, organization, popularization, communication, etc.—are
auxiliary to the *raison d'etre* of a scientist, the creation of new scientific knowledge, or the transfer of existing scientific knowledge
into new realms and applications. Scientific research is an end in
iteslf, a conversion of the creativity of scientists into new understanding and capability.

Research has many of the same external justifications as science
itself; hence, many of the points discussed in chapter 1 apply here
as well. For example, support of research can be justified on the
basis of its power to infuse into the people the spirit of innovation
as well as its material benefits in terms of economic well-being.

In the context of national development plans, or the plans of a
single company for that matter, research is often discussed in economic terms. Science is a powerful force in economic development.
However, research and development should be considered a catalyst rather than an ordinary input factor because of the subtle and
sometimes indirect relationship between research and production.
Research is inexpensive compared with the whole production process, and in LDCs the proportionate cost may be even less than in
ACs. Thus, it is advisable to institute research in LDCs even in the
early stages of development.

At this point, it is necessary to clarify the concepts of science
and technology. They are often mentioned together, and the distinctions are not always clear. This problem arises for two reasons.
First, when talking about science (basic and applied) and technology, we are to some extent dealing with a continuum of concepts
(or perhaps with a group of concepts which overlap and contain

borderline cases). This is a common occurrence in classifications; when a continuum is described in terms of a group of discrete concepts, there is always some objection. Second, the attempt is frequently made to classify these activities in terms of their results. Even an abstract piece of scientific research may eventually help make gadgets, and a direct technological development can contribute to the growth of abstract science.

Instead of classifying activities in terms of their results, therefore, one should classify them in terms either of the motivation behind them or the method used to pursue them. In terms of motivation, a scientist is interested in generating knowledge while a technologist is interested in creating a new product or process. In terms of method, publications in the sciences constitute an end product while in technology they are at best a tool. Thus, patterns of communication in science are quite different from those in technology (see chapter 4).

Similarly confusing is the interaction between science and technology. The exact nature and time scale of the interactions are the subject of debate. Some feel, for example, that the link is rather tenuous; many examples are cited in which technological advances were made in the absence of corresponding scientific understanding. However, the examples cited in support of this thesis are usually not recent ones. It is true that as long as technological products have depended on that part of science which deals with the small segment of nature directly accessible to our senses and experience, an empirical rather than a theoretical approach could often result in technological success. More recently, however, many technological products have come to depend on an understanding of natural phenomena not directly accessible to our senses and everyday experience. Studies must, therefore, be made in a systematic and theoretical way rather than by direct empirical manipulations. For this reason, the most significant technological achievements in recent years have depended heavily on relatively recent scientific research. The transistor, the laser, nuclear technology, and computers are but a few examples. In fact, the cycle of interaction between science and technology appears to be shortening: the time interval between a scientific discovery and its technological use may be only a year or two. Coupled with the fact that the most modern technological capability is often the economically most rewarding one, this circumstance adds special urgency to the need for LDCs to attain scientific autarky.

At the same time, research in science is heavily dependent on technology. As science explores realms of nature farther from direct human experiences, technical equipment and processes are needed to induce an experiment and to convert the results of that experiment into signals that our senses can detect. Thus, science and technology are interdependent. Unfortunately, a frequent problem in LDCs is the lack of a reciprocal relationship between science and technology. Building bridges between the two is therefore an important task for LDCs.

Classifications within science produce another set of concepts which are frequently classified by results rather than by the intention of the practitioner or the method used. Since this invariably adds to confusion, some critics call for the elimination of any distinctions. Yet, in practice, the use of certain distinctions makes it easier to build a well-balanced scientific infrastructure.

The most convenient classification is a dichotomy in which one concept is basic, fundamental, or "pure" scientific research. In terms of intention, basic research is characterized by the researcher's motivation of simply acquiring new scientific knowledge for its own sake. Of course, the researcher may hope that discovery will also benefit mankind materially through some technological applications, the method used in the work will not be determined by those hopes. Science is not a matter of cranking an automatic mechanism that spits out new discoveries. When engaged in research, a scientist must use judgment, make choices based on guesses, choose problems to work on, etc. In doing this, a person in basic research is influenced primarily by a thirst for new knowledge. The second concept is that of applied research in which an investigation is undertaken with some specific application as the ultimate goal. The judgment of the researcher is based on the attainment of this goal. The methods are not very different, but one can cautiously make some distinctions. Applied research tends to be broader in scope, more interdisciplinary, and more reliant on teamwork; problems in applied research are defined "from the outside" and are not likely to line up neatly along conventional disciplinary lines (see chapter 2).

In classifying research by intent, one must allow for the frequent possibility that what is basic research for one person is applied research for someone else. This situation has given rise to the intermediate classification of "oriented basic research" in which basic researchers are supported in work thought to be applicable by others (usually those supplying the funds). Since any science is likely to be eventually applicable, one gets into a discussion of intervals of time. With respect to method, however, this additional grouping contributes little conceptual clarification.

Given the concepts of basic and applied research, we are ready to approach the thorny question of how much of either an LDC should undertake. The situation is peculiar: from qualitative discussions of the issue one would think that the views of some debaters are miles apart. Indeed, a few claim that no basic research whatever should be done in an LDC. Most observers, however, agree that *some* basic research is appropriate. Some concede reluctantly, while others enthusiastically praise basic research. When the discussion gets down to particulars, however, there is a surprising degree of agreement. Of the total R & D effort of an LDC, about one-tenth can be spent in support of basic research.

Further confusion arises when one compares this recipe with what actually occurs in LDCs. Many commentators believe that LDCs perform only basic research, and applied research is almost entirely neglected. However, evidence indicates that most LDCs perform much more applied research than basic, the latter being 10-20% of the whole. Thus, the problem appears not to exist at all.

Yet the situation is not that simple. There are two reasons why seasoned observers of LDCs develop the impression that basic research is dominant. First, all too often the best indigenous manpower goes exclusively into basic research. As a result, the scientists who are conspicuous within the worldwide scientific community and are likely to be known by observers are in basic research. (Indeed, one often sees applied research done so poorly that it has no application; it then tends to be classified as basic research.) Second, though the ratio between basic and applied research is the desired one, the connection between the two remains undeveloped; hence, the effectiveness of both, particularly applied research, is greatly lessened. It is the improvement of quality in applied research and the establishment of links between basic and applied which should be the primary targets of attention, not the redressing of numerical ratios between the two.

Some approximate guidelines have been devised for the amount of support to be allocated to R & D as a whole and to basic research in particular: the estimates are 1% and 0.1% of the GNP, respectively. (This problem is discussed in detail in chapter 6.) Most LDCs fall far below these guidelines. If, in trying to reach these goals, basic research happens to forge ahead more rapidly than R&D as a whole, the former should not be penalized and held back. Progress is not made by restraining those who are successful but by encouraging those who have not reached their goal.

There is considerable discussion in the literature and in governmental pronouncements of the "relevance" of scientific research. What research is supposed to be relevant to is often stated in only the haziest terms. As a matter of common sense in scientific organization and administration, however, it is important to note that the best minds in science are repelled by very narrow constraints of relevance imposed on them. To maintain the creative activity of such people, it is necessary to minimize the actual enforcement of these constraints, though it might be permissible to voice them as part of political rhetoric or public relations. This has been widely recognized by science organizers from the General Electric Company to the People's Republic of China.

One may ask whether it would be better for some LDCs simply to import whatever science and technology they need. The conclusion in Chapter 1 was that if LDCs restrict themselves to importation, then their long-term development will suffer. Even the transfer of science and technology requires indigenous personnel trained in research who are capable of receiving the imported knowledge and adapting it to local conditions. Some types of science and technology needed in a particular LDC may not exist at all, and ACs may have no interest in developing them. In other cases, importing technology is only possible at a prohibitive price. If the special circumstances existing in a given country are to be properly dealt with, then an appropriate scientific infrastructure and technological complex must be developed. Thus, importation alone is not the answer.

Some importation is necessary and advisable. In the sciences, communication is an indispensable element in research (explained in chapter 4). The import (as well as export) of scientific ideas is part of the normal activity of any country including the most advanced ones. The transfer of technology is a more complex and selective process, but it is not the concern of this book (some sources are given in the references).

Scientific research is usually carried out in one of three types of institutions: universities, research institutes or laboratories, and industrial research centers. There is much debate over where research in LDCs should be located and how it should be distributed among these types of institutions. Again, there is more disagreement in principle than in practice. Many believe that universities should be the primary focus of scientific research because of their constant cantact with the next generation of scientists, their relative intellectual independence, and their often less cumbersome administrative structure. Yet circumstances often demand a different procedure. In some LDCs, universities are calcified skeletons with no organic content and little hope of change. In such a situation, a new organization must assume the task of developing the country's scientific manpower and undertaking scientific research. Furthermore, universities tend to concentrate on basic research; applied research must therefore be assigned to a different locale where interdisciplinary activities and teamwork are more compatible with the organizational structure. In practice, research in many LDCs is distributed among all three types of institutions. The bulk is usually concentrated in governmental research institutes and laboratories while the universities carry a much smaller fraction of the load, and industrial research is in a state of infancy.

The primary problem is again not so much the ratios between these segments as the lack of interaction among them. It is often a matter of absence of tradition: the various types of institutions may be far apart geographically which, in the absence of functional transportation, prevents frequent personal visits. Institutional channels for interchange of personnel are usually absent as well. In ACs, university scientists often serve as consultants to industrial or governmental laboratories. In LDCs this very seldom happens; when it does, it can create tension between the university and the industrial laboratory (the former claiming, sometimes with justification, that faculty members neglect university duties in order to earn additional income from consulting arrangements). Nevertheless, such consulting arrangements must be developed in some way in order to establish a durable rapport between academic and industrial science.

What should be the function of science in a university? Universities were once primarlly considered depositories of knowledge, not necessarily generators of the same. But a person who simply absorbs scientific knowledge without participating in research is a scientific scholar, not a scientist. In most ACs, universities have become centers for producing both scientists and science. This dual role of universities is not fully appreciated even in ACs. Some state legislatures in the US frown upon the pursuit of research in state universities. They tolerate it only because the Federal government makes huge payments to the universities (officially for "overhead") to support such research. In some LDCs, there is no enlightened federal government to foster this dual role; universities become intellectually moribund and lose their ability to provide functional education.

It is generally conceded that basic research is well suited to the university environment. There is more of a debate on whether universities should pursue applied research. Universities should not subordinate their teaching functions to the financial gains that might be derived from conducting industrial research. Yet, a judicious selection of applied projects can give breadth to the education of students who otherwise tend to develop one-sided views about various types of research. Similarly, support of academic research by local industry helps strengthen relations.

Governmental research laboratories and institutes have their own advantages and drawbacks. They are generally free of pressure for short-term applicability of research results, but they are often isolated from the criticism and standards of the international scientific community. In addition, they are saddled with an extremely complicated bureaucratic system and a type of career pattern deadly for doing science. Another drawback of such laboratories is the fact that they are devoted entirely to research; employees who are not suited or are no longer suited to that activity have no other outlet for their energies. This creates a severe problem of deadwood—some laboratories become overburdened with personnel who are scientists only in name. In principle, governmental institutions can play an essential role in creating an intermediate stage between academic science and industry; in some countries this has been achieved to some extent.

Industrial research in LDCs is usually insignificant. LDCs often attribute this to the fact that their industry consists primarily of subsidiaries of companies located in ACs. These companies prefer to do R&D in their main branches because of lower costs and availability of outstanding personnel. It is true that most companies have such a policy; yet, many LDCs have been developing locally owned and operated industries in addition to the foreign subsidiaries, and these lack research facilities as well. Furthermore, local governments have a fair degree of control over subsidiaries, and it would be possible to require by law that subsidiaries conduct a certain amount of indigenous research. The main difficulty, therefore, lies not in causes external to LDCs, but in the lack of local realization of the need for research in modern industrial processes.

International (or multinational) companies would be well-advised, from the point of view of self-interest, to strengthen their participation in the building of indigenous science in countries where their subsidiaries are located, even if a strict efficiency analysis did not recommend such action. Research is inexpensive and sponsoring it on the small scale that usually exists in LDCs is even less expensive. There are examples of international companies which sponsor local research.

How should an LDC decide which areas of research to develop? Some claim that no country can deviate significantly from the international pattern of scientific research: if it did, it would "give away" too much information in favored areas and would fall behind in neglected areas. This contention, however, seldom applies to LDCs. Instead, the following rules are suggested:

(1) Local advantages should be utilized. These may be geographical, climatological, astronomical, based on some easily available raw material, etc.

(2) Intrinsic costs should be compared; some areas of science are inherently more expensive than others.

(3) Potentials for application should be compared; some sciences, viewed from our perspective, are more remote from short-term application than others. However, such judgments are unreliable. Nuclear physics, extremely esoteric in the 1930s, suddenly produced one of the main technologies in the 1940s and 1950s.

(4) Educational objectives should be kept in mind. Some areas of science are better suited for educating students than others where, for example, specialization is too narrow.

(5) Attention should be given to the general considerations for determining scientific choices in terms of the extrinsic and intrinsic potential of the subdisciplines. These considerations also apply to science in LDCs, though they should not be the exclusive determinants in the selection of research areas.

These guidelines (and others mentioned in the second section of this chapter) can be used in making a list of preferred areas of research. There is, however, one consideration with which all these criteria pale in comparison—the availability of outstanding people. Scientific activity centers around creative individuals. Such individuals in the existing scientific manpower of an LDC are an asset that must be utilized. At the beginning, scientific activity is weak, critical mass is questionable, and the indigenous scientific community consists mainly of inexperienced researchers with a lack of leadership and direction. The presence of an outstanding person, able to serve as a focal point for exciting scientific activity, is invaluable and should largely influence the areas of research supported in that country. Such persons will generally have definite ideas of what scientific problems they consider interesting and should be supported in research on those problems unless it is financially impossible.

In this context, it is well to emphasize again the crucial role of equality. There is a strong temptation in LDCs to sacrifice quality for the sake of quantity in the hope that when quantitative targets have been met, quality can then be improved. Nothing is further from the truth. When a low standard has been established, it stubbornly perpetuates itself. Scientists are created who are unsure of themselves and try to maintain their positions by all available means. Second-rate research is not worth doing in any case. Some research may turn out to be second-rate, but to aim at this as a matter of policy is unpardonable. Part of the effort to improve quality has been the establishment of so-called centers of excellence in various LDCs, sometimes in countries with an already sizable infrastructure of universities.

People are the most important component of scientific research, but they are not the only requirement. Research cannot be done without equipment. This is seldom a major problem. Donor agencies from abroad like to supply equipment which represents a once-and-for-all expenditure, is easy to procure, and is conspicuous in terms of public relations. In laboratories in LDCs one often sees equipment standing idle either for lack of repair and spare parts or for lack of use (the result of quite different causes). There are cases where research in LDCs is hampered primarily by lack of equipment, but such cases are relatively rare. Lack of spare parts is a much more serious problem. Local supplies are not available, and purchasing spare parts from abroad involves foreign currency, an immense amount of red tape, and huge delays. This can be a serious obstacle to the pursuance of scientific research which is to some extent a competitive undertaking with potential competitors around the world. Facilities and personnel for repair of equipment are also often scarce in LDCs. Cultural preconceptions frequently inhibit the development of an ample supply of capable technicians: a number of LDCs note in their development plans that the ratio of technicians to scientists is much too low even for a small scientific community.

The communication of results is an integral part of research. In fact, publications are taken as a measure of the output of scientific activity (explained in detail in chapter 6). In applied research, however, patterns of publication are different from those in basic research. This is particularly true in industrial research where the end product is often not an article for a journal but an internal report. Such differences in patterns should be kept in mind when one compares the output of university publications with those of governmental laboratories or industrial research centers. In technological research, the result is often a patent, and patent counts are sometimes used to measure technological activity. Unfortunately, in all these measures, quantity takes precedence over quality.

Organizational aspects of research are often crucial to the effectiveness of the activity. This will be discussed in more detail in chapter 6, but it is appropriate here to comment on the civil service system in the context of scientific research. Job security and quality of performance are opposite ideals. Recently, the pendulum has swung far in the direction of the former. The civil service system accommodates the tendency perfectly: it is a one-way sieve which retains the incompetent and unmotivated while releasing the competent and ambitious who are eager to find more rewarding and challenging environments. In some types of activities, this results "only" in added cost and increased annoyance. In other types of activities which strongly depend on quality, the result is complete failure. In many LDCs, perceptive obesrvers have been urging that scientific manpower be placed outside the civil service system. In newer countries, with relatively little vested interest, this is still possible. In older countries, with a sizable manpower already under the umbrella, the task of reform has become practically impossible.

There are a number of international programs to assist research in LDCs. It is certainly true that ACs have paid relatively little attention to research problems of particular interest to LDCs (for understandable though not necessarily condonable reasons). Thus, international assistance seldom takes the form of actual cooperation in research in which LDCs are also interested. Instead, assistance consists of programs to foster research efforts in LDCs. (Much of this will be discussed in chapter 7; some specific items are presented in the second section of this chapter.)

Our ignorance of how to develop science far exceeds our ignorance in specific scientific disciplines. Yet, more effort is devoted to scientific research than to research on science development. Furthermore, most of the research on science development is carried out by scientists and other types of researchers in ACs. The number of people in LDCs who are seriously engaged in reserach on science development in LDCs is extremely small, as illustrated by the list of references in this book.

Background and Comments

The various roles of scientific research are often discussed in the literature. OECD 1968a (p. 139) emphasizes that research in the sciences is an end in itself, and production of knowledge is the result of such research (p. 15). SABATO 1970 (p. 192) stresses the element of creativity in this process while ZAHLAN 1972c values the spirit of innovation through research. GARCIA 1966 (p. 13) describes research as the "bridge [over] the gap that separates us from the rich countries." RAM 1968 (p. 6) points out the contribution of research to economic growth. PIRIE 1967 (p. 6) is more specifically utilitarian in saying that "useful research has three primary objects: to ensure that a country has a tolerable population, to ensure that the population can be properly fed, and to ensure that the people can live and move in reasonable comfort." Thus, there is a broad spectrum of justifications for research in an LDC. CLARKE 1971 (p. 6) contends that "the argument that all research ultimately benefits everyone is known to be false." I doubt that the argument ever existed in that categorical form. Nevertheless, the belief that virtually all good quality research will have some beneficial effect on most of us sooner or later remains the cornerstone of public support for research.

The particular function of research as an economic force is generally recognized by economists. PRICE 1965b (p. 53) talks of science as a directly productive force in society while UNESCO 1970b

(p. 12) points out the catalyzing nature of research. With regard to cost, it is noteworthy that while 92% of all scientists are in ACs, 98% of R&D expenditures originate in ACs (OECD 1971c, p. 57). The difference is perhaps attributable to the higher specific cost of research in ACs. DE HEMPTINNE 1963 (p. 243) estimates that the cost of research leading to a new products is distributed as follows: pure fundamental research, 1; oriented fundamental research, 3; applied research, 6; development work, 100. According to UN 1970b (p. 7), research accounts for 5-10% of the total cost of an innovation (though in some sophisticated industries, such as aircraft or electronics, the fraction devoted to research can be as large as 30%, WILLIAMS 1964, p. 96). RAY 1969 points out that in LDCs research may be an even smaller fraction of the total cost of a product because raw materials are likely to be more expensive. With regard to the financial return on research, NAS 1966 (p. 51) states that agricultural research in the US shows a 100% return *annually* on the cumulative investment in it. Contrary to this is the argument in COOPER 1971, for example, that the analytical methods and practices of economics are not appropriate for LDCs, because of the very different circumstances prevailing there.

Research may not show tangible effects immediately. WU 1970 (pp. 443-52, 458, 459) demonstrates that economic progress in the People's Republic of China has thus far depended very little on R&D performed in that country during the same time period. It is also conjectured that R&D will increasingly pay off in coming years.

That the concepts of science and technology are hazy in many people's minds is illustrated, for example, by GRUBER 1961 in which numerous contributors dwell on their ideas and expectations with respect to science and technology. (In fact, some of the disenchantment in ACs concerning science and technology can be traced to these false images and expectations.) Much of the development literature containing "science and technology" in the title deals exclusively with technology; "science" is attached either through ignorance or for decoration.

To clarify these questions, de Solla Price has repeatedly stressed the radically different attitudes of science and technology with regard to publications. He describes science as papyrocentric and technology as papyrophobic (PRICE 1969d, pp. 94-96; 1966, p. 91; and 1968). The terms are perhaps too restrictive—technologists do not dislike reading papers, just writing them, while scientists prefer writing articles to reading them.

The interaction of science and technology is rather subtle (NAS 1967, p. 13). Explanations can be found, for example in JONES 1971 (p. 6), PRICE 1972a, and 1965a (the latter concisely explains de Solla Price's somewhat extreme point of view on the separation of science and technology, p. 568). Some support for the latter is expressed in COPISAROW 1970 (p. 12). For differing views emphasizing instead the close interconnection, see NAS 1967 (pp. 29, 36-40) and GANDHI 1969 (p. 7) who assert that the innovation cycle is constantly shortening. Whatever the link may be, it is largely missing in LDCs, as stressed UN 1970b (pp. 4, 5) and RAM 1968 (p. 6). PHILIPPINES 1966 describes a workshop dealing with this particular problem. USMANI 1971 (p. 11) declares that the linking of science and technology must be a cardinal principle of any science policy.

In what order should scientific and technological activities be developed? NAS 1973a (p. xv) argues that the traditional sequence of research, development, and engineering might actually be reversed in an LDC. The country might first attain the capability of engineering an already developed product and later acquire the ability to develop with research being started at an even later stage. While this may be feasible, development of all three skills must start simultaneously since it might not take the same length of time to bring each to a functional level.

The practice of classifying science has a big literature. In UNESCO 1965b (p. 102), Auger defines pure, oriented fundamental, and applied research; the same classification appears in UN 1970b (p. 9). ZIMAN 1969 (p. 352) uses the terms "potentially applicable" for the intermediate class. IVIC 1971 shows that this classification is also used in practice. Others distinguish only basic and applied research, such as OAS 1972 (pp. 6, 10-23). That these are not altogether distinct is stressed in ZIMAN 1969 (p. 353) and NAS 1967 (p. 5); the somewhat parallel classification into extensive and intensive research is mentioned in the latter (p. 26). Some feel that there should be no such classification, or that it should be greatly deemphasized. Examples are WEISS 1973; NAS 1971b (pp. 1, 6, 10), dealing with Ghana; NAS 1965b (p. 1), in the context of Nigeria; GARCIA 1966 (p. 13); and NAS 1967 (p. 339) claiming that such distinctions are futile. Nevertheless, classification is widely used.

NAS 1967 (p. 15) points out that applied research is in greater need of institutionalization than basic, and applied research is more interdisciplinary (p. 260). Which is more interesting and challenging is a matter of personal judgment. PIRIE 1967 (p. 68) quotes William Hardy on the subject: "You know, this applied science is just as interesting as pure science, and what's more it's a damned sight more difficult." For a particularly eloquent and comprehensive essay by Teller on the nature of applied science, see NAS 1967 (p. 365). ZIMAN 1973 urges that the whole spectrum of possibilities be displayed to all young scientists so they can make their own value judgments.

In the context of LDCs, the distinction between basic and applied research may be in some ways academic. In SHAH 1967 (p. 376), Muherjee cites a remark by Stevan Dedijer, a seasoned and often perceptively witty researcher in science development, that even applied research becomes pure research in developing countries because it has no application.

Is basic research needed in LDCs? If so, what should the proportions be? There is a relatively small minority claiming that LDCs need no basic research. In GHANA 1971 (p. 14), a government official states that "pure" research projects are a luxury in a developing country. MURIEL 1970 (p. 39) calls pure physics in the Phillippines a luxury; ORLEANS 1972 (p. 865) uses the same word to describe basic research in the People's Republic of China. ALLENDE 1972 (p. 40) states: "Research for the sake of research is a luxury that our countries on this continent cannot afford." WU 1970 (p. 80) quotes Ma Hsu-lun, the Minister of Education of the People's Republic of China in 1950: "Education must not commit the same old mistake of 'knowledge for knowledge's sake.' " (Policy in that country, while undergoing large fluctuations, has not been altogether inimical to basic research and most recently appears to allow even activities like elementary particle physics.)

Others, while not absolutely negative about basic research, are willing to allow it only grudgingly. BLACKETT 1967 (p. 309), SHILS 1961, and JONES 1971 (pp. 27-28) are some examples. See NAS 1973a (p. 47): "LDC institutions should strengthen their emphasis on applied research and development, often neglected at present in favor of more glamorous, basic research."

Still others, in contrast, place great emphasis on basic research in LDCs. OECD 1971c (p. 68) states that every country requires basic research, even if only a small amount. UNESCO 1970b (p. 21) stresses basic research as something important in itself. A particularly eloquent statement appears in OECD 1968a (pp. 76-77):

Although exploitation may be in a place distant from the point of original discovery . . . part of the investment in fundamental research is nevertheless retained by the community which makes it; it has in fact the even more important role of producing at its source a level of scientific and technological consciousness, that makes possible the rapid exploitation and improvement of technology and invention wherever they may be in the world. A strong and balanced fundamental research effort in a country enables in fact a dividend to be taken from the totality of world research and not just from that nation in question. It might be urged that a small country would do well to concentrate on applied research and live on the exploitation of research produced by the larger countries of the world. Such a policy would be doomed to failure since the country in question would quickly lack a general scientific consciousness of world advancement sufficient to allow it to select for application those advances specifically significant to its economy. It would also lack trained research men for advanced applied research and development. In fact, by neglecting fundamental research, a country would be condemning its own industry to obsolescence.

For other comments in favor of basic research, see MORAVCSIK 1972a (p. 189), 1964c (p. 165), and ZIMAN 1969 (p. 351). UN 1970b (pp. 9-12) stresses that basic research is needed even in the early stages of development. Udgoankar, in INDIA 1970 (p. 307), illustrates the benefits of basic physics research for India. It is emphasized in some sources that basic and applied research both have a role in LDCs (see NAS 1968d, p. 1, and SHAH 1967, pp. 369-70). In fact, claims ZAHLAN 1969a (p. 8), neither can advance without the other.

There are even observers who think LDCs should devote a larger fraction of their total R&D effort to basic research than do ACs (e.g., UNESCO 1970b, p. 17). In UNESCO 1964c (p. 21), a plan for Africa, it is suggested that about 20% of R&D expenditures should be devoted to basic research, higher than the average for ACs. ZAHLAN 1972c suggests about 25% for the Arab countries. Those figures, however, are on the high side of the spread of recommendations. USMANI 1971 (p. 5) suggests 10%. BLACKETT 1968 argues that since it is 10% for Britain, India should have the same figure. NAS 1966 (p. 52) recommends the same 10% for Peru. (Incidentally, the same source repeats the recommendation [p. 13] with the added remark that "only economically powerful countries . . . can justify, on purely economic grounds, the tremendous expense of pure research," apparently unaware that the percentage in the US and other ACs is not much different.) WEISS 1973 suggests 5-10%. NAS 1966 (p. 52) records a different suggestion: "As much basic research should be supported as could be managed without sacrifice of needed applied research," which in practice would virtually assure no basic research at all. Various sources actually agree quite well on the percentage of financial support to be devoted to basic research.

In comparison with this recommendation, what is the actual situation? One finds (JAPAN 1972, p. 46) that in ACs the percentage fluctuates between 10% (for the UK) and 24% (for Japan), generally hovering around 15%. NAS 1967 (p. 6) quotes 5% as the average figure for industry in the US. As for LDCs, SALCEDO 1972 (p. 180) and UNESCO 1970e (pp. 27, 31) indicate a figure of about 11% for the Philippines averaged for 1959-66; recently it has been declining somewhat. The same ratio applies to Philippine industry. MORAVCSIK 1973g (p. 16) reports 20% for the Republic of Korea. The figures supplied by ROCHE 1966 (p. 54) for Venezuela are somewhat difficult to interpret: 11% basic research, 4% development research, 22% applied research, and 63% "oriented fundamental research," "perhaps too ready a niche in which to classify oneself," as Roche remarks. PERES 1969 (pp. 34-40), surveying 14 Asian countries (excluding Japan, India, and Pakistan), finds that about 16% of the manpower is in basic research, but two-thirds of those teach rather than do research. Thus, a realistic figure for basic research in those countries would be considerably below 10%. Figures for the People's Republic of China are not easy to come by. LUBKIN 1972 (p. 23) and HAMBRAEUS 1972 (pp. 140-50) suggest that there is a strong concentration on applied research with some resources devoted to basic research (of which the synthesis of insulin is given as an example). Thus, the ratio appears to be similar. According to UN 1970b (p. 10), "UNESCO statistical studies on R&D show that the lower the per capita GNP in countries, the higher tends to be the amount of fundamental research in the total national expenditure on research and experimental development"; however, no figures are given. The report applauds this trend and claims that it "corresponds to the actual needs of developing countries at the present juncture." The trend cannot be very extensive, however, since MORAVCSIK 1973g (p. 94) shows that Nigeria (a country with a very low per capita GNP) spends 7% of its R&D resources in universities and the rest in governmental institutions. This division must roughly correspond to the ratio between basic and applied research.

Both ACs and LDCs spend 10-20% of their R&D resources on

basic research. As mentioned, this is not the impression one obtains from the tenor of the comments in the literature. In some cascs, these comments are coupled with elaborate theories about the causes of the alleged neglect of applied research in LDCs. For example, VARSAVSKY 1967 (p. 22) claims that ACs want to retard LDCs in their development. This "scientific colonialism" results in problems of interest to LDCs "remaining ignored while local talent is oriented toward questions which are currently fashionable in the highest level international research centers."

One should not be overly preoccupied with debates on the proper ratio of basic to applied research. The serious problems are in quite different areas, namely, the quality of research, cooperation between the two types of research, and the total amount spent on research and development. A biting formulation of the same opinion appears in ZAHLAN 1972c: "It is my observation that the wordy controversy between the pure and applied scientists usually occurs where people are doing neither." However, Zahlan does not depreciate the importance of the question; he urges clarification of the terms involved.

The words "relevance" and "priority" have become very prominent. NAS1965b (p. 8) calls for research on "problems relevant to [Nigeria]." ALLENDE 1972 (p. 40) welcomes "any research which represents a contribution to Chile." But in neither case are these concepts made explicit enough to serve as bases for science policy. Priorities in research areas are frequently determined by the efforts of energetic and successful science organizers and managers. NADER 1969, for example, deplores the fact that between 1962 and 1967 Pakistan spent 10 times as much on nuclear research as on jute or fishery research (the latter two earn much foreign exchange). The reasons are rather clear if one investigates the Pakistani scientific community in detail. The chairman of the PAEC in that period was an exceptional organizer and administrator who launched a general program to upgrade Pakistan's scientific manpower and research capacity. In contrast, the researchers concerned with jute or fish did not have an equally outstanding spokesman. Under the circumstances, a substantially different distribution of funds would probably have resulted in considerable waste and few results.

JONES 1971 (p. 27) and NAYUDAMMA1967 point out that users of research results are an important link in the research-development chain and require serious attention. For further comments on research priorities, see SHAH 1967 (p. 367), Pakistan and India; GOWON 1972 (p. 57), Nigeria; and NADER 1969 (p. 191), Egypt.

Externally imposed, narrow constraints on research can bring about an alienation of scientists. As noted in NAS 1967 (p. 42):

> It is ... relatively easy to invent ... terminology to label fundamental scientific work with ... legitimate "applied-sounding" words. But the unfortunate aspect of this is that, usually, the less the ability and integrity of the scientist the more willing he is to invent expedient labels for his work, so that the net effect of providing support preferentially for fields or projects that have the appearance of immediate social utility is to drive the best and most creative minds out.... The more narrowly the objectives ... are defined, the more likely it is to drive out the most creative workers.

The desire for transfer of science and technology is strong everywhere. ALLENDE 1972 (p. 31) states: "That is what we are fighting for: the transfer of science and technology." For other examples of this sentiment, see CALDER 1960; BLACKETT 1967 (p. 308); OECD 1968a (p. 73), in the case of Ireland; JONES 1971 (p. 11); and USMANI 1970. More than simple transfer is required, however, as pointed out in UNESCO 1970b (p. 13), UN 1971a (p. 70), and SHAH 1967 (p. 379). A primary requisite is an environment capable of receiving such imported science and technology. OECD 1968a (p. 103) and SIDDIQI point out that during the period when Japan was importing huge amounts of science and technology, it was also conducting a vigorous program to develop its own research capability. The importance of such a capability is illustrated by the experience of the General Electric Company with the tunnel diode (NAS 1967, p. 46). Further emphasis on the importance of technical ability to receive transferred technology can be found in UNESCO 1970a (p. 141), RAM 1968 (p. 14), BLACKETT 1968 (p. 21), ZAHLAN 1972c, and UN 1971a (p. 72). According to WU 1970 (p. 459), the People's Republic of China has had more success borrowing technology in nonagricultural sectors than in agriculture partly because of problems of reception and adaptation. BLACKETT 1963 emphasizes that some science and technology necessary for LDCs may not even be available in ACs. Importation alone is financially weakening as demonstrated by the export-import chart of technology in JONES 1971 (p. 13). PHILIPPINES 1969a (p. 34) calls for more indigenous research to make exports more competitive. There is also the problem of missed opportunities to borrow technology. WU 1970 (pp. 451-52) indicates that the People's Republic of China was concerned with salinity in 1961-65. During that period, the same problem was solved in Pakistan (SALAM 1965c).

Examples of literature on technology transfer in particular are NAS 1967 (pp. 347-56), JONES 1971 (pp. 21-26), and BARANSON 1969. The more general problem of "research transfer" is examined in ZIMAN 1969 (p. 357).

Discussions of the best institutional location for research emerge in the literature in various contexts. GARCIA 1966 (p. 13) argues strongly for universities while SAAVEDRA 1969 and MORAVCSIK 1972a (p. 218) urge that research also be supported outside the universities. Jealousies that may arise on the part of universities are illustrated in BHABHA 1966b. Similar stories could also be told in the context of Pakistan, particularly with respect to the universities and the PAEC. Sometimes the opposite situation exists, as described in RAY 1967a. In general, universities are regarded as the centers of basic research while governmental institutions concentrate on applied research (UN 1971a, p. 66). In the People's Republic of China, the Academy of Sciences is for the most part in charge of basic research while applied research is managed by both the Academy and other governmental agencies (WU 1970, p. 60). A survey of 14 Asian countries in Peres, PERES 1969 (p. 34) gives the following distribution: 83% governmental institutions, 3% industry, 12% universities, and 2% other.

BLOUNT 1965 (p. 340) points out the lack of research tradition in Spanish universities. PRICE 1969c (p. 6) describes the university system as "paying for teaching, getting research free." UNESCO 1970a (p. 122) stresses the importance of academic freedom in research. An excellent summary of the role of universities in African research is provided by Njoku in UNESCO 1965b (pp. 100-105). GARCIA 1966 (p. 14) discusses the role of research in the South American university. UNESCO 1964a (pp. 45, 49) urges cooperation between universities and research institutes. Research in Turkish universities, rather scant and consisting mainly of theses, is described in a case study on OECD 1969 (p. 203). NAS 1973b reports the establishment of 10 research laboratory projects in Brazilian universities.

The question of whether applied or industrial research should be pursued in universities is discussed in NAS 1967 (p. 36). The conditions recommended were quoted in chapter 2. NAS 1965b (p. 16) suggests paid industrial laboratories for Nigerian universities. In Indian universities, BLANPIED 1970 reports research is almost always in the basic sciences. On the other hand, the primary center of excellence of the People's Republic of China, the University of Science and Technology, even has a Weapons Department (WU 1970, p. 412). In the Phillipines, industrial research at the universities quadrupled between 1962 and 1967 (PHILLIPINES 1969b, pp. 60, 71).

Prejudices between universities and industry certainly exist in ACs, as Chandrashekar illustrates with American examples in IN-DIA 1970 (p. 172). The conference at which the address was delivered, however, demonstrated in itself the deep division of the Indian scientific community since it was attended mainly by academic scientists. Similar observations can be found in MORAV-SCIK 1973e.

There is a wealth of material on the lack of interaction among universities, governmental institutes, and industrial research centers: Kaldo in NADER 1969 (p. 415); JONES 1971 carries some wieght because of Jones's long career at the interface of applied science and technology; OECD 1968a (p. 28), with respect to Greece; UNESCO 1970e (p. 30), with respect to the Philippines; NADER 1969 (p. 463); and MORAVCSIK 1972a (p. 222). Historical and chronological remarks can be found in UNESCO 1970a (p. 125) and NADER 1969 (p. 430). The absence of a liaison between universities and industry in India is deplored in RAY 1967b. PERES 1969 (p. 36) finds a similar situation in the rest of Asia. OECD 1969 (p. 228) complains that there is no mechanism for such interaction in Turkey.

The need for such contacts is, therefore, urged by JONES 1971 (p. 32), NAS 1967 (pp. 7,16), and NAS 1965b (p. 13). Various methods to accomplish such contacts are listed: geographical proximity (UNESCO 1970a, p. 47); foreign visitors from applied institutions (MORAVCSIK 1973f); organizational arrangements (RI-DEAL 1950, with regard to Spain); and consulting arrangements (MORAVCSIK 1972a, p. 222, and JONES 1971, p. 115, with reference to industrial and managerial consultants). Industrial support of academic research is advocated, for example, in CHINA 1972 (p. 48). BYUNG 1972 reports some success in the Republic of Korea. The Republic of Korea, Nigeria, Turkey, Indonesia, and Brazil are discussed in MORAVCSIK 1973g (pp. 25-27). In South Africa, following the British example, research associations involving leather, paint, fish-processing, sugar-milling, and wood-textile industries have been formed; these research associations are located at universities, thus promoting industry-universities (NAUDE 1959, p. 856).

Governmental laboratories also receive considerable attention in the literature. Definition of the tasks and criticism of the isolation of such institutions can be found in NAYUDAMMA 1967, UNESCO 1970e (p. 30), and UN 1971a (p. 18). The general problems of national laboratories are discussed in MORAVCSIK 1970a.

The nuclear program of the People's Republic of China is operated through the coordination of many agencies (WU 1970, pp. 412-14); it consumes about 2% of the GNP (at least as much as the total science budget). At the moment, however, only about 4% of the available scientific and technical manpower is employed in the program. When it was begun in 1962, all available relevant manpower was utilized (p. 457). BHABHA 1966b (pp. 334-35) describes the CSIR and the AEC of India and the differences between the two. Details on the CSIR are given in NATURE 1955. A good summary of CSIR, AEC, and the Indian Council of Agricultural Research is found in SINGH 1965; the National Chemical Laboratory is described in MCBAIN 1954. SWAMINATHAN 1954 reports the early history of Indian research. Various comments can be found in WILSON 1972 (pp. 390-94). The relationship of the PCSIR with industry is discussed in SIDDIQI. A similar liaison was established in Argentina, particularly in metallurgy, by the Argentine Atomic Energy Commission (SABATO 1963, p. 5, and 1968, p. 18). IRRI is an internationally supported institution in the Philippines doing about 70% basic and 30% applied research (SALCEDO 1972, p. 180). Although there are 35 nonprofit research institutes in the Philippines, 65% of their financial support goes to IRRI (UNESCO 1970e, p. 29).

Industrial research in LDCs is usually meager. CST 1970 (p. 95) complains of such a lack in India. Greece employs 58 research scientists in that capacity (OECD 1968a, p. 28). PERES 1969 (p. 35) reports that industrial research constitutes only 3% of the total research activity of Asia. Some international agencies have active programs to promote such research, such as the project in Central America reported in OAS 1972 (p. 33). The NAS is active in this area in Brazil (NAS 1968b). In the Philippines, on the other hand, where the total R&D expenditure is 0.22% of the GNP (an average figure for an LDC), 24% of that expenditure comes from private industry (UNESCO 1970e, p. 26). The industrial research in the Philippines is also evident from PHILIPPINES 1969a, 1969b, and

NAS 1969b. For a comprehensive study of industrial research in an AC, see JEQUIER 1970 on Japan. An interesting discussion of the various stages of industrial research in an LDC is given in RAHMAN 1973 (p. 124).

Subsidiaries of international companies practice a kind of "scientific colonialism," according to LOPES 1966 (p. 11). Suggestions for increased indigenous research in such subsidiaries are offered in MORAVCSIK 1971a (p. 64) and Patinkin in ADAMS 1968 (p. 92). An exhaustive study of this problem is presented in NAS 1973a with a good set of recommendations (addressed to companies, local governments, and AC governments). For example, the Philippines subsidiary of the Esso oil corporation does all its research in the US. On the other hand, the local subsidiary of the Dole pineapple company performs research locally, devoting 1% of its gross receipts to this task (PHILIPPINES 1969b, p. 80).

How should LDCs choose research areas? They can simply follow the world pattern as advocated in PRICE 1969c (p. 4) and 1964c. On the other hand, UN 1969 (p. 16) claims that the choice of research areas in ACs is strongly influenced by the country's national objectives. That this also occurs in LDCs is illustrated in UNESCO 1970e (p. 28) which reports that in the Philippines as much as 67% of research is in the life sciences, with only 4% in the physical sciences. THONG 1968 (p. 368) states that it is easy to foster biology in Malaysia but more difficult to support physics. Science in Latin America evolved from early activity in medical research which is still relatively strong there (ROCHE 1966).

Various criteria for choosing among fields are suggested in MORAVCSIK 1972a (p. 199) and MALECKI 1963 (p. 183). Not all fields can be pursued (NAS 1966, p. 52); uniqueness is desirable (UNESCO 1970a, pp. 51-53), and PIRIE 1967, p. 68), and local advantages must be utilized (COPISAROW 1970, p. 26, and SAAVEDRA 1973). Saavedra suggests, for example, that the availability of the Tololo international observatory in Chile made various abstract areas of astronomy and astrophysics very suitable for Chilean scientists (SAAVEDRA 1973). He also urges the support of good work already being done in an LDC; the same point is made in CLAF 1971 (p. iv). MALECKI 1963 (p. 183) stresses the importance of stimulating individual interests. Comments on internal brain drain (on "inappropriate" distribution of manpower within an LDC) can be found in UN 1969 (pp. 5, 16), UNESCO 1970a (p. 124), and BHABHA 1966b (p. 335).

Scientific and technological choices in LDCs are sometimes highly controversial. A prominent example is the question of whether LDCs should undertake a major effort in nuclear reactor science and technology. GREENE 1971 (p. 6) opposes the idea, citing Chilean scientists' description of the Chilean reactor as a white elephant. ALLENDE 1972 (p. 36) states the opposite opinion. DEDIJER 1958 (p. 14) quotes Oldham: "The establishment of nuclear reactors made in many poor developing countries is frequently considered to be one of the big follies of the later 1950s." On the other hand, ARGENTINA 1966 and SABATO 1968 (p. 14) argue that there are great benefits for a country in gradually mastering a complex area like nuclear technology. In these references, as well as in BHABHA 1966b (pp. 337-39) and WHITE 1966, the emphasis is on the transfer process, on gradually converting the building of reactors into an entirely indigenous process. USMANI 1969 elaborates on other benefits nuclear technology can bring to LDCs.

The necessity for a "critical mass" of researchers, discussed in chapter 3, is mentioned in JONES 1971 (p. 28), COPISAROW 1970 (p. 23), and MORAVCSIK 1973f.

I have dwelled at some length on the importance of quality in research. I am supported in this by SAAVEDRA 1973, SABATO 1970, and UN 1970b (p. 9) among others. JONES 1971 (p. 148) remarks that "there is no point in indulging in second-rate research, which is merely wasteful and demoralizing." Criticisms of poor quality are frequent. For example TURKELI 1972 documents a lack of quality in the Turkish research community. However, as NAS 1967 (p. 53) points out, measuring quality in applied areas is not easy. KOVDA 1963 develops an overall measure for scientific and technological potential; it is composed of six factors, four of which pertain to research (institutes, apparatus, documentation, and publications). But quality is not easily accommodated in such a measure.

Centers of excellence serve to enhance quality. Examples can be found in WILSON 1972 (p. 361), the Saha Institute in India; OECD 1968a (p. 29), the Democritus Center in Greece; AID 1970, the KAIS in the Republic of Korea; KHAN 1969 (p. 85), the PINSTECH in Pakistan; CEN 1970 (p. 32), the NAS chemistry project in Brazil; and WU 1970 (p. 102), the University of Science and Technology in the People's Republic of China. The FORGE project, which provides small amounts of support to outstanding researchers in Latin America (FORGE 1971) can also be considered as producing miniature centers of excellence. PRICE 1969c, very much in favor of such centers, nevertheless quotes Robert Merton's remark that such centers are based on the "Matthew Principle": "Unto him that hath should be given, and unto him that hath not should be taken away even what he hath." One can imagine that centers of excellence are not always popular locally among the rest of the institutions.

As mentioned above, applied research in LDCs is likely to lack quality. For a wealth of comments to this effect, see UNESCO 1970b (p. 21); SINGH 1965 (p. 43); JONES 1971 (p. 117) for industrial research; UN 1971a (p. 171); and SHAH 1967 (p. 390). SALAM 1965c (p. 39) provides an illustration of a local problem that should have been solved by indigenous scientists and technologists, but actually required international assistance: the problem of salinity in Pakistan remedied by the drilling of a system of tube wells. Thus, centers of excellence in applied research, as KIST was intended to be, are particularly important contributions to the scientific infrastructure.

Research has many ingredients. RANGANATHAN 1959 describes the great personalities in Indian science; KOPECZI 1972 discusses the encouragement of young scientists in Hungary. That equipment is not usually a major problem is affirmed in MORAV-CSIK 1964c (p. 171); 1965b; ZAHLAN 1970 (p. 14), with reference to the "inert possessors of equipment"; OECD 1969 (p. 213), based on a Turkish questionnaire; and ALLISON 1960 (p. 318). Equipment in the People's Republic of China is thought by most observers to be very good (WU 1970, pp. 433-37, and HAMBRA-EUS 1972, p. 152).

The problem of spare parts is generally recognized as much more vexing (UNESCO 1970a, p. 78; RIAZUDDIN 1970; SABATO 1970; p. 189; and ZAHLAN 1970, p. 15, gives an incredible example of incompetence in a case when funds for spare parts were in fact available). I have advocated centralized store rooms (MORAV-CSIK 1964c, p. 197) and have pointed out that bilateral links between institutions in ACs and LDCs can be used to obtain spare parts (MORAVCSIK 1971b). The lack of stockrooms in chemistry is deplored in NAS 1972b (p. 7). Instrumentation is discussed in UNESCO 1970a (p. 78) with a recommendation of inventory controls. Problems of repair and upkeep, suggestions for roving mechanics, and other remedies can be found in MORAVCSIK 1964c (p. 197), ALLISON 1960 (p. 320), and NAS 1971f (p. 6). Some research institutes lack laboratories altogether: OECD 1969

(p. 210) indicates that such is the case for 10-28% of Turkish institutions. The situation in India with regard to instruments and chemicals is reported in RAHMAN 1973 (p. 175).

Library and information services (mentioned in chapter 4) appear in discussions of research, such as MORAVCSIK 1964c (p. 197) and JONES 1971 (p. 15); UNESCO 1970a (p. 70) specifies the tasks of a documentation service as "to procure copies of publications (mainly journal articles) specifically requested by research workers; to draw the research workers' attention to literature likely to be useful to them, even though not specifically requested; and to provide translations of material published in languages unfamiliar to the research workers." Libraries are not everywhere available. OECD 1969 (p. 210) reports that only 39% of Turkish institutes in the natural sciences have their own libraries.

The communication of research results can be used as a measure of scientific activity. PRICE 1964a (p. 206) points out, however, that industrial scientists cannot be easily evaluated in such a way. Certain countries have used this measure for studies. Such efforts in Turkey are reported by Ozinonu in NADER 1969 (pp. 161, 162) and TURKELI 1972. ZAHLAN 1969a (p. 8) estimates on the basis of publication counts that scientific activity in the Arab world increased by 25 times between 1960 and 1966 (but is still at a very low level). In an unusually well-documented and useful publication, RANGARAO 1967, extensive data are provided on Indian patterns of publication. Productivity is very low, about 0.1 papers per scientist per year. The People's Republic of China has achieved large increases in activity; the publication count increased by nine times between 1950 and 1959 (WU 1970, p. 440). In a similar manner, patent counts can be used as a gauge of technological activities. Examples are given in MORAVCSIK 1973g (pp. 31, 109,110)—for the Republic of Korea; WU 1970 (p. 441) for the People's Republic of China; and RAHMAN 1973 (p. 132) for India.

Standards of measurement and metrology in general are important both in science and in technology, as remarked in UNESCO 1970a (p. 71), JONES 1971 (p. 15), and MATHUR 1947. The latter describes the National Physical Laboratory in India which is principally responsible for such matters in that country. The US NBS has provided assistance to LDCs in these areas (NBS 1971b and 1972b), as has the NAS (NAS 1968c, p. 13, reports on a seminar in Brazil). The availability of buildings to house scientific research is usually not a serious problem (MORAVCSIK 1964c, p. 171, and OECD 1969, p. 213).

An unusually eloquent article on the organizational problems of research is SABATO 1970. The author describes how research centers are initially supported by governments and brought to the point when they are about to become productive, at which point the support ceases. Sabato also points out the evils of the civil service system in scientific research. He explains how its system of promotion is antithetic to the rewarding of merit, demonstrating that a scientist who has been around long enough and has not done anything bad can become director of an institute. Civil service systems abound in regulations which often cramp the style of a creative person with an individual flair. UNESCO 1969a (p. 64) specifically urges that the civil service system not be used in science. GOWON 1972 (pp. 63-64) indicates that in Nigeria, for example, scientific manpower will be placed outside such a system.

The special problem of aging scientists is analyzed in MORAVCSIK 1970a. OECD 1969 (p. 216) alleges that there are too many older scientists in Turkey, but the statistics do not seem too serious (p. 201). In general, this malady plagues only those countries where science has existed for some time on a low and unproductive level. Other countries, however, will have to deal with it sooner or later.

The following are references on research in particular countries: MORAVCSIK 1973g deals with five countries: Republic of Korea, Indonesia, Nigeria, Turkey, and Brazil.

Turkey: OECD 1969 (pp. 181-237) and Ozinonu in NADER 1967 (p. 141).

Republic of Korea: KOREA 1972a (pp. 44-53, 168-74). This reference abounds in detailed statistics.

UAR: Sabet in NADER 1969 (pp. 187-236) and MITCHISON 1960.

India: WILSON 1972 (pp. 343-94); CST 1970; and RAHMAN 1973.

Thailand: NICHOLLS 1961.

Pakistan: KHAN 1969 (p. 85).

The Arab World: ZAHLAN 1970 (pp. 23-27), as well as other writings of Zahlan.

Phillippines: PHILIPPINES 1966.

Colombia: NAS 1968a gives a list of research institutions.

East Africa: WORTHINGTON 1948.

People's Republic of China: THOMPSON 1963; WU 1970 gives a table of research fields (pp. 563-92); and DEDIJER 1966, a bib- biography.

Republic of China: CHINA 1972 (pp. 8, 9-14) gives a detailed report on basic and applied research.

A few references should be mentioned here which describe in- ternational contacts aimed specifically at research activities. The NAS has been very active, mainly by organizing seminars (NAS 1965a, 1968c, 1969c, 1971a, and 1972a). The IAEA has its own in-house laboratory for research relevant to LDCs (IAEA 1973a, p. 31). As SALAM 1968 (p. 14) remarks, however, most UN ac- tivities are in applied research and technology.

Latin America fares better. OAS has an extensive program for support of basic, applied, and technological research. (See OAS 1972, pp. 6, 10-19 for descriptions of programs ansd OAS 1970 for a list of projects.) INTERAMERICAN 1969 records a loan of $134 million by the Interamerican Bank to Latin American insti- tutions, some of which will go to the upgrading of research. CLAF stimulates research in Latin America by emphasizing interaction among the separate national science communities and has taken a stand against the idea of large regional laboratories similar to CERN in Europe (CLAF 1971, pp. 3, 4). MORAVCSIK 1971a (p. 62) urges the establishment of joint research projects between sci- entists in ACs and LDCs. MORAVCSIK 1971b outlines channels through which research institutes in ACs and LDCs can interact. CLARKE 1971 (p. 46) proposes new worldwide goals for research which are more equitable to LDCs, an approach also taken by the UN World Plan (discussed in detail in chapter 7). KOVDA 1968 (p. 16) is an example of calls for an increased effort in research *on* development.

Six

Planning, Policy, and Management

The planning, organization, and management of science are in a less developed state than science in most LDCs. (These will be referred to as "providing for science.") This is a consequence of several factors. First, there are considerably fewer scientists in LDCs, and hence there are fewer candidates to participate in such activities. Second, interest in these matters within the scientific communities of LDCs is generally less pronounced. Third, there is a basic lack of knowledge in this area in terms of experience and familiarity with available literature. Yet, such expertise is needed in LDCs more than in ACs. "Providing for science" is therefore crucial to the building of science in LDCs.

Providing for science is not exactly held in high regard within the scientific communities of ACs. Most of the present generation of scientists matured in an era when science in the ACs was booming. A transition was being made from relatively small science to Big Science. Support was amply available, and mistakes in science-building were camouflaged by the explosive rate of development. Even in recent years when the great upsurge of science in the ACs has slowed, most scientists have clung to the belief that providing for science is something they do not have to worry about; some-one else will perform the task faultlessly and generously. Fortunately, there have always been some scientists who thought otherwise, who "saved" their colleagues by devoting themselves to providing for science. I suspect that even in the ACs, however, such a casual attitude toward providing for science will become increasingly untenable. The time is not far when these matters will be a standard part of the graduate education of a scientist.

Providing for science is both an art and a science. As usually

121

happens in such situations, it evolved first as a collection of individual, empirical accounts by pioneers in the field. To enhance this knowledge, attempts were made to collect factual (often statistical) descriptions of scientific structures and communities in various countries. Building on the anecdotal and statistical framework, a "theoretical" approach began to develop using methods of both the natural and social sciences. The new academic discipline created is often called the science of science or in some contexts the sociology of science. The present state of our understanding is, nevertheless, rudimentary indeed. We are far from being able to formulate guidelines for the building of science on the basis of what we know of the science of science; directives based on empirical evidence and experience are neither sufficient nor unambiguous. Thus, providing for science remains as much an art as a science, leaving considerable room for individual creativity, ingenuity, and judgment.

Analytical work on the science of science and on science development has evolved in several directions. For example, one of the important problems is how to establish criteria for scientific choices that arise in the daily work of a scientist as well as in the shaping of the scientific activities of a whole country. This problem is closely tied to the methodology, history, and philosophy of science. Other problems involve sociology and economics: economic aspects of studies of the growth of science and investigations of the economic aspects of scientific research are examples of work in this area.

The economic analysis of science has important limitations. Following a well-established method in economics, scientific activity can be considered as an input-output problem: certain necessary ingredients are invested, and certain results are obtained. This approach, as applied to science, works very well as long as one deals with the input. Manpower, equipment, money, etc. can be dealt with relatively easily in quantitative terms. In sharp contrast, the output of science, scientific knowledge, is very difficult to measure and evaluate. The usual "remedy" is apparently to ignore the difficulty and concentrate on a meticulous treatment of the input. This lends a striking aura of unreality to most discussions of science policy.

Measures of scientific output have been suggested. Since scientific publications are repositories of scientific knowledge, one might simply count articles as a measure. Among the many shortcomings of this method, one of the most serious is the absence of any index of quality. As an improvement, citation counts are sometimes used on the assumption that articles frequently cited are "better" and should be weighted accordingly. This measure also has severe limitations (for example, it cannot distinguish among scientific activity, productivity, and progress). In spite of these shortcomings, publication counts and citation ratings have developed into a useful tool for roughly estimating scientific output.

Two observations are appropriate here. First, even if providing for science were a perfectly developed procedure with clear directives about what to do and when, it is highly unlikely that the actual practice of providing for a particular scientific community would proceed according to such directives. As George Kennan remarked, the world is governed not by realities but by the shadows of realities. The actual development of science will at best be a shadow of the theoretical directives because of the emotions and imperfections of human beings involved.

The second remark pertains to any kind of development activity: it is more difficult to build than to destroy. This is the application of the second law of thermodynamics to human affairs, and illustrations are abundant. A long, arduous effort by many devoted people can be negated quickly by a dose of stupidity, ignorance, indifference, or, in some cases, bad luck. Rapid progress will be rare indeed, and repeated setbacks should be expected.

How can a practical framework be established for providing for science in an LDC? Here again, the beginning of wisdom is to know what is already being done. It is important to collect factual information of all kinds about existing scientific activity and the factors which may influence it. In collecting the information, definitions must be agreed upon, methods of reliable collection must be devised, the important parameters must be delineated, and so forth. It is important that this be done in a uniform way in all countries so that comparisons between countries can be made. International organizations, such as UNESCO and OECD, have contributed substantially to the streamlining of data collection.

After the diagnostic study, a scheme can be devised for providing for science. Such a scheme is often called a science policy. It is important at the outset to point out the double meaning of this term. Science policy can be regarded as the measures taken to assure creative and productive scientific activity, policy *within* science. However, science policy can also include those actions taken in a variety of areas with the help of science, policy *with* science. Considerable confusion occurs in public discussions and in the literature because of the double meaning of "science policy."

Part of the confusion is a result of claims that science policy must simultaneously consider methods of developing science and methods of developing with the help of science. Supporters of this approach argue that in order to shape science, one must know what one wants to do with it. Since the utility of science in LDCs is its applicability to practical problems, they say, science should be bent in that direction from the beginning.

I believe, however, that the distinction is an indispensable practical element in the building of science in LDCs. Experience with problems of science development in various countries indicates that a large majority of problems within science are universal, independent of geography, cultural and political traditions, and other specific influences. If we differentiate between policy within science and policy with science and concentrate on the former, we can make use of accumulated worldwide experience. Policy with science, in sharp contrast, depends on the particular country and time involved. Cultural traditions change, political systems come and go, public fads flare and vanish, "national goals" sometimes have lifetimes shorter than a rainbow; for all these reasons, policy with science changes rapidly. It is a tragic mistake, it seems to me, to impose such a burden on the long-term task of building science in which continuity is so important. This should not be construed as a denigration of the importance of policy with science which every country must pursue vigorously. On that subject, however, there is not much that an outsider can or should say. I will therefore concentrate on policy within science.

The distinction between policies within and with science is also important because it contributes to a separation of policy within science from politics. Some argue that science policy and politics must be closely linked. On the other hand, the relatively objective and long-range nature of science development has proven to be quite incompatible with the highly subjective, emotional, and variable nature of politics. There are innumerable examples of destructive political interference with science development. There are also examples of politically turbulent countries where mutual restraint on the part of both the government and the scientific community nevertheless assured the stability necessary to provide for science.

It is not difficult to enumerate some of the destructive effects of mixing politics and policy within science. Instead of the customary scientific procedure to determine whether or not a certain statement is correct, the criteria are ideological. In fact, the spirit of critique may be eliminated altogether because criticism is equated with sedition. Personal animosities which exist within a scientific community, even if it is nonpolitical, are escalated a thousandfold by the use of political weapons.

Fortunately, the majority of scientists resent political interference with scientific matters, especially if the politics are different from their own. In authoritarian countries where science must conform with the ruling ideology, political control is usually imposed in spite of the preferences of the local scientific community. In politically heterogeneous societies, where the intrusion of politics into other activities must be more subtle, some scientists are tempted to blur the distinction between politics and policy within science. As a rule, however, the separation is fairly well maintained.

The separation of politics from policy within science does not mean, of course, that scientists should not communicate with politicians. Nor does it mean that political leaders can afford to be ignorant and oblivious of science. On the contrary, political leaders must treat science similar to a city's water supply by maintaining it regardless of circumstances. In return, politicians can reasonably expect that the scientific community will remain nonpolitical and confine itself to the long-term tasks of science development. This requires restraint and a degree of sacrifice on both sides. Scientists in an LDC must realize that their role in the future of their country is likely to be much more effective if they devote themselves to science development rather than plunging into political skirmishes. If they try both, they are likely to lose both.

The distinction between policies within and with science has another advantage: the former can be examined more or less independently of the general development problems of the country. Progress by any group in any area has a variable pattern in that progress usually does not occur uniformly along a broad front, but in spurts. The more tightly the various participants are linked, the more difficult it will be for any one of them to make progress since strong coupling tends to pull everything down to the lowest common level. Specifically, a country with great difficulties in many areas of development may still make considerable progress in its building of scientific infrastructure if science is left to evolve by itself without being tied to other, more problematic areas. These principles are discussed more specifically in the second section of this chapter.

In any discussion of policy within science, the question immediately arises whether planning within science is possible at all. Isn't scientific discovery so unpredictable, and creative activity in science so inscrutable that planning for it is a contradiction in terms? There is a considerable difference of opinion. In some countries where planning has become institutionalized whether successful or not, science is also planned. In other countries, planning is frowned upon, and the law of the jungle is considered natural. In most countries, however, an intermediate approach is taken. Experience seems to indicate that while some planning of the input into science is helpful, planning invariably imposes rigidity on the scientific infrastructure, a detrimental effect. For example, if the training of manpower is planned quantitatively, employment opportunities must also be planned to accommodate the new manpower. Frequently, the result is that jobs are created whether necessary or not, and people are assigned to jobs whether they like it or not.

Whatever degree of planning is undertaken, certain general guidelines should be kept in mind. First, planning for science and policy within science are not substitutes for doing science. The proper function of planning and policy-making is to produce optimum conditions for indigenous creative scientific activity, a principle unrecognized in some LDCs. Like the "syllabusitis" mentioned in chapter 2, which prevents the improvement of educational methods, preoccupation with the formalistic aspects of planning can divert attention from the substance of development of a scientific community. For this reason, it is rather pointless to prepare an elaborate plan for science in a country where indigenous scientific activity is negligible.

Second, planning for science should be very flexible. Provisions must be made for continuous feedback into the plan itself so that it can be adjusted according to the requirements of the moment.

Third, planning for science must be consistent over an extended period of time. This is perhaps one of the most important functions of planning. It can make people aware of the necessity for continuous support for science on whatever level. It is more helpful to have a consistent, modest effort in science development than a more generous, stop-and-go pattern of support.

Fourth, policy within science must be developed locally, with the cooperation of the indigenous scientific community. Suggestions from abroad may be sought and considered, but the final product must have a local character. Unlike natural resources, or even manufacturing plants, science policy cannot be imported from a foreign country and "nationalized."

It is important to realize that LDCs need not re-enact all stages of science development that have occurred in ACs. In some respects the situation for LDCs is simpler. They can profit from the experience of ACs, and international cooperation and assistance are available. In other respects the situation is more difficult. Parity in science is more difficult to attain now than it would have been 40 years ago when science was done on a small scale even in ACs.

One of the primary differences between ACs and LDCs in doing science is that in the latter, almost every member of the scientific community must be occupied simultaneously with doing science and creating the conditions under which science can be done. Science in an LDC is eternally "under construction," with roadblocks, rough pavements, detours, and delays as part of the process. It is essential that the indigenous scientific community accept this as a natural part of the development process; too often it becomes an incentive to emigrate to the scientific communities of the ACs where the road may be smoother and the "irrelevant" obstacles fewer.

Providing for science has three parts: planning, making specific decisions, and implementing. As indicated earlier, large-scale planning may not always be advisable. Making specific decisions is unavoidable, however, and implementing decisions is essential. It is regrettable, therefore, that in many LDCs too much energy and manpower are devoted to planning while the making of specific decisions receives much less attention and implementation even less. The result is often a grandiose scheme on paper which proves to have only a tenuous relationship with realities within the scientific community. It is noteworthy that the US, presently the most advanced country in the sciences, has never had an overall science plan. Even countries with a predilection for planning, such as the USSR, when confronted with scientific problems of high priority, use more practical, ad hoc methods to achieve optimal results.

After these caveats and reservations, let me now discuss how policy can actually be formed. The ingredients are education, manpower, research, finances, auxiliary facilities, physical plant, and organizational structure. Of these, all but finances and organizational structure are discussed in previous chapters. The remaining two will be dealt with here.

The problem of finances has two important aspects: (1) What percentage of the total resources of an LDC should be allotted to science? (2) How should the funds allotted to science be distributed? I consider the second question more important than the first, and I shall therefore discuss it first.

Formalistic order has a certain esthetic appeal which prompts some to urge the creation of a centralized science administration in which a single agency distributes all funds for scientific activities. However, this neat system has several important disadvantages. The funding of science involves much judgment; to rely on the judgment of only one group of people in all cases is, therefore, inadvisable. Graft, corruption, and influence-peddling through personal channels, dangers in any country, are more likely to occur if a single agency wields all the funding power. Since scientific activities are diverse, centralized funding is likely to require an excessively cumbersome administrative mechanism. Lastly, the danger that politics will interfere with science is more acute when one central organization holds all the purse strings. It is therefore essential, even in countries in which a single agency is in charge of science policy, to distribute the power of funding among a number of agencies.

The importance of individual merit grants needs to be emphasized. The easiest, least quarrelsome, and also least productive way to distribute funds is to divide them equally among all possible contenders. A government may divide all available funds equally among its ministries, the Ministry of Education its share equally among all universities, each university its share equally among all departments, and each department its share equally among all faculty members. What is missing from this system is an acknowledgement of the importance of quality, perhaps the most important characteristic of a successful scientific community. An alternative system in which quality is recognized encourages all scientists to submit individual research proposals; each proposal is evaluated, using peer judgment, on the basis of the inherent merit of the proposal and the research proposed. (To arrange for impartial and competent peer judgment in the small scientific communities of most LDCs is not an easy matter. A possible solution is to involve members of the international scientific community in such refereeing as international journals do when judging papers for publication.) Exclusive use of the individual grant system also has its drawbacks, however, since a certain level of institutional development is needed before a good research proposal can be conceived and submitted. A combination of the two systems seems best, with funds being distributed both ways. In practice, however, the institutional system is used almost exclusively, a serious retardation of progress in science development.

A significant method of persuading institutions to cooperate in the distribution of funds for research is the system of "overhead payments." For example, some universities are reluctant to provide a research environment for their faculty even if research funds are furnished by an outside agency. In such situations, it is possible to induce change by making "overhead" payments to the universities, presumably as compensation for the cost of housing research. While this appears to be a good method for rejuvenating fossilized universities, it also has its dangers. It appears to establish the principle that universities need not pursue research on their own initiative, that it is a favor extended by them to the government when research is done at a university. Such difficulties have arisen recently in the US, indicating that the device of "overhead" payments should be handled with some care.

In attempting to establish guidelines for the allocation of financial resources to science as a whole, one runs into several difficulties. Statistics are often unreliable due to the difficulty of classifying expenses into categories, incompleteness of information, and the attempt in some countries to use statistics as a tool of political propaganda. In addition, the basis for setting financial guidelines is disputed. The most common benchmark used is the gross national product (GNP). It is sometimes claimed that the GNP cannot serve as an equally valid basis in countries with differing economic systems and stages of development. Yet, the GNP seems to be a useful tool for setting approximate guidelines, especially since the uncertainties about its validity appear to be much less than the discrepancy between the recommended and the actual science expenditures of LDCs.

Guidelines for expenditures on science are usually set in terms of a certain percentage of the GNP. These guidelines are then attacked by some as being to a large extent arbitrary. I tend to agree, though I also believe that the *way* allocations are spent is often more important than the amount spent. At any rate, setting definite targets in terms of percentage of GNP serves several purposes. First, the glaring discrepancy between even a modest target and present realities emphasizes that many LDCs have not done their share in building their own science. Second, an internationally accepted target can help (and in fact has helped) to spur LDCs into a competitive effort to reach the goal. Third, agreement on a worldwide quantitative target helps eliminate constant argument in governmental circles over how much should be allocated to science.

What are these guidelines? It is generally suggested that LDCs spend 1% of their GNP on R&D with 10-20% of that amount spent on fundamental research. The status of the latter figure is discussed in some detail in chapter 5. I shall comment here only on the overall figure of 1%. It was arrived at partly by comparison with ACs and partly by considering what LDCs can realistically be expected to attain in the immediate future. Leading ACs presently spend about 2-3% of their GNP on R&D, of which about one-third is for military research. Assuming, therefore, that LDCs do not spend money on military research (a quite unrealistic assumption) and considering the generally difficult financial state of most LDCs, the figure of 1% is obtained as a target.

One percent is indeed a small figure, and the major activities in an LDC, such as agriculture, certainly would not lose much if that amount were taken out of their own appropriations. Nevertheless, the actual figures for most LDCs are much lower, averaging perhaps 0.2%. To be sure, the percentage is increasing in many LDCs, some quite rapidly, but the figures are still considerably below the target. This is unfortunate since presumably the countries with the lowest standard of living need the most strenuous effort to "close the gap." Instead, there is a positive correlation between the standard of living already achieved and the percentage of GNP spent on R&D. The gap is increasing rather than decreasing.

In fact, the situation is worse than that. The absolute amounts spent by LDCs on R&D are very small compared to similar expenditures in ACs, but the cost of research per scientist per year is not very different in LDCs from that in ACs. There is a slight tendency for the expenditure per scientist per year to be lower in LDCs than in ACs, but it is not clear whether this is because research is cheaper in LDCs or because scientists in LDCs are not supported adequately. If we assume that the former cause is the case and gain, say, a factor of 3 in favor of LDCs, we are nevertheless confronted with the fact that per capita expenditure on R&D is about 300 times less in LDCs than in ACs. Even with this optimistic assumption, we find that the average American buys at least 100 times as much research every year as the average inhabitant of an LDC, a staggering discrepancy.

Salaries of scientists have about the same relationship to the rest of the population in LDCs as they do in ACs. Scientists tend to be in the well-paid segment of society, though very seldom in the top financial bracket. The absolute differences between countries can, of course, be large, and this induces some migration. Compared with the many other staggering problems confronting the building of science in LDCs, however, scientists' salaries do not appear to be one of the major obstacles. (There are exceptional cases where salaries need to be readjusted.)

In even shorter supply than funds is foreign exchange. Most LDCs have an unfavorable trade balance so foreign exchange is scarce. It is, therefore, important to include an adequate amount of foreign exchange in science appropriations to pay for international travel, importation of equipment not locally available, subscriptions to scientific journals, etc. Since foreign exchange is one of the most bothersome elements in the financing of science in LDCs, it is one of the prime areas where international assistance can be effective.

The remaining aspect of providing for science is organizational structure. Here again, formalistic tendencies often come to the fore with detrimental consequences. The purpose of organization is not to produce organizations but to facilitate the creative activities of the members of such organizations. For example, national science councils should serve not to honor scientists with long-standing careers but to facilitate communication between the scientific community and the government and to suggest ways to improve the conduct of scientific research and education in the country. Communication with the political community is of particular interest in an environment where the value of science is not generally appreciated and where decisions on providing for science tend to be made by groups entirely external to the scientific community.

The question of whether organizations should be centralized wherever possible (as the trend seems to be) can also be evaluated in a pragmatic context. The arguments against centralized decision-making in science are similar to those against centralized funding. On the other hand, if a national science plan is needed, the plan requires a central authority. Planning may, therefore, be centralized, but decision-making, funding, and implementation are handled better if they are decentralized.

A problem closely related to the lack of functional approach to organization is the phenomenon of sprawling bureaucracy. The coordination of activities which depend on creativity, intuition, improvisation, and flexibility with a support system necessarily steeped in the systematic, formalistic realities of everyday life is a sensitive task even with mutual understanding and a basic agreement on goals. Friction between scientists and administrators exists everywhere. The interaction can turn into a hopeless battle if the support system is bureaucratized by mechanistic, inimical personnel insensitive to the importance of time in the development process. (That bureaucracy can also seep into the scientific community is pointed out in chapter 5 in the context of the civil service.)

In comparison with the general nature of an organization, its exact structure is of secondary importance. In some countries, ministries of science and technology have been formed while in others the top organization for making policy within science is a national research council or similar group. In some countries, the academy of sciences plays a major role in such matters while in others the academy has no power at all. It is, therefore, futile to try to decide in principle which of the various possibilities is optimal for a given country. That will depend more on the personnel involved, on the ease of communication with other relevant governmental agencies, and on the influence exerted by the organization at the national level. The latter generally depends on the effectiveness of a few key individuals located at or near the top of the organization.

In most LDCs, the majority of scientific activity takes place in governmental research institutions, generally by default. Industrial research is still in its infancy, while universities are either few or inexperienced in research, or both. The problem of how to apportion research among these three types of institutions is discussed in chapter 5. It is clear that in many LDC, universities need strengthening in quality and in quantity. It is equally obvious in most LDCs that industrial research is in need of strengthening. Since governmental research institutions tend to be more bureaucratized than university research establishments (though not necessarily more than universities as a whole), the productivity of science could probably be increased by a more equal distribution of research among the three candidates. On the other hand, in a country with a very small scientific community, the requirement of a critical mass might necessitate the formation of science centers even at the cost of competing with university development. This is particularly true in applied research where interdisciplinary teams are an advantage. In all such institutions, the guiding principle should be strong leadership with maximum freedom for individual scientists.

Customs offices constitute a special organizational problem. Scientific activity depends on the international exchange of literature and equipment. In such exchanges, time is of utmost importance. If a journal arrives six months late, its utility is at best halved. If a spare part for research equipment takes months to clear the customs office, the resulting delays, when compounded from spare part to spare part, can be so huge as to exclude the possibility of meaningful research altogether. This is quite obvious; yet, problems with local customs offices are common in all LDCs. "Solutions" have been worked out by ingenious scientists involving a combination of persuasion and remuneration, but this is hardly the remedy. In this case, the blame must be placed squarely on the local government. The problem can be solved without new expenditures or any scarce commodities.

Throughout this discussion, I have suggested that the key ingredient in providing for science is the human element. Science planning bodies must be interdisciplinary, including economists, politicians, and industrial representatives. But the majority of members in such bodies should be scientists chosen for their high standing within the scientific community as well as for their interest and expertise in matters of science policy. No effective policy can be formulated without the consent of the community to which the policy will apply. It is an important requirement that the average scientist have confidence in the policy-maker. Science administrators should almost always be scientists themselves. Specifically needed are persons with scientific careers sufficiently satisfactory that they can communicate with fellow scientists without hidden feelings of inferiority. The emphasis must be on their personal satisfaction with their own scientific accomplishments, a satisfaction not closely related with the "absolute" standing of a scientist. There are outstanding scientists who feel insecure in spite of their distinguished accomplishments, and there are less eminent scientists who are nevertheless heartened by their own contributions to science. The latter have attained a certain serenity of mind necessary for smooth and effective interaction in a decision-making role. It is important that the administrators be scientists because scientists interact with other scientists much better than with "outsiders," whom they consider bureaucrats. Though such judgments are not necessarily justified, organizational contacts depend not so much on facts as on images. Yielding to the preferences of scientists in these matters is, therefore, a wise thing to do.

Middle-aged scientists seem to be the best choice for administrative positions. While they are perhaps not as creative in original research as they used to be, they have usually acquired through years of experience considerable knowledge of how to deal with scientific problems. They are also able to see scientific issues in a broader perspective than the particular technical aspect. A very large fraction of the science administrators in ACs have such a background, and there is no reason to believe that this practice would not work in LDCs. There is a danger, however, that administration will be construed by some scientists as a refuge from an unsuccessful career in research. In many LDCs, administrative posts carry higher social prestige than research positions which adds to the temptation. Scientists who obtain administrative postions as an escape from research seldom make successful administrators; they probably do more damage to the cause of science in LDCs than if they had remained merely unsuccessful researchers.

In providing for science one cannot overemphasize the importance of outstanding personalities, of exceptional individuals. In an AC, the scientific community is large, traditions have been established, and the process of further development is likely to be orderly and gradual. In contrast, science in an LDC is generally in a state of turmoil. Few people are in a position to take effective action, and even fewer have the ability to exploit such a position. Opportunity for an able individual is much greater in an LDC than in an AC. It is essential to give exceptional science leaders the opportunity to convert their energy and talent into accomplishments.

It is exciting to view the activities of some of these exceptional people but also sad to see how often they get embroiled in local feuding and personal battles within their scientific communities. Such infighting appears to be more common in LDCs. Perhaps the small size of the scientific community and resulting lack of opportunity for antagonists to avoid each other contribute to this phenomenon. In some countries where everything has been politicized, these personal battles take on political overtones with frequently ominous consequences. To an outsider such conflicts appear completely irrelevant and a sorry spectacle of wasted human resources.

We have enumerated the desirable qualities of science administrators. How can scientists be imbued with these desirable attributes? The education of science students in LDCs (or of students from LDCs being educated in ACs) should include discussion of problems providing for science. The sizable literature on this subject embodied in articles, reports, documents, and conference proceedings is virtually unknown to most scientists in LDCs, even to some very distinguished science administrators. While reading this material will not itself produce an expert in science policy, knowledge of experience elsewhere is helpful. Reference to international experience can buttress the arguments presented to local governments. Unfortunately, the material in question is not readily available to scientists in LDCs, a problem that must be dealt with by the scientific community in ACs and by international agencies.

Makers of science policy in LDCs must make a conscious effort to educate their successors by delegating some responsibility, a difficult task. In the midst of an exciting and exhaustive effort at science development, the most efficient method of operation often appears to be (and is) doing everything oneself. All too often, when brilliant science developers in LDCs retire from the scene, their achievements suffer greatly for lack of the continuity which they neglected to instill.

Evaluation of the results of efforts to provide for science should always be made through personal, extended visits by members of the international scientific community so that a consensus of well-informed views can be developed on the state of science in the country in question. It can be extremely misleading to come to conclusions simply by reading formal reports, input statistics, national science plans, publication counts, and the like. There is often a discrepancy between the elaborate complex of formal indicators and the reality within the scientific community as viewed by a knowledgeable but impartial fellow scientist. Providing for science is a necessary, difficult, and desirable activity, but it is futile without scientists who are energetic, competent, and motivated—qualities which do not appear in formal documents but are immediately evident to an experienced visitor.

Background and Comments

That providing for science is not well-appreciated in scientific communities is a well-known fact to anyone within such a community. It is mentioned specifically in NADER 1969 (p. 460), and the attitude is prevalent among my scientifically eminent colleagues at my university. Policy *with* science is understandably more popular since it appears to offer a legitimate outlet for scientists to deal with problems often far outside their competence. Policy *within* science is regarded as something that any scientist *could* handle but generally does not want to. Training for it, therefore, is considered unnecessary, and formal studies of the science of science are dismissed as feeble attempts by those outside the sciences to match the knowledge about these matters that scientists inherently have.

Nevertheless, the science of science and science policy have been developing quite rapidly in recent years. UNESCO 1971b gives a list (incomplete) of science policy research and teaching units around the world, covering both policy within and policy with science though not clearly distinguishing between the two. Some 340 individuals and groups are listed of whom a large number have interests in policy with science or in policy related more to technology than to science. Unfortunately, the peculiar classification of fields of interest (p. 197) prevents the reader from easily determining what fraction of those listed is concerned with policy within science.

There is no denying that the science of science and providing for science are still in their infancy. JONES 1971 (p. 16) remarks that "the theory of science for development is itself as yet underdeveloped." BROOKS 1967 (p. 27), discussing research on research, suggests that "there is still an absence of solid generalizations based on reliable empirical data." As early as 1959, DEDIJER 1959 (p. 368) pointed out the need for such studies, especiaaly in the context of LDCs. He quotes Kepler: "The road by which men arrive at their insights into celestial matters seems to me almost as worthy of wonder as those matters themselves." A prominent spokesman for the science of science has been Derek de Solla Price (PRICE 1964a, 1965b, 1965c, and 1966). International organizations, such as UNESCO, have been active in this area (UNESCO 1972b), but Price agrees that their studies are not yet major tools in the formulation of practical science policy (PRICE 1965c). The same point is emphasized in COPISAROW 1970 (p. 7).

Criteria for scientific choice constitute a problem of both conceptual and practical interest. UN 1970b (p. 11) urges better practical criteria, but it is not at all evident that the conceptual contributions to this problem, such as WEINBURG 1963 or MORAVCSIK 1974d, can easily be translated into practical recipes to be used by science organizers in daily decision-making.

The growth of science has received much attention. When agreement can be reached on the type of measuring stick to be used, quantitative results can be produced readily. PRICE 1969a (p. 102) reports, for example, that science grows exponentially with a doubling time of 7-10 years (and in fact has done this for about 200 years). As a result, 90% of all scientists who have ever lived are alive today. PRICE 1965c records Gerald Holton's picturesque expression of the same fact: "Today we are privileged to sit side by side with the giants on whose shoulders we stand." What the pattern of growth will be in the future is, of course, a matter of speculation. For a discussion of the factors determining future growth patterns, see MORAVCSIK 1974e.

That the measurement of scientific output is an unsolved problem is confirmed in BROOKS 1967 (p. 28). The author also points out that measurement of output is even more difficult in the applied sciences (p. 53). Christopher Freeman, an eminent contributor to economic studies of science and technology, agrees. FREEMAN 1969a gives detailed instructions for the collection of data to assess the scientific infrastructure of a country, but FREEMAN 1969b (p. 8), which deals with the theory of measurement of scientific and technological output, comments that "there is no *nationally* agreed system of output measurement, still less any international system. Nor does it seem likely that there will be any such system for some time to come. At the most, it may be hoped that more systematic statistics might become possible in a decade or two." The same conclusions can be found in UN 1970b (p. 14) and MORAVCSIK 1973g (pp. 3-7, 29-31).

Yet, there is a great need for evaluating science policy measures and specific scientific assistance projects. An interesting and laudable effort is made in NAS 1973c (pp. 39-65), for example, to gauge the effectiveness of the international programs of the NAS. Still, the yardsticks used in that attempt are all concerned with input items. KOVDA 1963 defines the scientific and technological potential of a country, but again all components of this index consist of input items.

Publication and citation counts have been used with increasing frequency as measures of scientific output. Details may be found in PRICE 1964c, 1969a (pp. 106-109), 1969c, and 1969d. The tables in 1969a are particularly interesting. ZAHLAN 1972a points out that the Arab countries combined have a publication count only one-third that of Israel alone. An interesting use of publication

counts can be found in TURKELI 1972 and MIRABOGLU 1972
which examine the low productivity of indigenous Turkish scientists compared with scientists of Turkish origin working abroad.
An excellent study is RANGARAO 1967 in which scientific research in India is analyzed using publication counts as a tool according to types of research institutions, fields of science, and mul-
tiplicity of authorship. Using the same tool, OECD 1968c (p. 196)
points out that in Greece, the cost of research per publication in
the "Democritus" research center is 200 times higher than the cost
of research per publication in the institutions of higher learning.
One cannot draw a conclusion from this fact alone without investi-
gating the circumstances in detail, but such figures call attention to
areas in which close analysis is needed. Publication counts have
some shortcomings, however, as pointed out in MORAVCSIK
1973h. "Rational" science policy may not govern what actually
occurs. As stated in SABATO 1968 (p. 24): "The obstacles preventing a given accomplishment are inversely proportional to the
degree of irrationality of the idea."

The process of collecting and classifying data on scientific activities has a considerable literature. UN 1971a (p. 32) singles out one
type of ambiguity in classification, namely, whether to include scientific and technical services in the definition of research and development. In order to standardize definitions, the so-called Frascati manual was developed (OECD 1963); nevertheless, some ambi-
guities remain. FREEMAN 1969a and UNESCO 1970d provide
manuals for collecting data. A number of sources, such as UNES-
CO 1969b (p. 14), urge the collection and analysis of such data.

A collection and analysis of a very different nature are con-
tained in GASPARINI 1969, a sociological survey of the Venezuelan scientific community. It is based on personal questionnaires
dealing not only with "facts" but also with the self-image of scientists in Venezuela. Such studies can be invaluable in assessing the
morale of a scientific community (see chapter 8).

The distinction between policy *within* and policy *with* science
is in general quite blurred in the literature. When OECD 1972b (p.
72) states that "science policy is a policy conducted by the structures responsible for science and technology within the framework
of an overall policy," it is referring to both kinds and throws in
technology for good measure. JONES 1971 (p. 16) also includes
both and claims that "science policy is much more than a policy
for scientific research, and cannot be treated in isolation." The

same point is emphasized in UN 1970b (p. 4): "Until a few years ago, many scientists believed that science policy was to be restricted to the development of science itself, and that state support of scientists was justified by the intrinsic value of science. This view was gradually abandoned when governments started to recognize that scientific activities can be effectively directed toward practical objectives." This seems to be a particularly fuzzy-minded statement (in an otherwise excellent document). The issue of policy with versus policy within science is merged with the issue of the justification of scientific research in general. It also gives the impression that policy with science is a recent phenomenon whereas it is several thousand years old.

SALOMON 1971 is closer to making the distinction between policy within and policy with science in a quote from OECD 1971a:

> If science policy is entering a period of uncertainty and reassessment, it is not so much due to the failings in science policy itself as to the fact that government policy in general and the goals of society, after a long period of consensus, are themselves passing through a period of uncertainty and conflict. . . . We [his committee] conceived it to be our task to take into account developments outside the traditional area of science policy. From the outset we decided to adopt a more comprehensive approach that would include goals that cannot be related exclusively either to the promotion of economic growth or to science for its own sake.

There is a suggestion that policy within science is concerned only with science for science's sake while policy with science deals only with practical applications. Salomon adds his own opinion: "Science policy is in a disarray because society is in a disarray." This can be expressed more simply in terms of the two concepts of policy within and policy with science. Policy within science continues to be valid. By its very nature, however, policy with science changes rapidly, especially at times when the external factors which determine it are also changing rapidly. We should, therefore, proceed with policy within science in the usual fashion. At the same time, we should reshape policy with science according to contemporary values. In doing so, we must also reshape the points of contact between policy with and policy within science.

In contrast, DE HEMPTINNE 1963 (p. 234) postulates the distinction very clearly by quoting Pierre Auger, one of the early figures in science policy. The names assigned to the two kinds of policy are not the ones used here, but the differentiation is similar.

In BLACKETT 1963, however, both policies are discussed without any indication that there is a duality.

Let us now turn to the question of politics and science. It is perhaps noteworthy that in some languages, such as Spanish, the words for "politics" and "policy" are identical, a circumstance that may contribute to the tendency in Latin American countries to mix politics with science policy. However, the theoretical proposition that science and technology have no political labels is reiterated in many quarters. ALLENDE 1972 states, for example, that "I do not believe that science and technology can be given political labels." BULLETIN 1950 (pp. 294-95), in a discussion of the Berkner Report on the international scientific responsibilities of the US Department of State, states that "science per se is incapable of creating any policy, for science is amoral. . . . There are formidable differences between problems of science and of international politics. They show that the method of science cannot be directly adapted to the solution of problems in politics and in man's spiritual life." DE HEMPTINNE 1963 (p. 236) describes certain pivotal features of science policy and states: "Investigations carried out by UNESCO show that the scientifically advanced countries tend to organize themselves according to the model described above, irrespective of the structure of the state and political system in power." Confirmation of this point can be found in DEDIJER 1964a. A point-by-point comparison exhibiting striking resemblances is made between the "science policy ideologies" of the US Republican Party and the USSR Communist Party.

All these arguments strongly indicate that science can in fact be treated independent of politics, a policy urged by a number of commentators, such as NADER 1969 (p. 461), LEWIS 1961 (p. 46), MORAVCSIK 1973e, and 1966a. The latter analyzes the reasons why scientists are particularly ill-prepared to become involved in political affairs. The opposite advice, that science and scientists must be strongly tied to politics, comes primarily from proponents of authoritarian or totalitarian political ideologies. In these systems, a certain political ideology is given a standing of absolute validity, and a neutral attitude is usually equated with a hostile one. In NADER 1969 (p. 476), the Brazilian scientist, Lopes, urges political involvement of scientists and adds: "If some prefer to avoid the discussion [of political issues] by proclaiming obedience to the higher ideal of working for mankind . . . let them know that this ideal would be seriously damaged by their refusal to contribute to the removal of the obstacles which impede the access of the greater part of mankind to the fruits and conquests of modern civilization" (see also LOPES 1966, p. 11). This is a relatively mild statement, and in the same article, Lopes presents a number of specific observations which are in fact useful for the building of science. A much wilder example is found in BAZIN 1972a which proclaims the inseparability of science and politics but gives no practical suggestions for the actual development of science in LDCs. Another example is BAZIN 1973. Such writing is greatly resented in the LDCs. For the later paper, Bazin was severely taken to task by the Chilean scientific community, regardless of political leanings.

Bazin's main inspiration seems to come from views in the People's Republic of China where the actual subjugation of science to politics is constantly emphasized. ESPOSITO 1972 (p. 37) quotes the bulletin of the conference of the Party Committee of the Academy of Sciences of the People's Republic of China: "Science must be regarded as a part of the proletarian revolutionary cause. . . . Any deviation, divorcing science from politics, must be resolutely opposed. The facade of the 'science for science's sake' advocated by capitalism (while in reality science in the capitalist world serves the interests of monopoly capital) should be exposed." HAMBRAEUS 1972 (p. 150), discussing the status of science in the People's Republic of China, quotes Chairman Mao Tse-tung to the effect that science cannot be separated from politics. Changes in science policy are decreed from a central authority, and within a short span of time one can witness a kaleidoscopic array of policies. Some are promising and even successful; others are doomed from the start. They follow one another in abrupt leaps and turns.

Specific detrimental effects of combining science and politics are listed in RYDER 1969a. Scientific criticism is interpreted as political dissension, the scientific community becomes involved in political squabbles which consume much time and energy, and individuals with great political power acquire undue influence in scientific matters. In fact, scientists generally resent political interference in scientific matters, points out Bruno Friedman, the editor of *Impact,* in his interview with Salvador Allende (ALLENDE 1972). It appears from that interview that Allende could not understand how that could be so.

There are numerous recent examples of political interference in scientific matters. SESHACHAR 1972 (p. 137) observes that

"[Indian] universities have become status symbols of politicians rather than training grounds of future generations of scientists and scholars." RYDER 1969b reports numerous appointments to leading scientific posts in Cuba of people with little scientific background but much political influence. TELLEZ 1966 describes the clash between the Ongania government in Argentina and the local *university* scientific community, an incident in which lack of respect for the separation of politics and science was evident on both sides. Further comments on the situation in Argentina may be found in FALICOV 1970 and BONFIGLIOLI 1972. DEDIJER 1957 provides some illustrations in the context of the USSR stressing in particular the impeding of channels of communication. A difficult problem in Peru is mentioned in NAS 1966 (p. 10): "The political activity of the universities [in Peru] is one of the biggest obstacles to the general and scientific development of the university, not only because of time loss and difficulty in obtaining adequate financial resources due to the unfortunate image presented to society, but also because it destroys the climate essential for the teachers and students to develop."

However, the best-documented case of political interference with science is that of the People's Republic of China. WU 1970 (pp. 42, 48, 71, 452, 472), CHANG 1969, ESPOSITO 1972, OLD-HAM 1968 (p. 484), LINDBECK 1969, HAMBRAEUS 1972 (p. 131), RANGARAO 1966 (p. 348), and ORLEANS 1972 (pp. 864, 866) describe in detail the total control of science by the Communist party, the harrassment of scientists to extort self-confessions from them, the requirement that all scientific progress be directly attributed to some quotation from Chairman Mao, the surveillance of scientific institutions by the Party and the military, and other instances. Some observers have suggested that it is only a show for purposes of propaganda, and science can actually function for the most part undisturbed. OLDHAM 1966 and HARARI 1968 (p. 82) are examples of this point of view. In the latter, for example, Pierre Piganiol, a seasoned commentator on science policy, asserts that "even when the Cultural Revolution was at fever pitch, scientific methods were never attacked. The manifesto of August 1966 even pointed out that, if these methods appeared to be influenced by suspect ideologies, they had to be reformed gradually and not attacked head-on." Harari contrasts this attitude with the Lysenko affair in the USSR in which Stalin imposed a certain genetic theory on Soviet biology for purely political reasons. However, the distinction seems dubious. In both cases, the issue was not scientific method as such but the supremacy of political considerations over purely scientific ones. That the Cultural Revolution was also anti-scientific and anti-intellectual is pointed out in HAMBRAEUS 1972 (p. 151). Reports that the Maoist slogan, "the lowly are the most intelligent, the elite are the most ignorant," were frequently sounded as recently as 1972.

Considerable confusion regarding the issue of science and politics is caused by the fact that some authoritarian governments are cognizant of the importance of science in achieving political power. They place great emphasis on the development of science, an action to be greatly applauded. In evaluating their performance, observers are so impressed with the energetic efforts toward science development that they overlook the detrimental effects of the political control of science. However, an active program of science development has no relationship to a totalitarian political system. There are many examples of totalitarian regimes with little interest in science development, and there are also examples of countries with heterogeneous political structures very intent on science development.

The separation of science and politics must be respected by both sides. For example, several US scientific organizations have made public pronouncements in connection with the Sakharov affair in the USSR, an episode not directly connected with matters of science or science policy. In spite of my personal sympathies in the matter, I consider such acts very regrettable.

One may reasonably ask whether it is possible to keep science and politics separate in view of the pressures from both sides. MORAVCSIK 1970b (p. 5) analyzes some factors which can produce a separation in practice. Moreover, documentation is available (SABATO 1968, p. 21; FALICOV 1970, p. 9; and BONFIG-LIOLI 1972) of the nonpolitical history of important governmental research organizations in Argentina, a country of turbulent politics and highly pitched emotions.

The separation of science from politics must not be taken to mean that political leaders should not understand science. SALCEDO 1972 (p. 177) mentions the increased interest in science shown by governmental leaders. *Ciencia y tecnologia,* by the Venezuelan politician Rodolfo Jose Cardenas, is a remarkably well-written and easily accessible discussion of problems of science and technology (CARDENAS 1970).

Earlier, I argued that science development need not be strongly tied to general development, and a separation is likely to be advantageous to science development. This point is disputed, for example, in NADER 1969 (p. 402). One argument I brought forward was that development is not uniform and dynamic sectors should be allowed to forge ahead. A similar view is expressed by Amilcar Herrera in SABATO 1968 (p. 32): "The changing forces of a society are never generated simultaneously at every sector and the relative advance of one of them can help to stimulate the others." Herrera concludes that in spite of stagnation in other areas of Latin American development, science and technology should be pressed ahead. The same dichotomy of views underlies part of the debate, presented in chapter 5, on whether LDCs should engage in research and development of nuclear reactors.

Is it possible to plan science in LDCs? Some commentators firmly believe that it is (e.g., UN 1970b, p. 42; FEDOROV 1963; and NAS 1965b, p. 3, with respect to Nigeria). Others are more cautious: in SHAH 1967 (p. 385), Mukerjee quotes D.S. Kothari to the effect that one can plan *for* science but cannot plan science itself. SHILS 1961 (p. 50) feels that planning is possible only to a limited extent, but that is better than complete randomness. DE-DIJER 1962 (p. 6) warns against the two extremes of anarchy and bureaucracy. On the other hand, in a thoughtful study of science policy in LDCs, ROESSNER 1968 concludes: "There is evidence of . . . a 'Western bias' regarding the necessity for and content of science policies in the underdeveloped nations; until attitudes and institutions become 'rationalized and standardized' in these countries, the concept of science policy seems useful only in the context of the developed nations." In the specific context of manpower planning, relevant comments can be found in ADISESHIAH 1969 (p. 70), UNESCO 1970a, (pp. 120-22), CIMT 1970b (p. 685), and WU 1970 (p. 105).

In spite of the formal emphasis on a central plan, most countries do not have one in practice. AID 1972a (p. 75) states that such is the case in Iran; OECD 1968a (p. 33) makes the same point concerning Greece. In general, the discrepancy between plans and policies on the one hand and realities on the other is evident everywhere. SESHACHAR 1972 (p. 136) illustrates this in the case of India. ZAHLAN 1972c mentions that at the 1966 meeting of UNESCO in Algiers dealing with science policy in the countries of Northern Africa and the Middle East, 21 recommendations were adopted. Six years later none had been implemented, not even the eight which should have been implemented by the UN agencies themselves.

I stressed in the first part of this chapter that organizational shortcomings are enormous in LDCs. MOREHOUSE 1967 (p. 374) considers them the biggest obstacle to the development of science in LDCs. ALONSO 1969 (p. 2) synthesizes a "development gap" from the gaps in education, science policy, and management. LOPES 1966 complains about such shortcomings particularly in the Brazilian context.

There are several good, general treatises on science policy which make particular reference to LDCs. SPAEY 1969 pertains primarily to Europe, covering both science and technology. UNESCO 1970a (pp. 99-158) has an excellent section on policy for LDCs, especially with regard to Asia. UNESCO 1967a presents a similar account in connection with the above-mentioned meeting in Algiers in 1966. Another excellent source, also originating with UNESCO, is DE HEMPTINNE 1972 which contains numerous statistics and a list of science policy-making bodies. JONES 1971 (pp. 34-52) is an additional source. MALECKI 1963 relates the Polish experience in this context. ROYAL 1968 (pp. 87-125) presents a kaleidoscopic view of science policies of the Commonwealth countries. MORAVCSIK 1970b surveys the problems of science policy discussed at a conference in Maryland in 1970.

More specific suggestions on how to formulate policy can also be found. NAS 1967 (p. 112) points out that moralizing and generalizing are not the same as forming policy. (An example of moralizing is found in LONSDALE 1969 and other Pugwash material.) NAS 1967 (p. 113) also stresses that policy formation is a matter of negotiation, either implicitly or explicitly, and policies imposed from outside are not likely to work. OECD 1972b (p. 15) presents a survey of analytical methods by which science policy may be formed, including social merit matrices and other auxiliary tools. While this report asserts that such techniques can be of some help in forming policy, it also emphasizes that sole reliance on such techniques at the present time would be foolish (see particularly p. 37). General awareness of the importance of a scientific infrastructure, advocated by DEDIJER 1963 (p. 65) and SAAVEDRA 1969, is undoubtedly essential for any progress.

Providing for science must be consistent and steady. This point is made by SABATO 1970 (pp. 185-86, 189) in the Argentinian context and WU 1970 (p. 28) in connection with Philippine policy. The latter advocates a special tax on foreign trade to provide a uniform degree of support. A negative example is described in ZAHEER 1968 (p. 11). During the Indian-Chinese conflict in 1962, one high-ranking official tried to cut off support for the CSIR on the grounds that the country needed cannonballs, not science.

Whether science policy should be formulated by scientists or by others is subject to varying views. SESHACHAR 1972 (p. 136) advocates the inclusion of people of broad vision and differing backgrounds. On the other hand, SALCEDO 1972 (p. 175) quotes Zhmudsky: "Scientists are the best informed members of society, capable of seeing where and how conquests of science can be best used in the interest of humanity as a whole." (I consider this a highly questionable assertion.) In my opinion, policy within science should be determined mainly (though not exclusively) by scientists; however, policy with science must be a broadly interdisciplinary undertaking.

It is frequently emphasized that LDCs need not recapitulate all the steps of development followed by the ACs (for example, in COPISAROW 1970, p. 20; CALDER 1960; KOVDA 1968, p. 15; and UN 1971b, p. 54). Time is short, and LDCs can and must leapfrog. UNESCO 1970a (p. 131) asserts that the LDCs are now where the ACs were 40 years ago. The statement is based on the fact that LDCs now spend about the same percentage of their GNP on R&D as the ACs did in the 1930s. The statement is highly misleading, however, for innumerable reasons evident throughout this book.

SABATO 1970 (pp. 192, 193) and 1968 (p. 22) are particularly emphatic in pointing out that the conditions for science in LDCs are very different from those in ACs. Sabato stresses the constant atmosphere of crisis in LDCs. He feels that it is unrealistic to demand "a coherent scientific policy as an essential prerequisite for the realization of a specific activity, in a society that was not able to determine even its municipal policy," or to ask "for order, security, and continuity that no country in crisis could offer." The same sentiment is voiced in ZAHLAN 1969a (p. 9) which refers to "a society in perpetual crisis," and the unrealistic expectation of "an ideal system within which the scientist spontaneously finds his equipment, his supplies, and his salary."

It is generally recognized that if overall plans are prepared, they must be flexible. CIMT 1970b (p. 682) discusses a "dynamic disequilibrium" to which plans must be adjusted. UN 1971a (pp. 4, 5) mentions a "dynamic process" and calls for plans to be "catalytic and not comprehensive." UNESCO 1970a (p. 104) suggests that progress can occur in the absence of a plan, and a feedback mechanism is in any case essential (p. 108).

My personal reaction to grandiose science plans is similar to my feeling when I was repeatedly presented with syllabi during visits to educational institutions in LDCs. Nothing is inherently wrong with formulating science plans, but if planning detracts from the actual development of the indigenous scientific community, and if producing a plan lulls people into a false feeling that they have gone more than halfway toward producing science, then such planning definitely becomes detrimental.

Other aspects of providing for science are mentioned in various sources. Self-reliance is discussed in WU 1970 (p. 73) and NATURE 1968; it is considered praiseworthy as long as it does not lead to isolationism. That early decisions are crucial in the development of science is also an important point. DEDIJER 1960 (p. 460) points out that because of the long-range aspects of science development, neglect of research at any time makes itself felt when it is too late to do much about it. According to UNESCO 1970a (p. 100): "For developing countries it is important to realize that the most significant and far-reaching science policy decisions are made during the years when the resources for scientific activities are in their rapid growth phase."

Channels of interaction between scientists and governmental decision-makers must be developed. Suggestions for improvement can be found in ECHEVERRIA 1972 (pp. 44, 48), SALCEDO 1972 (p. 180), NADER 1969 (p. 413), and UN 1970a (p. 108). The various stages of policy development and the various aims of policy are discussed in CSA 1971a (p. 79), UNESCO 1970a (p. 112), 1970b (p. 35), OECD 1965, and DE HEMPTINNE 1963 (p. 235).

I emphasized in the first section of this chapter the importance of funding based on individual merit. There are only a few examples in LDCs where this system of funding is used. PHILIPPINES 1969b (p. 41) and UNESCO 1970e (p. 17) report such funding in the Philippines; CHINA 1972 (p. 6) in the Republic of China (about 1200 awards per year); and CELASUN 1972 (p. 20) in Turkey by TUBITAK. On the other hand, NSF 1973 (pp. 89-90) lists as one of the major failings of the NSF-India science program the failure to establish such funding in India. NAS 1969b (p. 6) strongly urges that Colciencias, the funding agency of Colombia, *not* distribute its funds in a uniform way among all contenders without regard to merit.

The social status of scientists is a concern of science policy (see for example SHAH 1967, p. 370), a matter discussed in detail in chapter 8.

A few words are in order about corruption in administrative structures. This is a touchy subject, of course, and there is not much found in the literature about it (although ZAHALN 1972c discusses it at some length in connection with Arab countries). In my opinion, the primary curse of corruption is not that public funds are embezzled for personal use. Even in a relatively poor country, the total amount of public funds is large enough that only a small percentage of it can be stolen. The most significant effect of corruption is that posts are filled with people appointed on grounds other than merit, and decisions are made on irrelevant grounds. This type of corruption may, but need not, have financial motivations. The motive may be to maintain a certain social system, to honor a tradition of strong family ties, or to exhibit loyalty to a political ideology. The problem is immense, and scarcely any country is entirely free of it (ACs included).

The following is a list of sources where information about specific science plans and policies for particular countries can be found.

UNESCO 1970a (pp. 11-32): Afghanistan, Burma, Cambodia, Ceylon (now Sri Lanka), Republic of China, India, Indonesia, Iran, Japan, Republic of Korea, Laos, Malaysia, Mongolia, Nepal, Pakistan, Philippines, Singapore, Thailand, and Republic of Vietnam.

UNESCO 1966a: Algeria, Basutoland, Bechuanaland, Burundi, Cameroon, Central African Republic, Chad, Congo (Brazzaville), Democratic Republic of Congo (now Zaire), Dahomey, Ethiopia, Gabon, Gambia, Ghana, Guinea, Ivory Coast, Kenya, Liberia, Libya, Madagascar, Malawi, Mali, Mauritania, Mauritius, Morocco, Niger, Nigeria, Southern Rhodesia, Rwanda, Senegal, Sierra Leone, Somalia, Sudan, Swaziland, Tanzania, Togo, Tunisia, Uganda, United Arab Republic, Upper Volta, and Zambia.

ROYAL 1968: Australia, Botswana, Lesotho, Swaziland, Canada, Ceylon (now Sri Lanka), Kenya, Uganda, Tanzania, Ghana, Guyana, Hong Kong, India, Malawi, Malta, New Zealand, Nigeria, Pakistan, Sierra Leone, Singapore, West Indies, Zambia, and Rhodesia.

ZAHLAN 1972c: Iraq, Syria, Lebanon, Jordan, Saudi Arabia, Kuwait, Oman, Arab Emirates, Yemen A.R., and P.D.R. Yemen.

WU 1970 (pp. 466-73): People's Republic of China. For this country, see also DEDIJER 1965, a bibliography through 1964.

OECD 1968a and 1971b: Spain.

OECD 1968c: Greece.

UNESCO 1970f: Argentina.

UNESCO 1970e: Philippines.

MARTIN 1970: Nigeria.

NIGERIA 1970a: Nigeria.

INDONESIA 1969: Indonesia.

QUBAIN 1966 (p. 170): Egypt.

PERU 1970: Peru.

MEXICO 1970: Mexico.

CST 1970 and RAHMAN 1973: India.

TURKEY 1969: Turkey.

OECD 1969: Turkey.

BRAZIL 1971: Brazil.

KOREA 1970 and 1971a: Republic of Korea.

ODHIAMBO 1967: East Africa.

UNESCO 1972a gives a table showing the correlation between UNESCO science policy programs in a given country and local formation or reformulation of science policies.

Let us now consider the financial aspects of providing for science. An illustration of the unreliability of statistics are those on Pakistan presented in PAKISTAN 1968 (p. 28) and SIDDIQI (p. 62). The two differ in some instances by a factor of three. WU 1970 (p. 406) describes the use of statistics for political propaganda. FREEMAN 1969a urges uniformity, unambiguous definitions, and precise classifications in the collecting of statistics, and refers to the Frascati manual.

The quantitative financial data are numerous. Per capita GNP figures can be found in many economic reference books; some are given in SPAEY 1969 (p. 71). Absolute figures for R&D expenditures of countries in all parts of the world in local currencies have been collected in UNESCO 1970c (pp. 42-50). Additional figures for individual countries can be found in the following sources: CST 1970 (pp. 105-109) and SESHACHAR 1972 (p. 136) for India; MEXICO 1970 (pp. 378ff) for Mexico; NADER 1969 (pp. 193-96) for Egypt; OECD 1968b (p. 202) and 1971b for Spain; OECD 1968a (p. 27) for Greece; KOREA 1972b (pp. 44-47) for the Republic of Korea; UNESCO 1970e (p. 32) for the Philippines; UNESCO 1970f (p. 53) for Argentina; PERU 1970 (p. 44) for Peru; OECD 1970c (p. 194) for Greece; HAWKES 1971 (p. 1217) for Chile; CELASUN 1972 (p. 18) for Turkey; and OLDHAM 1968 (p. 485) for the People's Republic of China.

A more commonly used index of such expenditures is the ratio of funds for R&D to GNP, expressed as a percentage. UNESCO 1970c (pp. 51-55) gives a worldwide tabulation (with many gaps, however). SPAEY 1969 (p. 71) lists figures for the ACs and some LDCs. UN 1971a (p. 56) reports that the average figure for LDCs is 0.2%. UNESCO 1970b (p. 32) has data for some ACs. UNESCO 1970e (p. 25) and PHILIPPINES 1969b (p. 37) present a table for various Asian countries (the percentage for Thailand, for example, is 1.04). ZAHLAN 1972c reports that the percentage for the Middle Eastern Arab states is negligible, with Lebanon, one of the most advanced, spending 0.02% (ZAHLAN 1972a). UNESCO 1970a (p. 134) gives a table for 12 countries, both ACs and LDCs. Figures for the People's Republic of China are very difficult to ascertain. None are officially published, and the total must be estimated on the basis of fragmentary information from various sources. WU 1970 (pp. 408-10) cites data which amount to about 2% of GNP; OLDHAM 1968 (p. 485) gives a figure for 1960 of 1.54%. Both percentages are relatively high. The figure for the Republic of China is 0.8% (CHINA 1972, p. 5) but includes grants for subsidy of graduate work in the sciences. The figure for Mexico is given by TELLEZ 1968 (p. 47) as 0.07-0.1% and ECHEVERRIA 1972 (p. 44) as 0.13% in 1968. GOWON 1972 (p. 56) indicates an unusually large figure of 1% for Nigeria. SESHACHAR 1972 (p. 136) and CST 1969 (p. 60) agree on 0.4-0.43% for India (see also CST 1970, p. 109). According to PAKISTAN 1968 (p. 28), the figure for Pakistan is 0.17-0.13%, but according to SIDDIQI (pp. 63-67), it is 0.32-0.41% (both for 1963-66). OECD 1968b (p. 202) gives 0.25% as the figure for Spain (see also OECD 1971b, pp. 17, 19, 48), and OECD 1968a (p. 27) reports 0.23% for Greece. NAS 1966 (p. 55) states that in 1966 Brazil planned to achieve a figure of 1%, but informal sources indicated to me recently that the present figure is closer to 0.7%. For Argentina, UNESCO 1970f (p. 52) gives 0.32-0.34%. PERU 1970 (p. 20) gauges the expenditure of Peru at 0.17%. For Turkey, CELASUN 1972 (p. 18) gives 0.37%. HAWKES 1971 (p. 1217) estimates the figure for Chile to be 0.4-0.5%. In 1971 the figure for the Republic of Korea was 0.34% (KOREA 1972b, pp. 44-47).

Some LDCs have increased their R&D expenditures quite rapidly. OLDHAM 1968 (p. 485) reports figures of 0.01% in 1950 and 1.54% in 1960 for the People's Republic of China. WU 1970 (p. 411) states that R&D expenditures increased by 100% every year in that country in 1962-65. NADER 1969 (p. 196) reports a 23-fold absolute increase in Egypt between 1961 and 1967, though this represents only a fourfold increase in percentage of GNP. India's increase between 1958 and 1969 was fivefold in absolute figures or twofold in percentage of GNP (CST 1969, p. 60, and CST 1970, p. 107). UNESCO 1970f (p. 52) shows a great increase in Argentina between 1961 and 1966, but it represents mainly inflation. Other figures on the time development of such expenditures can be found in SPAEY 1969 (p. 76) covering ACs and a few LDCs, with a graph for the US (p. 77). KOREA 1972b (pp. 54-74) also gives data for ACs. PAKISTAN 1968 (p. 28) and SIDDIQI (p. 62) disagree again on the figures for Pakistan. UNESCO 1970e (p. 32) offers figures for the Philippines. UNESCO 1970b (p. 31) contains some comparative figures for the prewar and postwar periods in ACs.

In some sources, the percentage is given in terms not of GNP but of national income; examples are NADER 1969 (p. 199) for Egypt; OECD 1968b (p. 202) for Spain; KOREA 1972b (pp. 44-47) for the Republic of Korea and various ACs; and PHILIPPINES 1969b (p. 32) for the Philippines. In some cases, the percentage is given in terms of the national budget, in terms of governmental expenditures, such as in NADER 1969 (p. 196) for Egypt, in PHILIPPINES 1969b (p. 38) for the Philippines and some ACs, and in CST 1969 (p. 60) for India. These percentages are of little comparative value because of the different economic systems prevailing in different countries.

An interesting figure is the annual R&D expenditure per capita of population. Data are given in SPAEY 1969 (p. 71) for ACs and a few LDCs; in AID 1972a (p. 75) for Iran; in UNESCO 1970a (p. 135) for a number of ACs and LDCs; in CLARKE 1971 (p. 50) for an average number of LDCs and the UK; in UNESCO 1970e (p. 32) for the Philippines; in UNESCO 1970b (p. 81) for ACs mainly; in UNESCO 1970b (p. 158) for Japan; in UNESCO 1970f (p. 52) for Argentina; in DEDIJER 1960 (p. 459) for ACs and some LDCs; in DEDIJER 1963 (p. 62) for a number of ACs and LDCs; and in BHATHAL 1971a for Southeast Asian countries and Singapore. Typical figures are approximately as follows (projected for about 1970): US, $110; USSR, $50; UK, $50; some smaller European countries, $3-10; some more dynamic LDCs (such as Singapore, Iran, People's Republic of China, Argentina), $2; other LDCs, $0.1-1.0.

While the cost of research per scientist tends to be lower in LDCs the differences are relatively small. The cause may be partly the intrinsically lower cost of research in LDCs but partly the less adequate support given scientists in LDCs. The various figures given in the literature are difficult to compare. They are calculated from different years, and the cost of research is increasing rapidly everywhere (not only because of inflation but also because research is intrinsically more expensive as we explore natural phenomena farther removed from everyday experience). In any case, the highest figure that I found in consulting various sources was $60,000 per scientist per year for Switzerland (UNESCO 1970b, p. 81) while the lowest for a roughly comparable year was $5,200 for the Republic of Korea (KOREA 1972b, p. 50). For India the figure was $8,000 (RAY 1969) and for the US $50,000 (RAY 1969). Other figures can be found in OECD 1968a (p. 29), UNESCO 1964c (p. 19), UNESCO 1970a (p. 128), KOREA 1972b (p. 50), USMANI 1964 (p. 6), and UNESCO 1970b (pp. 81, 105, 166). At the most, the ratio between the highest and lowest is about 10. A more likely average figure would be a factor of three or five between ACs and LDCs.

The relative distribution of R&D expenditures is discussed and documented in chapter 5. The following additional sources discuss it in the context of budgetary considerations: SPAEY 1969 (p. 72); SESHACHAR 1972 (p. 139); OECD 1968b (p. 277); KOREA 1972b (pp. 46-49); PAKISTAN 1968 (pp. 28-33); SIDDIQI (pp. 62-67); CST 1969 (pp. 59, 61, 62); CST 1970 (p. 120); UNESCO 1970e (p. 33); UNESCO 1970f (p. 53); UNESCO 1970c (pp. 42-50); OECD 1971c (pp. 194, 197); OECD 1971b (pp. 25-26); and CELASUN 1972 (p. 18).

There are a number of possible relationships among the various manpower and financial indices of science development. A graph of GNP per capita versus population (e.g., JONES 1971, p. 3) shows no correlation: there are large and small poor countries, and large and small rich countries. WILLIAMS 1964 (Diagram III) plots percentage of GNP growth per capita versus R&D expenditures as percentage of GNP and finds no correlation. There are, however, four relationships in which the correlation is quite good.

(1) WILLIAMS 1964 (Diagram II) plots R&D expenditures as percentage of GNP versus GNP per capita and finds a proportionality between the logarithms of these two quantities valid within a factor of 2 from the means of the quantities themselves.

(2) DEDIJER 1964a (Figure 6) plots R&D expenditures per capita versus R&D expenditures as percentage of GNP and finds a proportionality between the logarithms of these two quantities also good in most cases to a factor of 2 from the means of the quantities themselves (this relationship is also mentioned in DEDIJER 1960, p. 460).

(3) PRICE 1969a (figure on page 106) plots for each country the number of scientific authors (as obtained from the International Directory of Research and Development Scientists) versus the GNP and finds a proportionality between the logarithms of these two quantities. In this case, the range of the abscissa is over four units in the logarithm and that of the ordinate over five units in the logarithm. Yet the relationship is valid, even at the worst part of the curve, within ± 1 unit in the logarithm, and in most places it is even more accurate. (In PRICE 1972a, p. 29, the same graph is reproduced and a curved line is superimposed drawn through some of the data points. Considering the scatter, however, the line appears to have no statistical significance.)

(4) RAY 1969 (p. 420, Table 1) lists R&D expenditure per scientist versus national income per capita (virtually the same as GNP per capita). Though only a few figures are given, they exhibit proportionality in the logarithms of these quantities.

It is easy to understand the origin of these relationships. Price's result is a direct consequence of three facts: (a) the cost of research per scientist is roughly the same (within a factor of 3 from the mean) in all countries since lower salaries in LDCs are offset by higher costs of equipment; (b) the percentage of GNP spent on publishable (i.e., unclassified) research is roughly the same (within a factor of 4 from the mean) for most countries; (c) the specific productivity of scientists (the number of publications per scientist per year) is roughly the same (within a factor of 3 from the mean) for most countries. Furthermore, there is a positive correlation between cost of research per scientist and specific productivity (in the sense that in ACs where research costs are high, scientists also tend to be more productive). Thus, the cost of research per scientific publication is probably roughly the same for all countries, perhaps even more accurately than a factor of 3 from the mean.

Within a factor of roughly 3 x 3 = 9, therefore, the more funds available in any country, the more will be spent on R & D, the more scientists will be supported, and the more publications will be obtained, as Price's relationship indicates.

One can, in fact, demonstrate this more rigorously and at the same time show that Dedijer's and Williams's relationships are equivalent by using a bit of algebra. Let us make the following definitions:

A = GNP in units of $$10^6$$
B = R & D expenditure in units of $$10^6$$
C = Population in units of $$10^6$$ people
D = Number of scientists in units of one scientist
E = Number of scientific authors in units of one author

The four relationships can then be written as follows:

Williams: $$\frac{B}{A} = 10^{-5} \frac{A}{C} \tag{1}$$

Dedijer: $$\frac{B}{C} = 10^{5} \left(\frac{B}{A}\right)^2 \tag{2}$$

Price: $$E = 2.2 \times 10^{-3} A^{4/3} \tag{3}$$

Ray: $$\frac{B}{D} = 3.9 \times 10^{-4} \left(\frac{A}{C}\right)^{3/5} \tag{4}$$

Equations (1) and (2) are the same since each of them may be expressed in the form $10^5 BC = A^2$. We have, therefore, three different relationships for the five unknowns. Let us now *assume* that the specific productivity E/D is the same for all countries, specifically that E/D = 0.3 (which is reasonable if we remember that the source for E used by Price includes only the *first* author of a paper with several co-authors). Combining (4) with (1) or (2), we get $D = 2.55 B^{2/5} A^{3/5}$; using (1) again to eliminate B, and inserting our assumption E = 0.3 D, we get $E = 7.8 \times 10^{-3} A^{7/5} C^{-2/5}$. Now the total range of C among the various countries is only about 100, and $100^{2/5}$ is only about 6. If we are willing to neglect factors of ±2.5 (which we can do since Price's relationship holds only within a factor of 10), we can replace $C^{-2/5}$ by its average value of 0.29. We then obtain $E = 2.2 \times 10^{-3} A^{7/5}$ which is for all practical purposes identical with (3). We see, therefore, that these various relationships are interrelated. Indeed, they are simple consequences of a few rather obvious facts about expenditures and manpower for science development.

DEDIJER 1964a and 1963 (p. 65) plot income per capita versus various other indicators of scientific acitivity, such as attendance at meetings and the existence of academies. Correlations are again evident.

Another financial aspect of science development is the issue of salaries. WU 1970 (p. 542) and UNESCO 1969c (p. 136) show that in the People's Republic of China, Venezuela, and the US the salaries of the highest and lowest ranking scientific workers differ by a factor of about 6. MENDELSOHN 1960 (p. 1263) reports that the ratio of the wage of a top scientist to that of an average worker is about the same in the People's Republic of China as in Britain. Though these are fragmentary figures, they reinforce the earlier suggestion that disparities in salaries are not a crucial problem in LDCs. Figures on Indian salaries can be found in RAHMAN 1973 (pp. 158-59).

There is an acute shortage of foreign exchange for science development in many LDCs, as mentioned in SABATO 1970 (p. 190). A few fortunate countries, such as Venezuela and Malaysia, do not face this difficulty.

UNESCO 1965b (p. 167) discusses ways of encouraging private financing of research, an acute problem in most LDCs, through tax benefits, research associations, patents, and governmental technical assistance.

Financial targets (as opposed to actual expenditures) for R & D are often given in national documents. Most countries consider it advisable to strive for the internationally established goal of 1% of GNP (UN 1971a, p. 56; UN 1970b, p. 17; UNESCO 1964a, pp. 53-54). ZAHLAN 1972c instead sets goals in absolute amounts for the Arab countries. CHINA 1972 (p. 5) sets a goal of 2% of GNP for the Republic of China. PERU 1970 (p. 20) urges the attainment of 1.3% in 20 years. OECD 1968c (pp. 219-20) projects an increase by a factor of 12 in industrial research in Greece between 1966 and 1975. Projections are seldom realized, but they do have a stimulating effect on development efforts.

Let us now turn to problems of organization. It is often instructive to view these matters in a historical context, and in fact there are a number of interesting papers in this vein. One of the most perceptive in BASALLA 1967 which establishes a general framework for the organization of science in LDCs. Another general, theoretical paper is DEDIJER 1962 which discusses what he calls the intellectual, economic, and political phases of the history of

scientific research. The situation in India is described in RANGA-
NATHAN 1959, RAHMAN 1973, and SINGH 1965 (p. 43) with
some remarks on the British role. East Africa is covered in
WORTHINGTON 1948. PRICE 1965c explains how the primary
emphasis in productivity has now shifted to the sciences.

Most countries lack the effective interaction of scientists with
government needed to assure a realistic policy within science. MO-
RAVCSIK 1973e and NATURE 1964a remark on this in a general
context. According to SESHACHAR 1972 (p. 139), this is one of
the main problems in India.

There are a number of warnings in the literature against strict
centralization of activities in science policy emphasizing that it
does not work. Examples are UNESCO 1970a (p. 126); NAS 1966
(pp. 57-58); and GLYDE 1973, in the context of Thailand. ODHI-
AMBO 1967 (p. 878), on the other hand, advocated increased centralization in East Africa.

An important aspect of science policy is the encouragement of
young scientists, as emphasized in SHAH 1967 (p. 394); KOPECZI
1972 (p. 669); NATURE 1964b (p. 529); RAM 1968 (p. 9) discusses democracy in laboratories.

The curses of bureaucracy affect science all over the world.
SHAH 1967 (p. 388) states with reference to India that "the extension . . . of a bureaucracy to the scientific field tends to accen-
tuate a false sense of prestige due to status and office." RAM 1968
(pp. 8, 9) urges more research and less organizing. SHILS 1961 (p.
51) asserts that "the organization of laboratories . . . will have to
make provisions to avoid the frustration of this scientific disposi-
tion by the dead hand of a desiccated and embittered older generation or by an unsympathetic and non-understanding bureaucracy."
The same problems are listed in ROCHE 1966 (p. 55) with respect
to Latin America.

A closely related subject, the civil service, is discussed in chapter 5. In ALLENDE 1972 (p. 39), this problem is glossed over by
the government, but GOWON 1972 (p. 63) expresses concern and
promises a remedy. SALCEDO 1972 (p. 181) reports that the situation is terrible in the Philippines. The most detailed and eloquent description of the problem, however, is that of SABATO
1970 (pp. 187-89).

Different countries have different formats for organizing science
policy. UN 1971a (pp. 91-94) and UNESCO 1972a present a large
table indicating the type of policy-making body for each country.

(A somewhat older listing can be found in EL-SAID 1969.) Examples of ministries of science and technology are given in KIM 1969 (p. 94), KOREA 1972b for most of the Republic of Korea, and BHATHAL 1971b for Singapore.

Organizations similar to national science councils are numerous. ALLENDE 1972 (p. 35) mentions Chile's CONICYT. ECHEVERRIA 1972 (p. 45) and MEXICO 1971 discuss Mexico's CONACYT. The activities of the Nigerian NCST are mentioned in GOWAN 1972 (pp. 56, 59), NIGERIA 1970, MARTIN 1970, and MORAVCSIK 1973g; the last two also deal with similar organizations in Turkey, Indonesia, the Republic of Korea, and Brazil. SESHACHAR 1972 (p. 140) concludes that the Indian COST is mainly a decorative organization. The Indian Science Advisory Committee is similarly criticized in PARTHASARATHI 1966 as being weak, susceptible to governmental pressures, and inconspicuous. The early history of Indian organizations can be found in SWAMINATHAN 1954. SALCEDO 1972 (pp. 178, 182) describes the structure of the Philippine National Science Development Board. NADER 1969 (p. 191) covers the Science Council in Egypt. WU 1970 (pp. 61, 403) reports on the Scientific and Technological Commission in the People's Republic of China. INDONESIA 1971 deals with the Indonesian Institute of Sciences, LIPI. The research council in South Africa is described in NAUDE 1959. SALAM 1970b finds the corresponding structures in Pakistan weak and ineffective. General discussion of research councils can be found in ZAHEER 1968 (p. 11) and NADER 1969 (p. 412).

Academies are another organ of science policy-making. SESHACHAR 1972 (p. 139) declares that the Academy in India is weak. On the other hand, in the People's Republic of China, the Academy of Sciences plays an enormously powerful and centralized role (WU 1970, pp. 51, 54, 402, 417, 423, 429, 546-54, 559-60, with tables of personnel and expenditure on pp. 546-55). The situation in Egypt in 1946 is described in MOSHARAFFA PASHA 1946. The state of affairs in Singapore is reported in BHATHAL 1971b. In NAS 1966 (p. 58), Harrison Brown (a distinguished member of the US NAS) expresses some reservations that academies' criteria for selecting members are ambiguous, control is excessively centralized, and there are difficulties in actually getting things done.

Organization in governmental laboratories is amply described in the literature. PRICE 1969c (p. 6) claims that this mode of research is often excessively expensive and clumsy. WU 1970 (pp. 416-20) describes the method by which such laboratories obtain support in the People's Republic of China. Governmental laboratories in India (CSIR, Atomic Energy, agricultural and medical research organs, etc.) are described in SESHACHAR 1972 (p. 134), NATURE 1955, RAHMAN 1964, SINGH 1965, BHABHA 1966a, and 1966b. The latter suggests a difference between the establishment of CSIR and Atomic Energy. CSIR first established a structure and then raided the universities to fill the created posts; Atomic Energy created the structure as the need arose, in terms of availability of qualified personnel, and thus avoided interfering with university development. (The author was a founder of the Atomic Energy programs, however, and may not be a completely unbiased observer.) The work of the Argentine Atomic Energy Commission is described in ARGENTINA 1966, SABATO 1968, and 1973. The Venezuelan IVIC, outlined in IVIC 1971, has an interesting structure in which researchers are grouped by disciplines but not divided into "basic" and "applied." SHAH 1967 (p. 365) provides information about Pakistani governmental laboratories under PCSIR and PAEC. SALCEDO 1972 (p. 178) describes the large governmental science center in the Philippines. Remarks about this center can also be found in MORAVCSIK 1971c (p. 36). NAS 1967 (p. 9) makes the general assertion that research institutions should combine strong leadership with a maximum amount of internal freedom.

The organization of university research is discussed in chapter 2. References are NADER 1969 (p. 350), the Middle East; AID 1970, the story of KAIS in the Republic of Korea (described in chapter 7); and GARCIA 1966, Latin America.

It is often useful to have a description or chart of the general organization of science in a particular country. The following is an incomplete but substantial list of such references. One of the most useful items is the Directory of National Science Policy Making Bodies (UNESCO 1966b). Other sources provide information on several countries together: UNESCO 1967a (Algeria, Iran, Iraq, Jordan, Kuwait, Lebanon, Morocco, Saudi Arabia, Sudan, Tunisia, Turkey, and United Arab Republic); UNESCO 1969c (Argentina, Bolivia, Brazil, Chile, Colombia, Ecuador, Jamaica, Mexico, Paraguay, Peru, Uruguay, Venezuela, Panama, and Central America in general); UNESCO 1969b (Burundi, Cameroon, Congo [Brazzaville], Dahomey, Ethiopia, Gabon, Ghana, Ivory Coast, Liberia,

Madagascar, Malawi, Mali, Nigeria, Rwanda, Senegal, Togo, Upper Volta, Zambia); and UNESCO 1965a (Australia, Ceylon [now Sri Lanka], Republic of China, Hong Kong, India, Indonesia, Israel, Japan, Republic of Korea, Nepal, New Zealand, Pakistan, Philippines, Thailand, and Republic of Vietnam). MORAVCSIK 1973g deals with Brazil, Nigeria, Indonesia, Republic of Korea, and Turkey. Turkey is covered in OECD 1969 (p. 181), a detailed account, and in CELASUN 1972. Organizational charts for the Republic of Korea and several ACs are given in KOREA 1972b (pp. 150-65). The People's Republic of China is discussed in WU 1970, OLDHAM 1968, and RANGARAO 1966. The organization of science in Cuba is the subject of RYDER 1969b. Information about India is voluminous: CST 1969 and RAHMAN 1973 (pp. 48, 52, 54, 57, 62, 83) give detailed accounts and can be supplemented by UNESCO 1967b (p. 34). For Pakistan, see USMANI 1971, PAKISTAN 1968, and SIDDIQI. Organization in the United Arab Republic is described in NADER 1969 (pp. 222-32), more sketchily in MITCHISON 1960, and in UNESCO 1967b (p. 67). East Africa is discussed in WORTHINGTON 1948 and ODHIAMBO 1967 (pp. 876-77). The Middle East and North Africa is the subject of NATURE 1964c. References for Singapore are BHATHAL 1969, 1971b, and 1971d. Mexico's organization is outlined in MEXICO 1970 (p. 142). NAS 1966 reports on Peru, GHANA 1973 (pp. 7-11) on Ghana, CHINA 1972 (pp. 3, 24) on the Republic of China, UNESCO 1970f on Argentina, OECD 1971b (p. 41) on Spain, and OECD 1968c (p. 185) on Greece. NAS 1968a lists institutions of higher education, research, and planning in Colombia. For comparison, UFFEN 1972 deals with the organization of science policy in Canada.

SABATO 1970 (p. 190) comments on the problems of customs offices: "The situation is even more serious in the case of a purchase from a foreign country, for then you have in addition all the business of import permits, availability of foreign currency, tax certificates, etc., ending up with the truly Kafkaesque world of customs." An international agreement (the so-called Florence agreement) has existed since 1950 to allow for greatly simplified importation of scientific equipment. Though it now has 68 contracting states, in most cases it has had little practical effect.

I believe that people involved in science development are a factor of pivotal importance in achieving success. In this context, some commentators ask whether economists can make a significant

contribution to providing for science. Doubts are expressed in
NAS 1965b (p. 83) and MORAVCSIK 1973g. ROESSNER 1968
doubts whether planning for science in LDCs can be done on the
basis of economic theory. A similar concern is implied in COOPER
1971. On the other hand, some outstanding persons in the field of
science policy have a formal background in economics, so one cannot generalize. UNESCO 1970a (p. 117) suggests that the membership of bodies concerned with science policy be two-thirds active
scientists of high quality and one-third nonscientists.

One cannot stress enough the importance of outstanding individuals. CIMT 1970b (p. 690) urges that exceptional measures be
taken to support the activities of exceptional individuals. SESHA-
CHAR 1972 (p. 138) flatly claims that "whatever development of
science there has been [in India] is largely due to the personalities
of some men of science in the past and the great influence they
were able to wield with the government." WEINBERG 1967 remarks (in the preface) that committees cannot produce wisdom—
they just use it.

Training of persons in providing for science has been neglected.
This has been emphasized by many observers, for example, in CO-
PISAROW 1970 (p. 21); BLACKETT 1968 (p. 23); MORAVCSIK
1964c (p. 168); 1964a, 1964b (p. 9), 1972a (p. 197), and 1973f,
in connection with visits of scientists to LDCs from ACs. RAY
1967a (p. 9) urges careful selection of science administrators.
UNESCO 1973b (p. 5) complains that UNESCO documents on science policy are not well enough known in LDCs, an unsurprising
fact since they are relatively expensive and not easily available
even in ACs. PRICE 1964a (p. 196) argues that critics of science
need not be scientists themselves, comparing them with critics of
art or music. As one of the latter, I can say that most respected
music critics have had a longstanding, active, personal involvement
with music in one way or another, even if they are not renowned
soloists or composers. The same must hold for science critics with
allowance for the exception that proves the rule.

OAS has supported study programs in science policy (OAS
1970, p. 18) while UNESCO has organized many conferences on
science policy which have been amply cited in this book. But talking about providing for science is not the same as doing it. New
practical activities are needed to make progress in that area.

Seven

International Aspects

It has been emphasized throughout that science has a strongly international character. International activities are a normal, mandatory part of the science of any country. In addition, however, international activities include scientific assistance between countries, particularly from ACs to LDCs. This is to a large extent a separate subject, though the two undoubtedly overlap in many places.

International scientific activities of the customary type in LDCs are discussed in chapter 4. However, there is a significant difference in this respect between LDCs and ACs. International scientific activities in ACs are a fairly balanced combination of formal programs arranged by large organizations, governments, etc., and of informal ties generated from within the scientific community through individual initiatives. The bulk of international activities in LDCs, on the other hand, are of the formal type. The most important international connections which really contribute to the advancement of scientific work are the *de facto* international ties among scientists on a working level, but these connections are scarcer in LDCs than in ACs. There are good reasons for this state of affairs: formal ties are easy to form, inexpensive to maintain, and a conspicuous demonstration of goodwill. In official reports and listings, therefore, one finds that both ACs and LDCs belong to the same international unions, United Nations agencies, etc. (though this fact is generally unknown to scientists in both types of countries). The situation needs much improvement; the initiative can come from either side, but it must come from within the scientific community itself.

The other aspect of international scientific relations, scientific assistance, will be dealt with in the remainder of this chapter. Scientific assistance is, of course, part of the international political relations among countries. In that sense, it has a huge literature which, however, is not our direct concern here. Instead, I shall discuss the more technical and organizational aspects of international assistance. Yet, I cannot begin without touching on the question of motivation for such aid.

As noted in chapter 1 in connection with the justification of science in LDCs, most successful causes have a broad range of justifications, among which people with highly differing thoughts and values can all find something to their liking. The assertion that an AC must provide scientific aid to a "friendly" LDC in order to assure that the LDC can withstand political or military pressure from "unfriendly" neighbors is quite compatible with the claim that ACs have a moral obligation to furnish scientific assistance to LDCs (on purely humanitarian grounds or as "reparation payments" for presumed past injustices). As long as these arguments agree on providing aid with the intention of building up indigenous science, the multidimensional justification should not be a impediment; it will undoubtedly be a stimulus. Whatever the motivation, however, the expectation of gratitude on the part of LDCs for assistance rendered by ACs is an unrealistic one and should not play a role in the administration of such aid.

Scientific aid has played a crucial role in the development of science throughout the ages, though perhaps not always as formalized as today. Civilizations have emerged and flourished at various times in various parts of the world, and whatever science they had to offer was propagated to "barbarians" together with the other components of those civilizations. The real mushrooming of science, however, began only about 300 years ago. The origins of science may be traced back to civilizations in Northern Africa and elsewhere, but in a functional sense, modern science is the product of Western civilization. Hence, scientific assistance has primarily emanated from Europe and North America. Whether a proper effort has been made in this assistance is frequently discussed now in the context of trying to place the blame for the present backwardness in science of most countries outside Western civilization. I personally find this question quite uninteresting because it argues over the past instead of being concerned about the present and, even more important, about the future.

Scientific assistance, like other forms of assistance, cannot provide the major part of the development effort in the recipient country. The lion's share of development must be indigenous. (The Marshall Plan for Europe after World War II constituted, in purely financial terms, only a small fraction of the total resources in postwar Europe.) The aim of assistance must be selective and catalytic action. The contact points of assistance must be strategically chosen so that small amounts of assistance can stimulate large amounts of indigenous activity in the proper direction. To attain this, one needs a significant understanding of the mechanism of scientific development and the infrastructure that will support it. The areas of assistance are much easier to delineate: education, manpower, communication, research, and science organization and policy. They are the same as the primary components of the building of science itself.

Scientific assistance is sometimes disapproved on the grounds that it provides a crutch to a country and impedes the attainment of scientific independence. The criticism is valid if scientific assistance is administered and used improperly. On the other hand, no country has yet managed to develop its own science without assistance. Thus, assistance properly used appears to be essential. Even with assistance, however, science development is a slow process. Judgments about success or failure must be made cautiously, and patience should prevail on all sides.

One of the problems in administering international scientific assistance is the shortage of appropriate personnel, particularly in ACs. This may seem incredible, considering the selective and catalytic nature of assistance, because 92% of the world's scientists are in ACs. Yet, largely because of the passivity of the scientific community in ACs (discussed later in detail), scientific assistance is in need of good people. Personnel involved in assistance should be taken from the scientific community of the ACs and rotated periodically to insure continued contact with science by those involved in assistance. Instead, a permanent staff often develops for the administration of scientific assistance and soon comes to be regarded as a group of bureaucrats rather than scientific colleagues, to the detriment of the assistance program.

Should aid be narrowly oriented toward a specific, often applied problem, or should it try to strengthen the broad scientific infrastructure? There is little doubt that both are needed. In practice, however, the distribution of scientific aid is heavily slanted in favor of narrow, problem-oriented projects; hence, demands for a more equitable balance are justified. This problem will be discussed later in connection with particular aid-giving agencies.

Scientific assistance is administered through a broad variety of organizations: governmental agencies, private foundations, scientific associations, international agencies, regional organizations, etc. Each has its strengths and weaknesses, and a multichanneled approach for scientific assistance is advisable. Here, as in most other realms of science policy and organization, a centralized, monolithic approach can be damaging.

Participation of the international scientific community on a significant level is indispensable for a successful scientific aid program. For example, if an international research institute is formed, it must be staffed with eminent people from both ACs and LDCs, and political difficulties must not be allowed to interfere with its work. For this to be accomplished, the institute must be operated and governed to a large extent by scientists themselves, as various positive and negative examples have shown. Scientific professional societies can play a significant role in channeling informal scientific assistance from country to country. Perhaps most important, influential and devoted scientists must find ways of influencing the governments of ACs so that scientific assistance is undertaken and carried out in an effective manner. Science development is a subtle, long-range task which has no natural constituency in a heterogeneous political arena. Its future, therefore, depends on the persuasive power of interested "experts."

Participation of the scientific community can take many forms, some of which have been discussed. Certain forms would not involve active steps, only the avoidance of involuntary negative contributions. For example, equitable distribution of preprints and reports mainly requires a realization of this problem on the part of every potential scientific author and a will to avoid violating equitability. Other actions may involve positive steps without a major change in living patterns. For example, scientists could take advantage of opportunities to work on problems of particular interest to LDCs in their spare time but in their home environment. Still other activities would involve some departure from present practices, such as spending some leaves of absence in LDCs interacting with the scientific community there. At the present time, however, the actual interest and participation in any of these categories is minimal.

International scientific aid plays a distinctly subordinate role

in the US governmental structure. Foreign aid as a whole is in fact
not very prominent: total international assistance, both governmental and private, is hardly more than 0.5% of the GNP, and the
fraction is not growing. But even within the existing program for
international assistance, science is a stepchild. The formal "reason" is that there is no US governmental agency within which scientific assistance can find substantial support. In the executive
branch of the government, even before the OST and the PSAC
were abolished, science in LDCs received very little attention.
PSAC rarely took any action on its behalf. OST had an official
concerned with international science, but he had to spend most
of his time on ceremonial links with other ACs and had practically no time for LDCs.

AID would ordinarily be expected to organize scientific assistance for LDCs. However, the overall task of AID includes economic, social, and technological assistance as well, and the mandate
is a staggering one. As an organization with high visibility, an almost impossible task, and a precarious position between the executive and legislative branches of the government, AID is the target
of frequent criticism from a multitude of quarters. I am not one
of those who fail to give AID credit for many specific projects well
done, nor am I an indiscriminate admirer of the organization. In
addition to problems of rigidity and heavy-handedness common to
most giant organizations, AID has two important shortcomings
from the point of view of science development: its almost exclusive preoccupation with short-term projects and its predilection
for large scale projects. AID admits and rationalizes both of these.
It claims that Congressional appropriations are governed by a desire for conspicuous short-term achievements, and that AID cannot
afford to wander into projects whose subtle benefits would not
be evident for a decade or two. (By no means would all congressmen agree with this characterization of the Congressional wish.)
AID also claims that it cannot afford to administer small and
experimental projects since the cost of administering projects is
largely independent of their size, and they have only limited personnel. Whatever the reasons, the fact remains that because of
these shortcomings and the general background and orientation
of its personnel, AID is heavily slanted toward technology as opposed to science.

If the US scientific assistance program were significantly multichanneled in terms of organizing agencies, the specific prejudice

of AID would not matter so much. In fact, however, the overwhelming majority of US governmental scientific assistance depends on AID for funding, so AID's imprint can be felt across the field.

In part, the realization of this unbalance prompted the creation of the so-called Peterson Commission charged with making recommendations for restructuring the US international assistance program. The commission suggested that an independent entity (International Development Institute or IDI) be established to deal with scientific and technical assistance. Science might still be subordinate to technology, but at least a second, independent opportunity would be offered for science to assert itself. The proposal was forwarded by the President to Congress where it has sat for the past three years with essentially no chance of being acted upon.

Science development fares rather badly in the US Congress. Most of the work in Congress is done in committees and within them by staff members. Unfortunately, Congress has never provided itself with adequate staff, either in quantity or versatility. Staff members are overworked, and with backgrounds predominantly in law, social sciences, or humanities, they have little natural inclination toward science, particularly the international variety. Since international science has no domestic constituency, few congressmen care to devote a major part of their time to it. Even within the Subcommittee on International Cooperation in Science and Space of the Committee on Science and Astronautics of the House of Representatives, international assistance to LDCs occupies a less-than-distinguished position. It is highly unlikely that Congress will take the initiative in championing the cause of science in LDCs. Perhaps select congressmen can be persuaded to pay more attention to this subject.

Federal agencies dealing with science, such as the USAEC and NSF, are not doing much better. The AEC has an international division, but its mandate is limited to matters of atomic energy, and in practice it is concerned mainly with nuclear technology. Since it deals primarily with ACs and UN agencies, the amount of activity that reaches LDCs is infinitesimal.

The NSF has an Office of International Programs with a broader mandate as far as science is concerned. It is burdened with many routine chores involving formalistic ties with other ACs, and hampered by a lack of manpower. Yet it does have some activities concerned with LDCs. It administers some Public Law

480 funds (counterpart funds for US agricultural products locked into local currency in various countries and used by mutual agreement of the US and the particular country for the benefit of that country). Unfortunately, such funds are available only in a very few countries, though sometimes in huge quantities. NSF also administers the SEED program which provides grants for individual scientists and engineers either for travel to an LDC (up to nine months, salary not provided) or for a stay of nine to twelve months in an LDC involving research and teaching (salary provided). Since it is funded by AID, however, it is slanted toward short-term considerations. NSF has recently established a Cooperative Science Program in Latin America for cooperative research projects, joint seminars, and scientific visits between US and Latin American scientists. It is too new to be properly assessed as yet, but it appears to be well-suited for strengthening scientist-to-scientist interaction.

The NAS is a semi-governmental agency supported primarily by the US government; it is perhaps the most active organization in the US government in the area of scientific assistance to LDCs. Its main tools are the study group, seminar, and workshop which it organizes either within the US or in an LDC in cooperation with local counterpart organizations. It also operates a bilateral program designed to upgrade and broaden the chemistry community in Brazil. The proceedings of the meetings and study groups organized by NAS are published and often constitute interesting documents.

Some shortcomings of NAS activities stem from the fact that much of NAS's support originates with AID. The topics chosen bear the AID hallmark of short-term gains and an orientation toward technology. NAS has also been rather unsuccessful in recruiting the rank-and-file of the US scientific and technological community for activities in science development. Over the past decade or more, study groups, meetings, workshops, and other programs in science development have involved only about 600 US scientists and engineers, less than 0.1% of the total US manpower in science and technology. Workshops, seminars, reports, and general advising are helpful, but they are somewhat moot without assistance in the implementation of the ideas developed. The Brazilian chemistry project is an instance of implementation, but it is the exception rather than the rule among NAS activities. As we will see, lack of implementation is also a problem in scientific assistance provided by international organizations. However, it is perhaps too much to ask of "official" organizations that they become organically involved in local implementation of science development. It is often a sensitive political subject that really should be left to the scientists themselves.

The US governmental laboratories play a very small part in international scientific assistance. From time to time they host scientists from LDCs sent under the auspices of other agencies, but they have no particular programs aimed at LDCs. Oak Ridge National Laboratory, with AID funds, has assisted some LDCs, for example Pakistan, in activities determined by the usual AID preferences. The National Bureau of Standards has on occasion been used by AID to organize a conference or conduct a study. The NBS also receives a dozen long-term visitors each year from LDCs; however, their salaries and expenses are not paid by NBS. NBS maintains some cooperative research in India and Pakistan using "special foreign currency" funds (P.L. 480, etc.). The total investment in the scientific component of these projects has been about 0.5 million dollars. The cooperation involves some two dozen Indian institutions. A substantial fraction of the research appears to be rather routine, neither close to the forefronts of basic or applied science nor specifically geared to Indian economic development. One has to conclude in spite of these exceptions that the potential of governmental laboratories to assist in science development has hardly been scratched.

Canada, whose population is about one-tenth that of the US, is in some respects more advanced in the area of scientific assistance to LDCs. Canada spends almost 1% of its GNP on international assistance, about 1.5 times the percentage for the US. It has a counterpart to the proposed US International Development Institute called the International Development Research Centre. The Centre is much smaller (even proportionately) than the planned US IDI. It is mainly research-oriented and not designed to manage large action programs, but it is already in operation, active primarily in technology and in certain applied sciences which closely border on technology. AID's counterpart in Canada is the Canadian International Development Agency.

Most other Western countries have their own scientific assistance programs. In France, for example, compulsory military service can be replaced by service in an LDC, a policy which has provided some helpful scientific visitors to those countries. In former colonies which have continued to maintain close cultural ties with the colonizing country. Programs of scientific assistance by the latter are often better adjusted to local needs than programs of other ACs. For example, British programs in West African countries have broader conception, greater variety, and more flexible management than the corresponding American programs.

In many Western countries, most notably the US, the private sector of the economy could play a part in science development. However, the task is approached without much more energy and resources than the effort of the US government. I have already touched on the role private industry could play in LDCs by sponsoring local scientific research through its subsidiaries, a role seldom performed. Private industry could supplement the education in ACs of students from LDCs by offering them temporary positions during summer vacations or by financially supporting summer seminars at which these students would be introduced to particular aspects of science useful in their home countries.

Private foundations in the US could also play a significant role, though their financial resources are small compared with those of the US government. Opinions differ as to whether foundations play a significant role. In science development, they certainly do not. Very few foundations are active in international assistance in the first place; those that are active generally concentrate on educational and social projects in the mistaken impression that science development in LDCs is taken care of by the government. Foundations fail to utilize their opportunity to stimulate novel and experimental projects. The list of foundation-supported science development projects is usually filled with useful but unimaginative items. In view of the monolithic funding of US governmental activities in science development, this lack of innovation in privately funded science development projects is perhaps the most regrettable shortcoming.

Turning from national to regional science development projects, we encounter different types of difficulties. The intent of a regional project is to combine the resources of many LDCs (sometimes invoking the help of an AC in the same geographical region) and to aid the exchange of information and experience among countries facing similar problems. The difficulties begin with the fact that countries geographically close are not necessarily similar culturally or politically. It is difficult to imagine a regional project for the Indian subcontinent, while a regional grouping in Latin America is not only possible but already in operation. Africa is intermediate: animosities may not be significant, but differences in culture, background, and language often are. Even if a particular region is homogeneous enough to allow a cooperative configuration, differences in size and development among participants may be a problem. In Latin America, for example, Brazil has such a long lead in science over neighboring countries that the regional efforts of OAS or CLAF are handicapped by most countries' fear of being overpowered.

Nevertheless, regional cooperation can be beneficial, and the results are generally appreciated, particularly in Latin America. In that region, there are several different types of organizations. The OAS has its own Department of Scientific Affairs and runs an extensive program based largely on exchanges of experts among the member countries. It is also active in science education, science policy matters, and other areas (details can be found in the second section of this chapter). OAS is an intergovernmental organization and has relatively ample resources but a ponderous organizational structure. In sharp contract, CLAF and similar organizations in other scientific disciplines are "scientists'" organizations with activities directly related to the daily work of scientists but with very small financial resources. A third type of regional organization, of a general nature but with implications for Latin American science, is the Interamerican Bank, which has furnished huge loans to institutions for science education and research.

Europe has many regional organizations with relevance to science and technology, but most do not affect the European LDCs. An exception is OECD which has helped Greece, Ireland, Spain, and Turkey. The activities have primarily involved meetings, study groups, and science policy literature (the latter is of high quality).

In the Middle East, CENTO engages in scientific activities. In South Asia, the Colombo Plan represents a regional association. The former British colonies still maintain contact by Commonwealth ties; conferences are occasionally held to exchange knowledge and experience among those countries on various topics, including science.

Moving from the regional to the worldwide level, we encounter international organizations, particularly the UN and its agencies. At first sight, universal international organizations appear to offer great advantages in administering international scientific assistance. One would think that all charges of political motivations behind assistance programs would disappear, and world resources could be pooled effectively. One might also think that the prestige of such organizations would help stimulate progress. These factors are indeed at play, but they are counteracted by a number of negative factors greatly inhibiting the work the UN can do.

First, neutrality of an organization with a heterogeneous membership can be tantamount to passivity. The UN includes countries with many different philosophies, including some who do not believe in international assistance precisely *because* it does not deliver a political payoff. UN operations must be sufficiently bland and noncontroversial to pass the innumerable committees and officials who review them.

Second, the detrimental effects of a civil service system are evident in the UN and are, in fact, raised to the n-th power. In order to keep the UN and its agencies "balanced," elaborate geographical quotas are used in filling posts. Thus, the merit system is suppressed even below its usual level in a civil service structure.

As a result, UN activities in science development, though by no means without merit, have been effective only in certain circumstances. An effective illustration of both the strengths and the problems is the UN World Plan of Action for the Application of Science and Technology to Development (usually referred to as the World Plan). It was prepared in the late 1960s through a series of studies and committee deliberations within the UN with the help of some outside consultants. Much of the preparatory theoretical work was of high quality, and the analysis of the deficiencies of science in LDCs is, on the whole, a sound one. The final document was prepared by ACAST as part of the Second United Nations Development Decade. It states general goals in terms of contributions from ACs and LDCs and lists sample problems which might be attacked by this international effort. (Quantitative details of the Plan are provided in the second section of this chapter.)

Unfortunately, the matter seems to have ended there. Nothing was said in the Plan on how to implement it, and as we approach the middle of the decade during which the Plan was supposed to have been realized, it becomes increasingly evident that nothing will actually be done. There are substantial differences of opinion about the advisability of aid to LDCs and the form which aid should take. Such differences can be swept under the rug during the preparation of a plan, but they emerge when it comes to actually doing something. Furthermore, the World Plan was prepared without the participation of rank-and-file members of the worldwide scientific community (though some eminent scientists are members of ACAST). The Plan is, therefore, largely unknown to and almost completely ignored by that community. Since science development will not take place without the enthusiastic and active participation of a significant part of the scientific community, implementation of the Plan is not likely to occur.

The UN has an Office of Science and Technology dealing for the most part with worldwide agreements concerning issues with scientific and technological content. Most activity in scientific areas, however, takes place in the special agencies of the UN, such as UNESCO, IAEA, and WHO.

UNESCO's main scientific interests are science education and science policy. It also sponsors research in politically fashionable scientific areas, such as ecology, oceanography, and natural resources. Its educational programs range from the beginning of schooling to advanced training including support for research at universities. Some regional groups, such as CLAF (see above), are subsidized by UNESCO, as are some ceremonial organizations, such as ICSU. UNESCO's science policy division holds meetings and publishes studies aimed at assisting LDCs in policy-making. Again, emphasis is primarily on planning activity; achievements in implementation are less pronounced.

UNESCO's leverage in affecting science development has been considerably increased by the institution of the UNDP. Unlike other UN organizations or the UN itself, UNDP is supported by voluntary contributions from countries. Any country can contribute without a similar contribution being demanded from other countries. UNDP then supplements the funding of other UN agencies. Much of the bread-and-butter research support provided by UNESCO to institutions in LDCs comes from UNDP funds. In fact, 70% of what UNESCO spends for science comes from that source.

The IAEA is a more specialized agency similar to WHO and FAO. Its concerns are nuclear research and technology, and it helps LDCs to advance in these areas. Its program consists mainly of sending experts to LDCs, offering fellowships to scientists and future scientists in LDCs for further training, and donating equipment for research in LDCs. It also deals with organizational and legal matters pertaining to nuclear energy. IAEA performs research of its own and contracts for research to be done for the benefit of LDCs. It has an information service which generates and distributes material on nuclear energy and related matters.

A special project which has been supported in part by both IAEA and UNESCO is the ICTP (mentioned in chapter 4). The two agencies are to be commended for supporting ICTP, but it should be noted that the creation and maintenance of ICTP would never have been undertaken by these agencies in the absence of heroic efforts by a few individuals within the scientific community. (Though these efforts were contributed by a number of people, the lion's share came from Abdus Salam, an eminent Pakistani physicist who is the director of ICTP.) In fact, the financing of ICTP, to which UNESCO contributes a relatively small part, remains a perpetual problem. Furthermore, ICTP is limited in its coverage of scientific fields and can accommodate only a limited number of people. It has been suggested that in other areas of science, the same aim could be achieved simply by instituting visiting positions at scientific institutions in ACs to be filled by scientists from LDCs. Such a network of positions would require a negligibly small addition to the existing scientific structure of the ACs, but nothing has been done to realize this suggestion.

UNESCO has benefited from the so-called associate expert scheme in which ACs supply younger scientists from their own manpower supported by their own scientific budgets. These associate experts cooperate with regular UN experts in various projects in LDCs. Unfortunately, the number of associate experts is small, and only a few countries have offered them so far.

The so-called World Bank (International Bank for Reconstruction and Development) has recently established the post of science advisor so the scientific and technological content of its projects can be evaluated more reliably.

A particular form of international scientific assistance that is often discussed is the bilateral link, a somewhat vague term. It is sometimes used to designate any scientific assistance program arranged between two countries. But bilateral links can be developed on many levels: government-to-government, institution-to-institution, laboratory-to-laboratory, or even one research group to another. The great advantage of bilateral links should be the elimination of red tape through direct contact between the participants, instilling a sense of personal responsibility for action.

To achieve this, the links must be structured in small units. For example, institution-to-institution links are usually not small enough for this purpose since they can easily be made ineffective by the interference of the perniciously sterile patterns of institutional (particularly university) administration.

While many activities within bilateral links can be undertaken with no new financial resources, others can be greatly aided if outside funds are available. The organizational task is to find ways for large organizations to assist many small bilateral links, all generated by the participating scientists themselves. Present patterns are not optimal in this direction. AID, true to its style, has dealt with whole institutions or even with groups of institutions primarily in technology. Some bilateral links have utilized P.L. 480 funds while others have found support through OAS. The key is vigorous campaigning for funds on the part of the scientific community.

To summarize the status of international scientific assistance at the present time, it is insufficient in quantity, not catalytic enough to have sufficiently large multiplying power, and not CSIK 1973g, such activities are listed for Nigeria, Turkey, the Re- the originating or at the receiving end) to be sufficiently effective in actually building science in the LDCs. Much of what is being done has value, but in the face of the enormity of the problem, the response has been altogether inadequate.

Background and Comments

Information on the formal international scientific activities of LDCs can be found in virtually all of their national plans, reports, and official documents, as well as in other accounts. A few examples will suffice. Sabet in NADER 1969 (p. 215) discusses international scientific ties for the United Arab Republic. In MORAVCSIK 1973g, such activities are listed for Nigeria, Turkey, the Republic of Korea, Brazil, and Indonesia. UNESCO 1970e (pp. 21-22) covers the Philippines including some of its bilateral links with neighboring countries. MEXICO 1971 reveals that CONACYT has a special section dealing with international cooperation. CHINA 1972 advocates more informal ties involving visits of scientists, particularly of Chinese origin, within the framework of a formal cooperative agreement with the US (pp. 15-23, 95-113, with a list of participants on pp. 113-17). NATURE 1968 discusses the delicate balance in the People's Republic of China between the desire for international contacts and the tendency toward isolationsism and "do-it-yourself" attitude. RAHMAN 1973 (pp. 140-48) gives an exhaustive list of formal international ties for India.

Turning to international scientific assistance, let us consider a few of the numerous comments on scientific assistance as part of the general question of international relations with LDCs. MORAVCSIK 1972c surveys this topic commenting in particular on the political consequences of *not* assisting LDCs in the development of science and technology. The same question is discussed in ZOPPO 1971, particularly with respect to nuclear science and technology. Both studies conclude that *not* assisting is an unrealistic alternative. An earlier essay on the role of science in foreign policy is NOYES 1957, but, like many early discussions of this subject, it contains little about LDCs. The same is true of SKOLNIKOFF 1967. BULLETIN 1950 describes the so-called Berkner report on science and foreign policy with practically no mention of LDCs. It appears that during the past 20 years at least some awareness has been generated about the problems of science in LDCs.

Awareness was certainly accelerated by articles of emotional eloquence, such as SALAM 1963 and 1964a. Salam's plea is based on historical accounts, such as SALAM 1964b (in 1835, Lord Macaulay strove to give India the best Britain could offer in the way of an educational system, but this did not include science and technology; later developments on the Indian subcontinent never quite caught up with this initial deficiency, p. 3).

One of the most comprehensive discussions of scientific assistance in a historical context is BASALLA 1967. WU 1970 (pp. 15, 20, 32, 33, 57, 64) describes international scientific assistance received by the People's Republic of China and its predecessors. For example, Kyo Mo-jo, President of the Chinese Adacemy of Sciences, states that it was essential for the People's Republic of China to take advantage of the advanced scientific experience of the Soviet Union to further Chinese national construction (p. 56).

That international assistance is always small in quantity compared to the resources of the country to be aided is demonstrated in THOMPSON 1972 (p. 7); even at the peak of the Marshall Plan, the flow of aid never exceeded 4% of Europe's capital needs. RAHMAN 1973 (p. 152) reports that in scientific and technological research, about 10% of India's development is contributed by foreign aid. OAS 1972 (p. 29) stresses that its assistance in Latin America represents only a small fraction of the resources allocated by the countries of the region for scientific and technological development, but it acts as a catalyst. In view of this, the report offers some guidelines for criteria of selection of such aid projects (p. 36).

There are a number of other general discussions of international scientific assistance dealing with guidelines, principles, and methods. Much discussion overlaps extensively with the arguments mentioned in chapter 1 justifying science in LDCs. OECD 1968a (pp. 223-39) and BUZZATI 1965 are examples; the latter attempts to establish an optimal size for scientific infrastructures considerably larger than those of some LDCs. MITCHIE 1968 examines the problem from the point of view of education and educational exchange. Further comments can be found in DEDIJER 1962 (p. 7), ALLISON 1960 (in the context of Egypt), and DILLON 1966. MORAVCSIK 1973a outlines some of the conceptual bases for scientific assistance as well as some of the practical difficulties in administering it. A concise, practical, and remarkably perceptive set of guidelines for international collaboration with LDCs in mathematics is JONES 1970 (pp. 1-12). It deals with the choice of components, conferences, seminars, and courses, consultants and short-term visitors, writing groups, local training, evaluation, and some general pitfalls. I regret that these guidelines are too lengthy to be quoted in full.

The view that assistance from abroad might be a hindrance to development is expressed, for example, in PARTHASARATHI 1966: it might be an impediment to independence and socially detrimental. On the other hand, BHABHA 1966a and 1966b illustrate how judicious use of foreign aid can accelerate the attainment of independence. The author cites the reactors at Trombay as examples.

The specialized question of using local currency for international assistance projects is discussed in MORAVCSIK 1974f.

The expectation of gratitude in international aid projects is unrealistic, mentioned in MORAVCSIK 1973a and TASK 1970

(p. 2). Many commentators stress the importance of trying to think in terms of the LDCs own priorities (for example, TASK 1970, p. 3). That even a successful assistance program requires patience is amply stressed (for example, in TASK 1970, p. 9, MORAVCSIK 1973a, and most succinctly in THOMPSON 1972, p. 18; the latter quotes the anonymous saying that foreign assistance often involves a struggle to meet 20-year needs with a 3-year program, 2-year personnel, and 1-year appropriation).

The shortage of high-quality personnel from ACs to participate in international scientific assistance projects results in a lowering of standards in some instances. ZACHARIAH 1973 claims, for example, that long-term educational experts sent to LDCs are, on the whole, useless. ZAHLAN 1967 (p. 11) believes that many experts loaned by UN organizations or AID are mediocre, though he speaks highly of the personnel of British assistance projects. TASK 1970 (pp. 29-30) argues that rotating temporary personnel might help raise quality.

Because of the short-term orientation of most assistance projects, strengthening of the scientific infrastructure in an LDC is frequently neglected in favor of specific projects which assume the existence of such an infrastructure. Numerous appeals in the literature urge that more attention be paid to building solid foundations for indigenous science. TASK 1970 (p. 29) stresses the importance of scientist-to-scientist contacts for this purpose. CIMT 1970b (p. 457), with regard to Latin America, urges assistance for general research and training. A similar argument is put forward in MORAVCSIK 1964c and 1974b. BURKHARDT 1966 advocates visits, scholarships, and fellowships for graduate students from ACs to do thesis research in LDCs in cooperation with local scientists. For the same reasons, TASK 1970 (p. 29) recommends channeling more scientific assistance through universities, scientists' organizations, and other bodies with direct access to the scientific infrastructure in the US.

This theme of utilizing the scientific community appears in various other contexts as well. UN 1970b (p. 19) states: "There is a great doubt that the growth of an indigenous scientific community can be effected without active participation by the international scientific community." This point has been emphasized in MORAVCSIK 1972b (aimed at the US physics community), 1974c (dealing with communication problems), 1971b (on the role of research institutes in scientific assistance), and 1964a, b (in more general contexts). International research centers are the subject of NATURE 1964a. The CERN laboratory in Geneva, the primary focus of Europe-wide scientific cooperation in high-energy physics, is often mentioned as the paragon of success in international cooperation. Its success appears to be largely the result of its being organized and operated almost entirely by the scientific community itself. It was, however, relatively easy to establish such a laboratory in Europe where indigenous expertise was already present and differences among countries were not great. It is not clear whether the CERN pattern can be easily transferred to LDCs.

There are international laboratories involving LDCs. The cosmic ray laboratory on Chacaltaya Mountain near La Paz, Bolivia, which originated in a Brazilian-Bolivian collaboration a number of years ago, now houses local as well as international researchers. The astronomical observatory on Tololo Mountain in Chile was created by a US consortium of universities but is operated as a joint venture between that consortium and the fledgling Chilean astronomical community. Since at its remote location it must be completely self-sufficient in supplies and repair facilities, the observatory also serves as a high-quality training ground for Chilean technical personnel.

Professional scientific societies are not active in science development. The American Institute of Physics, for example, and its affiliated societies have no program pertaining to LDCs except the CIEP of the AAPT. On a minuscule budget, CIEP has fostered programs, such as visitors' registries, the Physics Interviewing Projects, and surplus journal projects. The recently formed European Physical Society is also unconcerned with science development. The American Association of the Advancement of Science is considering orienting some of its activities toward LDCs. A few active members of the scientific community take a personal initiative to create science development projects. An outstanding example is Carl Djerassi's center-of-excellence programs (DJERASSI 1968) in Mexico (TELLEZ 1968 and ROMO 1973) and Brazil (CEN 1970). Organizations concerned with development in general are often quite active (such as the Society for International Development), but their orientation is seldom toward the sciences. Scientists sometimes get involved in politics, as in the Pugwash meetings, and in that context formulate pronouncements about science development. But they usually do not get beyond the stage of pronouncements (GLASS 1968 and UNESCO 1969a, pp. 92-93).

An interesting program within the framework of the scientific and technological community in ACs is VITA which recruits members of this community to work in their own locales on problems of relevance to the development of LDCs. The results of this work are then forwarded to LDCs wherever needed. It has had some 5,000 volunteers from dozens of countries. Its primary thrust is in the direction of technology, but it includes social sciences, home economics, medicine, economics, and other fields. VITA is mentioned, unfortunately with some erroneous details, in UNESCO 1969a (p. 90).

Another interesting product of the scientific community is ICIPE, described eloquently by its director in CSA 1971a (pp. 99-106) with further mention in BULLETIN 1972. Its beginnings are related in ODHIAMBO 1967 (p. 881). Founded with the collaboration of local African scientists and their colleagues from ACs, the center provides a locale for collaborative basic research in an area of considerable potential applicability to Africa. Located in Nairobi, it can house some 30 researchers. The financial support of ICIPE is as precarious as that of ICTP. Established with an initial capital investment of about 3 million dollars, the institute operates on about 1 million dollars per year.

A different undertaking of the scientific community, barely off the ground, is the ISF. Brief comments can be found in CSA 1971a (p. 47) and MORAVCSIK 1970b. It is based on the fact that funding of worthwhile research projects on the basis of individual merit is largely absent in LDCs (mentioned in chapter 6). ISF would act as an international funding agency to fill the gap. As visualized by its promoters (prominent members of the scientific communities of ACs), the organization would be operated entirely by scientists but would draw huge sums of money from various governments. Such an idealistic structure does not exactly square with political realities, and the project has not aroused much interest among potential contributors.

Another proposed institution is the World University (see SALAM 1970a). It would be a regular educational and research institution with a heavy emphasis on the involvement of scientists from LDCs (both students and staff).

As noted above, US governmental activities in science development are rather feeble. Science development is certainly of only peripheral interest in discussions of science and international affairs. For example, SKOLNIKOFF 1967, an excellent survey entitled *Science, Technology, and American Foreign Policy*, devotes about 14 out of 330 pages to the discussion of science in LDCs (pp. 152-59, 195-203). As we will see, governmental documents exhibit a similar pattern.

Total US governmental international assistance is around 3 billion dollars per year (UNESCO 1969a, p. 89, reports 2.5 billion dollars in economic aid and 0.4 billion dollars in military aid for 1968). This includes many items not related to science and technology but excludes extragovernmental contributions. The amount of scientific and technological aid apparently is not well-known. AID 1973b gives a rough estimate for fiscal year 1972 as follows: (1) R&D explicitly for the benefit of developing countries: AID, 100 million dollars; US contributions to multilateral organizations, 70 million dollars; US foundations, 40 million dollars; (2) other R&D in developing countries: through other US governmental agencies, 90 million dollars; private industry, 20 million dollars; (3) other R&D of potential short-term benefit to developing countries: governmental agencies, 500 million dollars; private industry, 30 million dollars.

The last category is research done in the US which might also have incidental benefits for LDCs. As such, it should not be strictly counted as scientific assistance. The first two categories amount to about 320 million dollars, about 1.3% of the R&D expenditure of the US. The three categories together constitute about 3% of the US R&D budget. However, this includes all kinds of research, and the lion's share of it is in technology. There is no estimate of the science component of this amount.

Let us now examine the status of science development in the various branches of the US government. The deliberations of PSAC are not public, but informal evidence suggests that PSAC was not much concerned with this problem. TASK 1970 is the report of the so-called Peterson task force mentioned in the first section of this chapter (*none* of its 16 members were from the scientific community). The report is, in many respects, to the point. It recommends an initial annual budget of one billion dollars for the proposed International Development Institute (IDI). The President's message which accompanied the recommendations stresses the importance of long-term funding for IDI to ensure continuity of programs (NIXON 1970). In the 1971 annual report to Congress on the foreign assistance program, there is no mention of these new proposals (NIXON 1971). Except for matters of health and agriculture, there is no mention of science at all. Another interesting feature of this document (in fact, an annual report by AID, not the President) is the listed membership of AID's advisory committees. If we exclude university administrators and those in health and agriculture, there is not a single scientist among the 120 members of the 10 advisory committees.

There subsequently appeared a number of commentaries on the proposed IDI, the structure and function of which were left undefined by the Peterson report. One was NAS 1971d, the result of a project sponsored by AID and administered by NAS. Again, apart from health and agriculture, there was not a single active representative of the US scientific community among the 13 members of the committee that prepared the report. (The committee did, however, include ex-officio member Harrison Brown and regular member Alvin Weinberg, both with roots in the scientific community.) A different, individual commentary on the proposed IDI is MORAVCSIK 1974b. The two views partly overlap and partly complement each other. They agree in stressing the long-term aspects of scientific and technological development; both emphasize the need for sponsoring intensified research on development. The NAS report contains very little discussion on science, concentrating instead on technology; proposals to strengthen scientific infrastructure occupy only about 1% of the report. The organizational structure suggested for IDI is similar to the present structure of AID, excepting size and flexibility. My commentary, on the other hand, deals mainly with the scientific development of LDCs, stressing the importance of infrastructure and urging the involvement of a broad segment of the US scientific community.

Interest in science development in Congress is weak for reasons outlined in the first section of this chapter. CSA 1967 reports on scientific affairs in the 89th Congress: of its 127 pages, 0.3 are devoted to LDCs (p. 107). Another document of the House Committee on Science and Astronautics is entitled *Policy Issues In Science and Technology—Review and Forecast* (CSA 1968). It consists of 54 pages, of which 9.5 are devoted to international science; of that, only a fraction of one page deals with LDCs. The House Committee on Foreign Affairs produced a document entitled *Science, Technology, and American Diplomacy—The Evolution of International Technology*, a valuable work prepared by

Franklin Huddle of the Library of Congress, but it deals with practically no science (CFA 1970). A better effort is CSA 1971a and 1971b, records of a hearing on international science policy. Featuring some eminent and knowledgeable people, about 20% is devoted to LDCs. The hearings were obviously of an educational nature, however, not intended to produce specific action programs, and apparently none have emerged from them. The Senate Committee on Foreign Relations has issued a volume containing MORAVCSIK 1973a. It presents various individual views on foreign assistance policy in general, but most of the volume does not deal with science.

AID is the central governmental agency for the administration of US international assistance. The organization within AID that deals with science and technology is the Office of Science and Technology (OST—not to be confused with the now-abolished OST of the executive branch of the government which was attached to the President's Science Advisory Committee). A fairly comprehensive summary of OST's activities is given in AID 1973a. While AID is not completely void of support for science, such projects are very few in comparison with projects of technological orientation. Some science programs supported by AID are: NSF's SEED program; a program for secondary school education in Southeast Asia in mathematics and science; the project to improve science education in India operated by NSF (described later); the building of centers of excellence in Kanpur, India and Kabul, Afghanistan; the Korean Advanced Institute of Science (KAIS); the Asian Institute of Technology (AIT) in Thailand; and an Asian Research Program providing funds for "short- to intermediate-term" research at Asian institutions "to increase their contributions to the development of Asian nations." Recently, AID decided to contribute to FORGE. AID has also supplied the funds for the NAS-CNPq chemistry project in Brazil.

As can be seen from AID 1973a (pp. 13, 15), which lists the various AID projects having scientific and technological content, the programs mentioned above are few in comparison with the many others which are purely technological or industrial in nature. Furthermore, even those mentioned vary greatly in their scientific content. The NAS-CNPq projects are indeed legitimate scientific assistance programs. On the other hand, KAIS has become a technological training center. This was evident in AID 1970, a survey report on the establishment of KAIS; KAIS has begun to operate, and the tendency appears to have been realized. This is regrettable since KAIS was supposed to be a scientific counterpart to the Korean Institute of Science and Technology (KIST), also an AID project. KIST was established some years ago to serve as a focus for research directly utilizable by Korean industry. AID's investment in KIST was massive (for example, almost 4 million dollars in 1967 and almost 3 million dollars in 1968). It was supposed to become self-supporting from indigenous industrial revenues within a few years after its establishment. However, KIST is now supported primarily by the Korean government. Its work is overwhelmingly in technology, and not very high-grade at that. The lavish treatment of KIST caused displeasure within the Korean scientific community, particularly among university people. KAIS was, therefore, supposed to be to some extent a university-type scientific counterpart of KIST. It is somewhat ironic (though perhaps characteristic of AID's philosophy) that institutions like KIST or KAIS are often hailed as "the local MIT." MIT, whose name does not even mention science, is one of the great scientific educational and research institutions in the world. KAIS, whose name does not even mention technology, is a technological training center. Further information on the Korean situation can be found in NAS 1969a.

Another difficulty with AID is its mode of operation, which can be illustrated with a typical example. Early in the 1960s, AID commissioned a report on the existing and potential relationships between AID and US universities. The result was the so-called Gardner report (GARDNER 1964) presenting a sound analysis and good recommendations. About four years later, AID commissioned another study whose aim was to apply the criteria established by Gardner for selection of universities to participate in AID projects assessing on that basis the university resources in the US for international development (ALTER 1968). The resulting report sampled a fairly large number of universities (land-grant universities, large private universities, junior colleges, etc.). It then tried to determine whether the Gardner criteria hold for these groups. It concluded, not very surprisingly, that some groups fulfill some criteria and not others, and that in general there is a tremendous potential available with the US university community. The conclusions are quite obvious to anybody who has lived in the US university community for any length of time. The total cost of this second report was $99,877. The reader may decide, after reading ALTER 1968, whether it was worth that amount. In my own view, this heavy-handed, wasteful approach to development projects represents another major hindrance to AID's becoming a truly effective organ of science development.

However, the point I am making is not that the bulk of present AID operations are useless. AID is virtually the *only* source of governmental funds for science development projects. Its philosophy and mode of operation, which may be quite suitable for other types of development projects, are nevertheless a serious impediment to US efforts toward science development. Assigning only 10% of AID's funds to an independent agency specifically concerned with development of science in LDCs would make an enormous difference.

Other critiques of AID's scientific activities are NAS 1966 (p. 61), NSF 1973 (pp. 84, 85), EKUBAN 1973, and MORAVCSIK 1973a. KIST is mentioned briefly in KIM 1969 (p. 95). The US AEC's international activities, mainly oriented toward ACs, involve reactor technology, exchange of technical information, visits and exchanges of personnel, conferences, exhibits, IAEA, isotope technology, and other areas.

The National Science Foundation (NSF) is discussed in the first section of this chapter. Details of its Science Education Improvement Project in India are available in NSF 1973, a comprehensive, substantial report on that program. Over 1967-73, it cost 4 million dollars plus 19 million rupees in local currency (pp. 19, 20, 93, 94). The program involved summer institutes, college development, secondary school development, materials development, and special projects such as conferences. The idea of summer institutes was in fact conceived by the Indians themselves several years before the NSF project began (NSF 1973, p. 4). A critical essay on these institutes is HAFNER 1967.

As indicated in chapters 3 and 4, exchange of scientific manpower is a very important tool of science development. US efforts in such exchange activities have been commendable, though not enormous. The total cost of US *governmental* contributions to educational exchange (in all fields, not only science) grew from about 4 million dollars in 1947 to 28 million dollars in 1966 but was down to 17 million dollars in 1971 (BFS 1971, p. 34). The exchanges sponsored under these programs received only 53% of their funds from the US government; 34% was contributed by nongovernmental sources, and 13% by foreign governments (p. 24). The total number of participants between 1949 and 1971 was about

104,000, about two-thirds as visitors to the US and one-third Americans going abroad (p. 28). About one-third of the exchanges were with LDCs (p. 87). Unfortunately, there is no breakdown by field of study so the science component cannot be determined from this report. It is noteworthy, however, that during 1946-71, the Board of Foreign Scholarships which operates the exchange program had 73 members, two of whom were in the natural sciences (pp. 68-69). Additional statistics covering 1972 can be found in BFS 1972.

A more detailed statistical profile is given in STATE 1971, covering a broader group of exchanges (the total number of persons exchanged in the US between 1949 and 1971 is given as about 140,000). This source gives a breakdown into disciplines for the 1971 program indicating 10% for the natural sciences. There is also a breakdown by countries, but since there is no classification by disciplines *and* countries, the science component pertaining to LDCs cannot be ascertained. GREENE 1971 (p. 10) comments on exchange programs in Latin America.

Even with the limitation mentioned above, the work of NAS in science development is impressive. NAS 1965b (p. 1) explains the quasi-governmental nature of NAS. The best overall summary of its activities is NAS 1973c which lists the 12 countries where NAS has been active, records the hundreds of scientists and technologists from around the world who have been involved in NAS activities, and presents some evaluation of the various programs. Recent details can be found in NAS 1973d. Some NAS studies deal with certain areas of technology of general interest to LDCs (e.g., NAS 1972a on solar power). Other studies cover specific problems pertinent to a whole geographical region (e.g., NAS 1965a on animal diseases in Africa). Work has been done on organizational problems of science in specific countries (e.g., GHANA 1973, NAS 1971a, and 1971b dealing with science in Ghana; NAS 1969b pertaining to Colombia; and NAS 1973e dealing with Brazil). More specific projects are described in NAS 1970c (visiting teams in Colombia); NAS 1970a, b (Argentine scientific communications); NAS 1971f (Colombian chemistry); and NAS 1971c (East Pakistan Land and Water Development in Agriculture). A general report on technical cooperation with the Republic of Korea is NAS 1969a. (This list is not a complete compendium of NAS reports.)

In addition to these workshops, seminars, and studies, there is the NAS-CNPq chemistry project, described in a series of reports (NAS 1970a, 1972b, and 1973b). The cost has been shared, with

Brazil contributing over one-half million dollars. Some organizational problems have been successfully solved (e.g., the importation of chemicals, described in N AS 1972b, p. 6). It appears that after US assistance ends, Brazil will take over entirely on its own, which speaks well for the program.

US national laboratories have contributed very little to science development in LDCs. The activities of NBS mentioned in the first section of this chapter are described in NBS 1971, 1972, and 1973.

Details on Canadian activities can be found in SCHROEDER 1973 (pp. 8, 19) and IDRC 1971. The International Development Research Centre has a budget of 1-2 million dollars per year, a small-scale operation for a national effort. GREENE 1971 comments on the French program.

A prominent example of the scientific assistance program of a small but affluent AC exists in Sweden. The Swedish program is, in fact, similar to that found in the US, though on a smaller scale. As in the US, international assistance programs are centralized in one organization, SIDA. It is structured in 10 divisions and within them in 29 sections (SIDA 1972b). No section is explicitly concerned with science. Among other activities, SIDA supports research programs of benefit to LDCs. In 1970-72, this support amounted to about 7 million dollars, of which about 5% was spent on scientific projects primarily in science education (SIDA 1972a). Like AID, SIDA subcontracts projects through educational institutions. For example, SIDA 1973b lists courses and seminars cosponsored by SIDA (with UN agencies) in 1973-74. Of the 46 courses and seminars, five were in the sciences. Support of ICTP is an important factor in the scientific aid projects undertaken by SIDA. Sweden at one time had a scholarship program for students from LDCs, but it has now been terminated (SIDA 1973a, p. 10). Since the amount of funds available is relatively small, Sweden wishes (probably wisely) to concentrate on aiding a few countries. The choice of these countries is strongly influenced by political considerations (as is AID's choice). Like AID, SIDA has been deficient in recruiting a significant fraction of the scientific community for active participation in science development projects (SIDA 1973a, p. 11). Even the general rhetoric explaining the basis of Swedish international assistance sounds similar to AID documents enunciating the basis of US international assistance.

The involvement of private industry in science development in LDCs has been discussed recently. Two large studies have been released (NAS 1973a and UN 1973b) on the role of multinational corporations in the development of LDCs, and there have been frequent references to the necessity of industrial companies sponsoring local research in LDCs (e.g., MORAVCSIK 1971a, p. 64). AID 1973c lists developmental activities in LDCs sponsored by multinational firms, such as the Creole Foundation in Venezuela, the Gillette Foundation in Argentina, and the support of FORGE (described below) by a number of companies. It also mentions local subsidiaries with R&D facilities (though not necessarily for scientific research), such as the United Fruit Company's facilities in Honduras, the General Tire subsidiary (FATE S.A.I.C.I.) in Argentina, G.D. Searle pharmaceutical research laboratories in several Latin American countries, and the Firestone laboratory in Liberia. Yet, the examples are rather sporadic. Some LDCs have developed links with industrial organizations in ACs (RAHMAN 1973, p. 135), but the links primarily involve collaboration in the production stage, such as building plants and machinery, designing plants, and designing production processes.

The two reports on multinational companies are quite extensive (NAS 1973a and UN 1973b). They generally stress the important role companies can play and to some extent have played in the development of LDCs, but they also present an extensive list of possible actions, some to be taken by international firms, some by host countries, and some by international agencies and agencies of ACs. It is evident that much remains to be done in this area.

The role played by private foundations in science development can be illustrated by considering briefly two large US foundations, Ford and Rockefeller. Private foundations seem to assume that science is well taken care of by the government; hence, their interest in the natural sciences is rather weak. In 1971, the Ford Foundation distributed a total of 220 million dollars in grants. Of that, 2.8 million dollars, 1.3%, was spent on science development in LDCs including science teaching. Of the latter amount, 60% went to six projects: International Rice Research Institute; birth control in India; University of the Philippines; birth control in El Salvador; education at the University of Chile; and the Middle East Technical University in Ankara, Turkey. (The above figures are approximate since the line items in FORD 1971 are not always specific as to the scientific content of projects.) There have been suggestions (e.g., RAO 1966) that the Foundation should broaden its efforts in science development both in quantity and variety. The existing projects are in part short-range in their perspectives. Ford activities in India are described in ODHIAMBO 1967 (p. 878). The grant to the University of Chile was primarily for the University of California-University of Chile bilateral program. GREENE 1971 (pp. 11, 12) comments on Ford's performance in Latin America.

The total value of grants awarded by the Rockefeller Foundation in 1971 was about 33 million dollars (ROCKEFELLER 1971, p. 162). (One should keep in mind the scale of private foundations as compared with governmental programs. Since its establishment in 1913, the Rockefeller Foundation has appropriated a *total* of about 1.1 billion dollars which corresponds to about four months of US governmental international assistance.) Of the 33 million dollars, it is difficult to ascertain the fraction spent on science development. Rockefeller's primary approach in science-related areas has been its University Development Program (6.6 million dollars in 1971) aimed at "training professional people, scientists and scholars, in the applied disciplines" (ROCKEFELLER 1971, p. 46). Support under this program has been primarily concentrated on five groups of institutions: University of Valle (Colombia); University of the Philippines; University of Ibadan (Nigeria); Mahidol University, Kasetsart University, and Thammasat University (Thailand); Makarere University, Kempala, The University of Dar es Salaam, and the University of Nairobi (East Africa). A detailed description of this program can be found in THOMPSON 1972. The Rockefeller Foundation also supports the International Rice Research Institute and is in fact famous for its support of various agricultural projects aimed at developing better varieties of wheat and rice. The Foundation's role in India is described in RAHMAN 1973 (pp. 148-50). The Rockefeller Foundation's annual contribution to science development is approximately 2 million dollars.

Other private foundations are much smaller, though some are more oriented toward LDCs. For example, the Asia Foundation's program for science and technology development is sketched in ASIA 1972a (p. 39). Its project grants in the fiscal year 1970-71 totaled about $880,000 (ASIA 1972a, p. 90), of which approximately 16% was for science projects. The Foundation also provides individual grants to Asians for study outside Asia. These grants numbered about 120 in the fiscal year 1970-71; about 7% were in science, science teaching, and science policy. The Foundation also maintains the Books for Asia program discussed in chapter 4. Examples of its projects are given in ASIA 1971.

Most other US foundations are not active in science development in LDCs. For example, the Kellogg Foundation spends 19 million dollars annually; about 11% is devoted to Latin American health and agriculture (KELLOGG 1972, p. 23), but most of that fraction is spent on social services and technology. The Danforth Foundation has a general interest in international education and supports ASAIHL (see chapter 2), but its programs are not aimed at science as such (DANFORTH 1972, pp. 40-42). Of the more than 1300 fellowships awarded by the Guggenheim Foundation during a recent four-year period, not one was for work in science development. Even private organizations specifically oriented toward developmental problems in LDCs frequently have very little feeling for the crucial role indigenous science could play. A recent 200-page publication of ODC (HOWE 1974) with the impressive title, *The US and the Developing World—Agenda for 1974,* makes no mention at all of science development.

Supported by US private industry, and more recently by AID as well, FORGE distributes small research grants to promising, usually young, scientific researchers in LDCs (primarily in Latin America) (FORGE 1971). The small merit grants are designed to establish high-quality scientists in research so they can then acquire local support. An organization with beautifully simple administrative machinery, it operates in the best tradition of catalyzing indigenous science.

In the field of science education, IIE serves as a switchboard for educational personnel traveling to and from LDCs (IIE 1971). CIEP of AAPT operates the Physics Interviewing Project which interviews students in LDCs to evaluate their capabilities for graduate education in the US. CIEP also plans to organize a summer seminar for science graduate students from LDCs being educated in the US; it will cover aspects of science and science policy not usually touched upon in US graduate schools, but which are important in LDCs. The first attempt to organize such a seminar in the summer of 1973 failed for lack of financial support. Various suggestions for activity in these areas can be found in MORAVCSIK 1971a (pp. 56, 57, 60, 61) and SCHROEDER 1973 (p. 19). The Creole Foundation is described in CREOLE 1966.

There has been much discussion of regional organizations for science development. CERN is usually cited as the shining example; ZAHLAN 1967 (p. 10) analyzes why it works so well. KING 1957

mentions CERN but does not think its model would work opti-
mally in the context of LDCs. Some regions have little cooperation, such as parts of Asia (PERES 1969, p. 41). KIM 1969 (p. 97)
suggests means for Asian cooperation in personnel exchange, regional meetings, documentation, and production and repair of
instruments. RAHNEMA 1969 (p. 60) contributes some general remarks. GRESFORD 1964 is another commentator on the situation
in Southeast Asia. NAS 1965b (p. 9) urges regional cooperation
for Africa to overcome the legacy of separatism and to tackle common problems. It advocates national development which can be
coordinated with a regional plan (p. 53). Comments on East Africa
can be found in BANAGE 1967, WORTHINGTON 1948, and
ODHIAMBO 1967. Africa is discussed in WORTHINGTON 1960.
NBS 1972 (p. 11) points out that standardization of measures and
processes must be regional in Latin America. Also in the context
of Latin America, MORAVCSIK 1973e and ROCHE 1966 (p. 60)
urge regional cooperation. JONES 1971 (pp. 29, 52) appeals for regional collaboration but emphasizes that a national base is necessary to realize the advantages of such cooperation. A detailed, perceptive discussion of the principles of organizing and operating regional programs appears in UN 1970b (pp. 58-60). UNESCO 1968
(p. 18) and 1971a express UNESCO's views on regional organizations.

The OAS has a Department of Scientific Affairs for science development projects. The Department's deputy director presents a good
survey of the relevant problems in Latin America in ALONSO 1969.
A factual summary of OAS activities is given in OAS 1972. OAS
supports exchange of personnel (between LDCs in Latin America
as well as with ACs), seminars, fellowships, and research. Between
March 1968 and December 1971, the OAS Regional Program col-
laborated with 150 scientific and technological institutions in Latin
America and dealt with about 1600 specialists, professors, and researchers in Latin America and other parts of the world. In the process, the Program spent over 11 million dollars including science
and technology (p. 29). The breakdown shows a fairly balanced distribution among basic sciences, applied sciences, technological
development, "supporting actions," and scientific and technological planning. A detailed list of projects of OAS for the fiscal year
1970-71 is given in OAS 1971, illustrating the intertwining links
among all countries of the region. A similar document is OAS 1970.
OAS projects are in good standing with the Latin American scien-

tific community, though there are some problems. For example, in some Latin American countries, assistance from another Latin American country is considered "second-class help"; a Peruvian student would much rather be trained in the US than, say, in Chile (GREENE 1971). Another source of difficulties is the bureaucratic inefficiency of OAS causing projects to be postponed, travel grants to be allocated after the fact, and so forth.

This might be a proper point to comment on the general problem of bureaucracy in scientific assistance. OAS is certainly not alone in this respect. Other international and national governmental agencies are not very different. With some exceptions, the time lag between input and output is many months. Particular individuals are usually not responsible for such clumsiness. It is, rather, the "system," the procedure used to do anything. Apart from the loss of time, serious enough in many cases, the massive bureaucratization of science development raises the cost of any project. AID, therefore, refuses to consider "small" projects (anything costing less than $100,000). Thus, there is a third detrimental effect: in addition to loss of time and added cost, there will be automatic rejection of small, novel, and experimental projects in favor of huge, routine, and frequently unexciting ones. Those in developmental assistance agencies often speak disparagingly of the slowness and inefficiency of the administrative machinery in LDCs. They might discover, however, that their own operations are not much more efficient than, say, an LDC customs office.

CLAF is quite a different organization. Operating on a shoestring compared with previously mentioned agencies and foundations, it has an annual budget of perhaps $100,000 which fluctuates wildly from year to year. Details and evaluation can be found in CLAF 1971. Recently, CLAF has been receiving support from UNESCO.

Other regional organizations are discussed in the following. The Interamerican Bank is described in INTERAMERICAN 1969 and Ismael Escobar's concise summary in NBS 1971 (p. 345). Examples of OECD's work can be found in OECD 1971a, a report of 110 pages of which about five are devoted to LDCs. OECD has published a number of reports quoted in this book. The relevance of the Colombo Plan to India is discussed in RAHMAN 1973 (pp. 143, 144, 149, 150). Scientific activities of the Commonwealth are described in COMMONWEALTH 1973 and ROYAL 1968.

As an introduction to UN programs, I strongly recommend

KOVDA 1968. Kovda first establishes the size of the UN's annual expenditure on science and technology: at that time it was about 100 million dollars, or 5 cents for each citizen of LDCs (p. 14). An immediate conclusion is that without national efforts to supplement this sum, not much will be done in the LDCs. Kovda then shows that even that expenditure has been rather ineffective having been used mainly for collection of data (p. 15). (Since science as such does not even exist as a line item, it is difficult to trace expenditures for it. But 50% of the amount was spent on salaries and 25% on transportation [p. 15].) Kovda goes on to make some specific suggestions for further action. KOVDA 1963 is interesting in that it is a much more abstract and cautious essay.

Overall figures for UN expenditures on science are given in SALAM 1968: 30 million dollars by FAO, 50 million dollars by WHO, 30 million dollars by UNESCO, 10 million dollars by IAEA, and 100 million dollars through UNDP. However, much of this is for technology rather than science—the actual science figures are not separated here. Salam remarks that the scientific effort supported by the UN has been mainly in applied science.

The UN must operate strictly on an egalitarian basis, a restriction greatly disapproved of in LEWIS 1961 (p. 47): "Members of the General Assembly are egalitarian and, if permitted, would distribute aid on some simple per capita basis which took no account of what was likely to be done with the aid."

The UN (through its Office of Science and Technology and apart demand the sponsorship of an organization such as the UN. (The UN Office of Science and Technology also deals with international this publication serves as an introduction to computer science for science administrators. It was prepared by an illustrious international panel of experts, though there is nothing in it that would demand the sponsorship of an organization such as the UN. (The UN Office of Science and Technology also deals with international treaties, such as that pertaining to the exploitation of sea beds.)

An illustration of the UN at its worst is UN 1973a, the report of the first session of the UN's COSTED.

The UN World Plan has been extensively discussed. For some time, the opinion had been expressed (for example, BLACKETT 1967, p. 311) that ACs should make a greater contribution to science development in LDCs. The actual flow of international assistance can be ascertained from such sources as SID 1973 and COOPERATION 1973. "Official development assistance" as percentage of GNP is 0.1% for the "negligent" European countries (Italy, Austria); 0.3-0.4% for US, Germany, UK, and Japan; 0.5% for Sweden; 0.6-0.7% for the "diligent" European countries (e.g., the Netherlands or France); and an exceptional 1.5% for Portugal. The total flow of assistance (including all official assistance, private flows, and grants by private agencies) is 0.4-0.6% for Germany, Sweden, US, Switzerland, Denmark, Austria, Italy, and Norway; 0.8-1.1% for Belgium, UK, France, Australia, Canada, and Japan; and again an exceptional 2.1% for Portugal. The corresponding percentage for the Soviet Union is 0.25% and for the People's Republic of China between 0.3% and 0.6%, depending on how one estimates the GNP. SID 1973 gives other figures for flow *among* LDCs as well as the amount for the People's Republic of China. As mentioned above, the science component of these assistance flows is generally not indicated.

Partly because of dissatisfaction with such assistance figures, studies were undertaken to formulate a world plan for the assistance of LDCs by ACs. UN 1969 (pp. 22-42), 1970a, and 1970b are some of the documents which preceded the final version of the World Plan. They are expertly composed, interesting contributions to policy for science development. The final plan is stated in UN 1971a.

The World Plan is designed to be catalytic, not comprehensive (UN 1971a, p. 5). Bilateral links are emphasized (pp. 50, 69, 88), and the necessity of cooperation with the international scientific community is recognized (p. 58). In terms of financial targets to be reached by 1980, it makes the following proposals (CLARKE 1971, p. 51, or UN 1970b, Table 1): (1) LDCs should reach 1% of their GNP as their expenditure for research and development (including scientific and technological public services); (2) ACs should reach 1% of their GNP as the total international assistance to LDCs; (3) of the previous item, 5% (0.05% of the GNP of the ACs) should be spent specifically for assistance to science and technology in the LDCs; (4) of the previous item, 40% (0.02% of the GNP of the ACs) should be allotted to supplying financial aid and equipment to the LDCs and 60% (0.03% of the GNP of the ACs) to sending experts from the ACs to the LDCs; and (5) in addition, 5% of the nonmilitary R&D of the ACs should be devoted to problems of primary interest to LDCs.

Some of these figures have substantial implications. For example, 0.03% of the GNP of the ACs could support about 20,000 scientists and technologists from ACs for work in LDCs. Since the number of LDCs is roughly 100, this procedure would supply an average of 200 experts per LDC, a significant number. The targeted amounts are not exorbitant. For example, the total international scientific and technical assistance of the US is estimated to be about 320 million dollars; the targeted amount of 0.05% of the GNP would be 500 million dollars. In general, the targets are a factor of 2-3 above present levels. Since the target date is 1980, the goal seems realistic. A brief mention of the Plan is made in JONES 1971 (p. 30). The main difficulty with the Plan is not that its requirements are unreasonable, but that no provisions are made for its implementation. In particular, no procedure is suggested to involve the scientific community itself. This criticism of the Plan is also presented in ZIMAN 1973.

In discussing UNESCO, it is interesting to follow its history by examining references chronologically. NEEDHAM 1948 and BOK 1948 describe the optimistic beginnings. (The latter mentions that on the long list of official advisors for UNESCO, there is not a single scientist.) The same optimism is revealed in STAKMAN 1952 with its long list of planned programs. ZWEMER 1957 is a rather generalized essay. However, at this time critical remarks begin to appear: KING 1957, for example, remarks on the heavy hand of international bureaucracy and on UNESCO's remoteness from the scientific community. Perfunctory comments on UNESCO can be found in NOYES 1957 (p. 236). An outline of UNESCO's situation in the early 1960s is presented in RODERICK 1962. Its activities at that time involved communication, documentation, science policy, education, and fellowships. The two-year budget for the natural sciences was 4.3 million dollars (compared with 15 million dollars 10 years later). An additional 10.8 million dollars in 1962 came from "extrabudgetry funds" (compared with 35 million dollars from UNDP 10 years later). The breakdown of these amounts in RODERICK 1962 shows that most of the funds going directly into the scientific structure of LDCs came from the "extrabudgetary funds." Other general outlines of UNESCO's structure are given in MAHEU 1963, BULLETIN 1964, UNESCO 1964b, 1968, and 1969b (the last two describe situations not very different from the present one). At about the same time, ZAHEER 1968 (p. 11) criticizes UNESCO for spending too much on itself while RICHARDSON 1969 finds fault with performance as opposed to plans and with efforts made to recruit experts. ZAHLAN 1972c and 1972d are critical along the same lines claiming, for example, that six years after the UNESCO-sponsored conference in Algiers in 1966, none of the resulting recommendations have been implemented. The present effort of UNESCO in the natural sciences is described clearly in UNESCO 1973a. The section of UNESCO called "Natural Sciences and Their Applications to Development" has a budget of 50 million dollars (30% being regular UNESCO funds, the rest from UNDP). Of the total, about 70% is spent on salaries of project personnel. There are three main groupings: Science Policy and Promotion of Scientific Communication (9% of the funds); Scientific and Technological Research and Higher Education (61%); and Environmental Sciences and Natural Resources Research (25%). The remaining 5% is divided between field offices and the office of the Assistant Director General.

Many UNESCO documents are valuable sources of information on science development. Examples are UNESCO 1970g (educational research institutes in Asia), 1966b (world directory of science policy organs), 1967b (a general study of science policy), 1969e (a specific study in biomedicine), 1970b (a theoretical work on economics in science development), 1969b (dealing with a region, Africa), and 1970f (dealing with a single country, Argentina).

According to UNESCO 1972b, the Science Policy Division conducts normative activities, cooperative activities, research activities, collection and diffusion of information, coordination, exchange of information, some training, and occasional operational programs on request from LDCs. An example of the latter is the case of Nigerian science policy being developed through efforts of UNESCO (MARTIN 1970).

A good summary of IAEA activities is IAEA 1973b. IAEA spent a total of 44 million dollars on assistance in 1958-72 (pp. 60-61). The annual amounts have been increasing; in 1972, the budget *for assistance* was 8.5 million dollars. The total budget, however, was about 15 million dollars in 1972 (not counting UNDP funds). This total was contributed by some 100 countries in proportion to their abilities. Roughly speaking, the US contributed one-third; the USSR, West Germany, France, UK, and Japan contributed one-third; and the rest of the world contributed one-third (IAEA 1973a, pp. 66-67). Expenditures for assistance are about equally divided among experts, equipment, and fellowships (IAEA 1973b, p. 30). The organizational structure of IAEA is described in SZASZ 1970. Other information on activities of IAEA can be found in IAEA

1972 (publications), IAEA 1973c, and USMANI 1969, the latter stressing the role of IAEA from the point of view of an LDC.

Information on ICTP can be found in ZAHLAN 1967 (p. 10) which advocates locating such institutions in LDCs; in many papers by Abdus Salam, such as SALAM 1965a, 1965b, and 1966; and in ZIMAN 1971 which describes the so-called "Winter College" pioneered by ICTP. SAAVEDRA 1973 pays eloquent tribute to ICTP: "After a couple of years back in Chile I felt like a squashed lemon. I just could not be of any further help, and I thought the only honest thing to do was to give up and to return to Europe. At that time the International Centre for Theoretical Physics was opened in Trieste, and it was given to me the possibility to stay there for three months every year, for a few years (this is the scheme called 'Associateship'); it was thanks to that that I could remain in Chile."

It is too early to say much about the scientific activities of the World Bank since they have just begun. A comment from some time ago is in LEWIS 1961 (p. 47).

The documentation of bilateral links can be found in much of the literature. Regarding the country-to-country level, TASK 1970 (p. 22) states that US scientific assistance should, if possible, be channeled not into bilateral activities but through multinational or international agencies. COPISAROW 1970 remarks, however, that even in that case assistance will be basically bilateral in nature because an expert of definite nationality will still work in one particular country. MORAVCSIK 1973a urges a mixed approach in which bilateral aid is combined with assistance through international channels. On a smaller scale, institution-to-institution or even research-group-to-research-group, such links are likely to be more effective, as stressed in MORAVCSIK 1971a (p. 57). THOMPSON 1972 (p. 9) offers a critique of AID's bilateral approach calling it poorly implemented. AID's bilateral program (in all areas) in 1967 amounted to 166 million dollars. Participants included 71 US universities and 39 LDCs (UNESCO 1969a, p. 90). An example of such a program with some scientific content is found at Cornell University directed by chemist Franklin Long. A good general discussion of bilateral links, examining both assets and dangers, is UN 1970b (pp. 57-58).

The "theory" of bilateral links is well-treated in GLYDE 1972, an intelligently conceived analysis of bilateral links between Britain and Thailand (its main conclusions are listed in chapter 4). Glyde's work supports the position that bilateral links should be organized in small units in which the contact between scientists is direct and the administration decentralized.

Another valuable document on bilateral links is UNESCO 1969a, a summary and tabulation of a worldwide survey of bilateral links in science and technology. It reports on 584 links between 84 "recipient" countries and 21 "donor" countries. Of these, 85% involve four "donor" countries: US, 179; West Germany, 155; France, 112; and UK 59. Of the 179 US links, about 16 are in the sciences; the rest are in technology, social sciences, and other areas. MORAVCSIK 1973g (p. 107) lists the disciplines in which bilateral links have been established in Nigeria, Brazil, Turkey, the Republic of Korea, and Indonesia. Many informal bilateral relations exist which are not reported in such documents. CIEP is in the process of establishing some in Latin America with the help of OAS. OAS also assisted the University of Texas in making arrangements with the University of Mexico. Other references and descriptions are SCHROEDER 1973 (p. 58), a Brazil-Canada link; AID 1972a (pp. 76, 80-82, 104, 115), links with Iran; and NICHOLLS 1969 (p. 81), links with Thailand.

There is a substantial link between the University of California and the University of Chile. It was perhaps stimulated by contacts between California and Chile developed during a rather unsuccessful general bilateral AID project in the mid-1960s (described, for example, in DVORIN 1965). The new link was established in the late 1960s, and in its first six years of operation spent about 6.5 million dollars. Its main categories of activity are agriculture and veterinary medicine, arts and literature, sciences and engineering, and social sciences. The expenditure for sciences and engineering in the first six years was about 1.8 million dollars. Some of its actions have been controversial, such as the donation of a cyclotron (proton accelerator) to the University of Chile by the University of California at Davis and the subsequent exchange of staff members in connection with research on this machine. This example of "Big Science" is disapproved of by some Chilean scientists (GREENE 1971, p. 7), but it is not at all clear that this feeling predominates in Chile.

Eight

The Big Intangible

Previous chapters discuss those elements of science development required by even the simplest model of "scientific method": education, manpower development, communications, research institutions, organizational matters, and international connections. These can all be discussed in fairly objective terms and, as far as input is concerned, even in quantitative terms. The measurement of output is, as we saw, a more subtle task, but even certain rudimentary yardsticks can be used, at least for a general orientation.

This chapter is concerned with a different element in science development. It cannot be pinpointed in objective terms, it cannot be measured quantitatively, and it usually does not appear at all in theoretical discussions of scientific method. Yet, it is perhaps the most important ingredient in science development by holding the other elements together and making the whole structure move. I refer to the factor of morale.

The importance of this ingredient results from the fact that scientists must be taken care of as human beings before they can function effectively as scientists. In addition to obvious material needs, psychological needs must be accommodated.

What motivates people to work as scientists? It appears that a combination of elements are usually present simultaneously in the "philosophy" of every scientist, though in ratios which may vary with the individual and, for a single individual, with time. These motivations are:

(1) Scientists have a curiosity about nature, about the unknown, about the esoteric. In evolutionary terms, this seems to be a favored trait: human curiosity throughout the centuries has "paid off" in material dividends. Fascination with new and unknown things is

certainly not confined to scientists. In their case, however, it takes
the form of an interest in the laws of nature. There is hardly a scientist of any substantial achievement who cannot recall the excitement of gaining understanding of some part of the structure of nature. This excitement is present even in cases when the discovery is
purely personal (that is, when the law of nature is already known
to others and it is a "first" only for the person in question). I stress
this because excitement over a discovery is distinct from the joy of
discovering something for the first time, that is, winning the "race"
with other scientists.

(2) Most human beings have an innate urge to convert whatever
talents they may have to actual accomplishments. Presumably this
also is favored by evolution, and it too is widespread whether we
are considering an athlete, a lawyer, a farmer, a doctor, or a scientist. In the last case, the urge can manifest itself in achievements in
scientific research, science teaching, science organization, or related
activities.

(3) Humans are competitive. Scientists are motivated by the satisfaction of being the first human being ever to grasp the laws of a
certain part of the universe. Science is a particularly suitable arena
for competition because the rules are very well-prescribed and the
judges are, on the whole, quite objective.

(4) Scientists are motivated by recognition of their work. Because of the relatively objective nature of scientific research, recognition is awarded according to fairly clear rules. The form of the
recognition depends on the community which awards it. Within
the scientific community, the best forms of recognition are frequent
references in other scientists' work to the person's scientific papers
and awards of leading roles in international conferences. Outside
the scientific community, the most appreciated form of recognition
is appropriate support for the scientists' work and the freedom to
conduct research according to the scientists' best judgment. Special
medals, prizes, and honorary awards are also used for this purpose,
but they make less of an imprint on the scientific community than
the daily expression of support for research.

(5) Scientists are motivated by the conviction that science is an
intellectual and material contribution to humanity. The cumulative
structure of scientific knowledge makes use of even small contributions by second-rate scientists. (In contrast, for example, the work
of second-rate artists appears to have less long-term justification.)
While this may appear to be a strong motivation to those outside

the scientific community, within the community it is generally not very important. In particular, it appears to play a rather minor role in determining a young person's decision to go into science. It is, in fact, double-edged since the uses of science, like the uses of anything else, can be either beneficial or detrimental depending on the user and on the values of the viewer. Nevertheless, scientists responsible for research leading to widespread technological applications are usually proud of having played a role in that development.

If scientists are to become creative, and remain so, it is essential that their motivations to do science are tended to satisfactorily. In a society typical of many LDCs, scientific curiosity will be on a collision course with the resistance to change and novelty and with the fear of plunging into the unknown prevalent in static societies. The scientists' desire for free exploration and the opportunity to turn talents into accomplishments may be suppressed by ideological orthodoxy which prescribes the path each individual must follow. Such obstacles will put scientists to a test and may cause weakened motivations.

Recognition of scientific work is hindered in LDCs for several reasons. The scientific community is likely to be small, and small scientific communities tend to have more internal strife and infighting than large ones. In many LDCs, bitter personal conflicts rage in the midst of the scientific community preventing the awarding of normal scientific recognition for significant contributions. Recognition from society is often lacking partly because of plain ignorance about science and partly because of antiscience attitudes rooted in cultural, religious, or political preconceptions. In many countries, science is still considered esoteric without much social prestige, societal influence, or communal respect. Even the pragmatic aspect of science remains unappreciated either because no connection is made between the efforts of scientists and improvement in the country's living conditions or because the connection is perceived as negative.

So far, I have discussed psychological factors in the motivation of scientists which can be related to specific shortcomings in the scientists' environment. They cannot be measured quantitatively, but they are amenable to specific remedies.

There is, however, an additional factor, a truly intangible one which plays a decisive role in the creativity, productivity, and vigor of a scientist. Different words have been used to describe this factor: high morale, will, personal strength, optimism, self-confidence, and positive mental attitude are only some. I will use the term "morale" to describe this characteristic which is so pivotal to the welfare of a scientific community.

Morale is intangible because, at this stage of our knowledge, its state cannot be predicted solely on the basis of the numerous factors discussed previously. For example, one may encounter two LDCs with virtually identical external factors influencing science and scientists. In one country productivity is flourishing and steady progress is being made while in the other stagnancy seems to prevail. During my visits to various countries, I have witnessed scientists working under the most adverse conditions and yet working with enthusiasm, energy, determination, and purpose and achieving correspondingly. On the other hand, I have seen scientific communities with good physical and social environments which were nevertheless demoralized and unproductive. I have known scientists from LDCs who produced admirably while temporarily in an AC. When they returned to their own countries, the physical facilities there were at least equal to those they had just left behind, and their social status was higher than in the AC. They nevertheless stopped functioning as creative scientists because, they said, "in our country you just cannot do science."

Morale is, of course, a familiar phenomenon. Each of us knows people who can overcome the most severe obstacles—material, psychological, or social—and reassert their faith in their goals and activities. We also know people with no internal strength who buckle under the slightest misfortune. But low morale is particularly damaging in the sciences because of the highly collective nature of scientific research. Low morale can be extremely contagious and can spread from scientist to scientist. One of the crucial requirements for an LDC, therefore, is high morale among its scientists. Without it, the best of plans will fail.

In sum, then, the detrimental psychological factors which can hamper the development of science in LDCs are the following: suppression of curiosity through fear of the unknown or through dogmatic cultural or political attitudes; impeding scientists' efforts to make use of their talents through resistance to change or negative social or political pressure; societal indifference or hostility to scientific achievements because of ignorance or the fear that knowledge may be misused; resorting to nonscientific criteria and personal animosities in allocating recognition within the scientific community itself; and low morale, a lack of belief that certain goals are worthwhile or attainable, and a general demoralization which degrades the values and personal satisfaction found in pursuing science.

However, there is an important point to be brought out here. Does the above list of maladies characterize science only in LDCs? Definitely not. In many ACs, there has recently been a decrease of interest and confidence in science, an upsurge of antiscientific sentiments, and an increasingly strong claim that science is "irrelevant" to our age. Fears are frequently expressed of the consequences of new scientific knowledge. There is a more prevalent belief that change is usually for the worse, and a widespread weakening of personal initiatives and motivations to explore new forms of creativity and to undertake new and complex tasks.

But the decrease of public morale is perhaps not the most important phenomenon. The most significant signs are evident within the scientific community itself. Legitimate concern with the uses of science is increasingly degenerating into an antiscientific attitude toward scientific and technological issues. The attitude is seldom exhibited with respect to the scientist's particular program (though there are instances of scientists directly involved in experiments using rockets and space vehicles who oppose the space program; they argue that funds should not be wasted on space research while other, allegedly more important problems remain unsolved). It is increasingly common, however, for scientists to oppose scientific and technological expenditures affecting areas other than their own or to object to proposals for experimental determination of unknown effects in applied sciences (such as the building of prototype supersonic commercial aircraft to test the claims of an altered ozone balance in the upper atmosphere). Scientists more frequently advocate the "when in doubt, do nothing" approach to public issues with scientific or technological components. For example, some claim that since the precise effects of extremely low-level radioactivity on human beings are not known, all nuclear power generation must be stopped. Or they demand that the distribution of new drugs badly needed be postponed until "it has been proven that there are no side effects," a condition that is patently impossible to satisfy. Other scientists are swayed by the argument that the elimination of war can only be achieved by de-emphasizing science and technology; hence, they begin to feel guilty about practicing science as a profession. Still others are troubled by the claim that the modern world has been dehumanized by science and technology; they are becoming dubious about science because of its presumed role in suppressing human values and relationships.

It is not my purpose to argue the merits of these claims and concerns. Whatever the merits are, the point is that such tendencies greatly contribute to a weakening of morale with respect to the pursuit of science. For quite different reasons, psychological problems now exist in ACs and LDCs.

It is indeed possible that the psychological factors working against science development will become more intense in the ACs but will lessen in the LDCs. If so, the LDCs would have an exciting opportunity indeed. If one disregards the psychological factors and considers only the tangible constituents of science development, one could easily conclude that the gap between ACs and LDCs will continue to increase in the foreseeable future. If, however, one includes the factor of morale and hypothesizes that morale will continue to sink in the ACs and continue to rise in the LDCs, one can conceive that purposeful and strong-willed LDCs might rise to scientific leadership in the world in a relatively short time. From a historical point of view, there is precedent for a reversal of roles. Civilizations rise and fall; invincible giants collapse and vanish while "lowly barbarians," deemed outcasts forever, become the new leaders of emerging civilizations.

However, new civilizations are generally based on new values, ideals, and areas of excellence. If LDCs were to assume the leadership of the world, it is not obvious that they would also adopt the predilection to do science, the system of values in which the exploration of nature has a prominent role. There are two reasons, however, why the transmission of a scientific civilization appears rather likely. First, scientific and technological excellence have become closely related to political and economic strength. The cultivation of science, therefore, seems a necessary prerequisite for the evolution and survival of a new civilization. Second, and perhaps more important, science has a substantial degree of objectivity which should make it compatible with different value systems. Throughout this book, I have emphasized the international character of science. Scientists from any combination of countries, no matter how different their cultural, traditional, religious, ideological, or other backgrounds may be, can easily accept, discuss, and pursue the same kind of science. This aspect of science might enable it to be transmitted from one age to another.

Though much of this is speculative, one might ask what LDCs

should do to take advantage of a possible opportunity to close the gap. The answer is simple in principle though probably difficult in practice. LDCs must acquire an increased purposefulness, a determination to develop their science in the most rapid and effective manner possible, and they must do this in the face of opposite trends in the ACs. They should adopt and adapt as much scientific know-how and organizational skills from the ACs as possible. At the same time, they must reject the fears, insecurities, doubts, and negativism to which they may be exposed through contact with the ACs. This is, of course, a supremely difficult task requiring scientists with rare qualities. Yet, the opportunity is so momentous and exciting that this task deserves the primary attention of the whole scientific community of LDCs.

The specific provisions for science that were discussed in chapters 1-7 are necessary for building an indigenous scientific community in LDCs. However, these provisions will produce results only if they are generated in a satisfactory psychological environment. A crucial psychological factor is high morale which will give the members of the scientific community the purposefulness and strength to tackle the challenging task of science development.

Background and Comments

By its very nature, the problem of morale has received much less attention in the literature on science development than the tangible inputs, such as funds, manpower, and organization. Intangibles do not appear in development plans, quantitative estimates, or budgets; furthermore, morale is a sensitive issue in political, human, and interpersonal terms. Whenever the matter is brought up in the open literature, it becomes controversial. As a "debate" develops, positions harden and little is accomplished. In many aspects of human development, secret diplomacy has no equal, and problems of morale might belong in this category. In that sense, it may be unwise to discuss the subject here. On the other hand, since morale is such a decisive factor in science development, and the present discussion does not castigate any particular country or individual, I felt it necessary to include this problem.

The importance of morale is emphasized often in the literature, though the terms vary from commentator to commentator. Skyes in NADER 1969 (p. 553) talks about the right "mental attitude." MORAVCSIK 1964a, 1964b (p. 9), 1964c (p. 197), 1965b (p. 19), 1966c (p. 389), 1971c, 1972a (pp. 198-99), 1973e, and 1973f examine the importance of morale to local development (in the sciences and elsewhere), its bolstering through international exchange, and its manifestations in specific instances. In the context of the latter, MORAVCSIK 1965b (p. 19), MURIEL 1970, and MORAVCSIK 1971c illustrate the type of controversy that can arise. DEDIJER 1963 (p. 68) gives examples of statements indicating low morale in the context of science development in LDCs. Both COPISAROW 1970 and LEWIS 1961 (p. 46) use the term "will" and suggest ways to improve it. SNOW 1964 uses the term "optimism" contrasting what he perceives to be "individual" tragedy with "social optimism." While the context is not identical, many of Snow's ideas have applications in science development. BHABHA 1966b (pp. 337-39) describes the construction of the first reactors in India and remarks on the resulting pride and self-confidence generated in the indigenous scientific and technological community. Psychologists and sociologists have undoubtedly discussed the problem of morale in the general development literature, but to delve into that would take us too far afield.

The question of what motivates scientists has also been extensively treated. It may suffice to cite a few discussions by people involved in science development: DEDIJER 1963 (p. 69); LONSDALE 1968 (p. 373); MORAVCSIK 1974a; and PRICE 1968. The last is of particular interest since it makes the following claim: "Science and technology are both creative occupations. They both set a premium on those who can combine thoughts in interesting ways that simply would not occur to other people. Edison and Einstein can agree completely that the biggest part of their motivation is indeed 'getting there first, before the other fellows.' Contrary to popularly held beliefs that they are beset by natural curiosity or by the hope of doing good, it appears from many modern researches that it is competition that holds first place in incentive." Unfortunately, the "many modern researches" are not cited in PRICE 1968.

Social and political factors impeding science development have been mentioned throughout this book. A few additional references should be noted. ZAHLAN 1972c discusses the problem of insecurity in LDCs as a consequence of perpetual crises (mentioned in previous chapters). Instances of political control of thought are recorded in WU 1970 (pp. 42, 48, 50, 56, 81, 83, 95, 97, 100, 460). JONES 1971 (p. 22) emphasizes the need to overcome resistance to change. The fear of plunging into the unknown is characterized aptly in CLARKE 1971 (p. 5): "How then are we to proceed? We must first beware of false fears—because, as one wit put it, 'if we had stopped to think through all the implications of inventing the wheel, we would probably never have done it'." "Desacralization," used by Skyes in NADER 1969 (pp. 555, 557), represents an intolerance of taboos which hinder the exploration and utilization of nature for the bettering of human life. BASALLA 1967 (p. 620) comments on nationalism and science: "While I do not hold with the Nazi theorists that science is a direct reflection of the racial or national spirit, neither do I accept Chekhov's dictum that 'there is no national science just as there is no national multiplication table.' . . . In emphasizing the international nature of scientific inquiry we have forgotton that science exists in a local social setting."

The social status of scientists is a frequently discussed aspect of morale. SHAH 1967 (p. 370) urges explicit social recognition of the importance of science, and the conspicuous inclusion of scientists in prestigious social functions. He argues further that industry should pay tribute to the role science can play in its development, and explicit attention should be paid by senior science administrators to the psychological needs of scientists. UNESCO 1970a (p. 37) discusses the social status of science and scientists complaining that administrators have more prestige than working scientists (p. 38). It also points out that the negative social implications of manual labor in certain societies constitute a handicap to the development of science. ROCHE 1966 (p. 60) observes:

> Social intercourse [in Venezuela] is based most often on the use and abuse of a quick wit which loves to destroy, a mocking irony as distinguished from the soft humour of the Anglo-Saxons, and a very basic doubt as to our capacity for real achievement. In such an atmosphere, the serious-minded and constructive scientist cannot but suffer. Progress has been made, and the research worker no longer feels as a complete social outcast; he is beginning to integrate into the social purposes of the country. Yet there is still a long road to be travelled in that direction.

The social role of science and society's approval (or lack thereof) is also the subject of DEDIJER 1963 (p. 68), BASALLA 1967 (p.

617), and Katzir's remarks in GRUBER 1961 (p. 227).

Various devices may be used to reassure scientists about their place in society. Prizes are common in many countries. For example, in the People's Republic of China, prizes and medals are awarded for research work or academic writing. The monetary value of a prize can reach several times the yearly salary of the recipient (WU 1970, p. 62).

An unusually interesting sociological survey is GASPARINI 1969. It is study of the Venezuelan scientific community, not only in terms of technical facts but also in terms of the self-images which Venezuelan scientists have of themselves. On the basis of individual surveys of several hundred scientists, it gives an extensive tabulation of opinions (pp. 117-84) on certain questions: Is Venezuela in the process of modernization? What is your role in such development? What are the main obstacles to such development? What is your general image of Venezuelan scientific investigation? Do you think that most Venezuelan scientists are incompetent? Do you think that most Venezuelan scientists are neurotic? These opinions are cross-correlated with the age, length of career, number of papers published, and other characteristics of the respondent. This is perhaps the only systematic way to ascertain the general morale of a scientific community, and it should be pursued in many other countries.

It was suggested in the first section of this chapter that a marked decline of morale in the ACs and a marked strengthening of morale in the LDCs could produce a relatively quick reversal of roles in scientific leadership. This possibility is discussed by Skyes in NADER 1969 (p. 588), MORAVCSIK 1973d, 1973i, and FLEMING 1967.

Nine

Where Do We Go From Here?

The previous chapters summarized the present state of science development. It is now appropriate to consider the future. To do that, however, a brief glance at the past is necessary. Prior to World War II, science everywhere was a small undertaking. There were scientifically advanced countries but in a sense very different from that of today. Even among the scientific leaders, the scientific community was small and intimate, the material requirements of science very modest, and the operation of science rather inconspicuous. Science and technology were much less closely linked than today; hence, the technological leaders of the world were not necessarily the scientific leaders.

At that time, many countries now called LDCs had already begun some indigenous scientific activity though usually on an even smaller scale than that of the scientific leaders of the day. Some of those countries were under colonial rule, and some had independent governments. China, India, and Argentina are examples. Other countries now considered LDCs had at that time no science whatever, such as some of the African countries.

There is little doubt that World War II served as a tremendous stimulus for the development of science. It was during 1938-48 that the present scientific leaders developed "Big Science," increasing their manpower and percentage expenditure in science by a factor of 10. At the same time, science became more intimately associated with technology and acquired public prominence in terms of national policies. A similar phenomenon began to occur in LDCs approximately a decade later. The delay was partly because LDCs in general were not involved in the war, partly because some of the upsurge of scientific activity was a result of decolonialization, and

209

partly because it takes time for a new idea to spread around the world. In a way, this delay of a decade was costly for the LDCs. They were generally unable to expand science as rapidly as the ACs had done. This is particularly true with regard to quality; the rapid expansion in LDCs often resulted in an infrastructure of mixed excellence, constituting a burden difficult to shed.

During this time the development of science was primarily a private or perhaps national undertaking. International scientific assistance was, on the whole, not practiced beyond the usual international scientific interaction. The few exceptions were those under colonial rule where the ruling powers undertook programs for science development in the colonies.

International scientific assistance to the LDCs began only about 25 years ago in the early 1950s (or perhaps late 1940s). During the 1950s it was inconspicuous and directed mainly to a few LDCs which already had some science. In the meantime, however, more and more new countries were coming into being, and "closing the gap" between LDCs and ACs was proclaimed as an objective in scores of LDCs. Nevertheless, the gap did not close but appeared to widen, at least in terms of standard of living and access to the benefits of technology.

The 1960s might be called the decade of awareness-building. It was necessary to impress upon the governments of LDCs the importance of science in the modernization of their countries. It was also important to persuade the ACs of their proper role in science development. At the same time, there was need for theoretical discussion of how science should be developed. Thus, the 1960s were a period of conferences, workshops, symposia, science plans, and so forth. If one compares a conference held at the beginning of the decade, such as the Rehovoth conference in 1961, with a meeting held several years later, such as the UNESCO conference in New Delhi in 1968, it is apparent that progress was made. Awareness was created in a general way, and on a purely theoretical level considerable clarification was achieved.

Spending 10 years on preliminary activities, though perhaps necessary, can also seem rather wasteful in time. It was, therefore, natural that by the end of the decade a feeling of urgency gripped some involved in science development, both in LDCs and in ACs. An expectation developed; after the preliminaries it was time to enter a decade of action when many of the ideas previously formulated and propagated could be converted into reality, activity, and actual development.

While it is, of course, premature to judge the decade of the 1970s, so far those expectations have proved completely futile. Except for a very few countries which seem to have "taken off" toward self-propelled scientific development, the LDCs continue to struggle with their problems as they did in the 1960s. International assistance aimed at promoting and accelerating science development is as inadequate in quantity, quality, and effectiveness as it was in the 1960s.

It would be gratifying to be able to blame this state of affairs on a few influential villains who conspire to prevent science from spreading around the world and keep its benefits to themselves. If that were so, the task would be easy: identify the villains and slay them. Suddenly, science would be evenly distributed worldwide, technological differences would vanish, and standards of living would equalize. Though the contention here is an extreme one, conspiracy hypotheses of this type are often voiced in connection with science development. Depending on whom you listen to, you will be told about different villains: the imperialists, the communists, AID, the local government of an LDC, the senior scientists in power in an LDC, the scientific community in ACs, UNESCO, etc. The suggestion is usually that if we could only do away with that obstacle, science development would suddenly blossom with unprecedented intensity.

Unfortunately, the reality is quite different: blame for the paucity of results must be shared among almost all participants in the process. This statement can be supported by conclusions reached in previous chapters concerning the shortcomings of present efforts in science development. I must first emphasize the assertion that should not be construed as a personal criticism of the many dedicated and energetic individuals in LDCs and ACs who have devoted themselves during the past decade to science development. They are pioneers in an exciting and immensely challenging field. But we have now passed the stage where isolated pioneer work could constitute the whole of international scientific assistance. ICTP, ICIPE, and IRRI are valuable institutions, but they address themselves only to specialized needs. There has been no action on a large, general scale during the 1960s and early 1970s—a condition I deplore.

In the LDCs, governments have generally been negligent in realizing the role of science, in arranging adequate organizational frameworks for its development, and in devoting sufficient funds to it. Instead, they have allowed bureaucracy and politics to play havoc with the little that has been established. Society in the LDCs has been equally remiss in not providing a suitable environment for science and in making no effort to assimilate science. In particular, the technological and industrial sector in the LDCs, however rudimentary, should have established better links with and better utilization of indigenous science.

The scientific communities in LDCs have been, on the whole, too lethargic in reforming their educational systems, in building their own scientific institutions, and in educating those around them on the needs of science. These communities have often been dominated by scientists of lesser accomplishments who are reluctant to share policy-making with their more deserving colleagues.

Scientists from LDCs have been too timid in presenting their cases to the international scientific community. It is ironic that a large fraction of the people involved in international scientific assistance programs, in writing for science development journals, and in making oral pleas for this cause have been scientists from ACs. Some voices from LDCs have been ineffective because of the nonfunctional, general nature of their message. It is extremely rare that a realistic international scientific assistance program originates from LDCs, proposed by the indigenous scientific community. Since I have been involved in science development for the past dozen years, I get ample correspondence from many LDCs. Rarely does a letter contain novel, specific suggestions for programs. This is regrettable if only because eminent spokesmen from LDCs, personally pleading their case before the scientific or even political community of ACs, could be much more effective instruments of science development than scientists from ACs pleading the same case. The dictum that nobody is a prophet in his country is applicable here.

The ACs, however, do not fare any better than the LDCs with respect to sharing the blame for past inactivity. Governments of ACs have supported programs generally inadequate in size, crippled by bureaucracy, and short-sighted in scope and purpose. Science development has been almost entirely ignored by society in ACs. Private industry takes little interest, private foundations ascribe low priority to it, and educational institutions neglect it in the face of local problems. One might say the issue is treated as a matter of charity. The extent of involvement is determined not by the magnitude of the task, but by how much the donor chooses to spend on charity.

International agencies must also share the blame. They are insufficient in size, overbureaucratized, and timid in approach. Too much of their funds is spent on routine, often ceremonial items, and their mode of operation keeps them distant from the working scientists they are supposed to aid.

These are general criticisms. A list of specific needs would require repetition of much of the previous chapters. Instead, I will list a few particular problems that I consider exceptionally urgent.

(1) Scientific assistance programs place too much emphasis on discussion instead of action. Conferences, seminars, workshops, and symposia were in order in the 1960s, and it was appropriate that they constitute the bulk of the programs. They must now be the exception rather than the rule, and programs must be oriented toward action.

(2) Personal contacts arranged within science development programs are usually too brief. Hurried visits by experts, though useful in certain contexts, must not supplant opportunities for extended research, work, or consultation.

(3) Scientific contacts are not sufficiently and directly channeled through scientists; the scientist-to-scientist relationship is impeded by intermediary organizations and channels.

(4) Relatively little assistance is awarded directly to the deserving scientist in the LDC. Before funds reach the working scientist, they are delayed, decimated, and misdirected by a complicated array of national and international organizations and officials. Excellence tends to become a secondary consideration as creativity and initiative are dampened to produce deadly mediocrity. The result is a scientific infrastructure which only *appears* to function.

(5) Scientific assistance is generally overbureaucratized at all stages, national and international alike. Decisions even in the simplest and least controversial cases take many months; meanwhile, science moves onward at a rapid pace in ACs. This disparity is a serious cause of demoralization among scientists working in LDCs.

(6) The education in ACs of students from LDCs needs improvement. Techniques of selecting students must be refined; their curriculum must be made appropriate for the conditions awaiting them on their return to their country; ways must be found to maintain contact with them after they have returned so they

receive assistance during the most difficult period when they establish themselves as scientists.

(7) There are few opportunities in ACs for scientists from LDCs to visit periodically for a year or so in order to mitigate the isolation they may experience in their own countries. Visiting positions should be awarded to scientists from LDCs after, say, five years of domestic service. A minute increase in the number of scientific positions in ACs (e.g., 1%) would generously satisfy this need.

(8) Patterns of scientific communication involving journals, preprints, and conferences tend to ignore scientists in LDCs. The patterns should be adjusted so as not to handicap these scientists.

(9) Only a small fraction of the scientific community in ACs takes an active interest in science development. A much larger percentage must become actively involved if anything significant is to be accomplished.

(10) Individuals and agencies are sometimes surprisingly intolerant of approaches to science development which differ from their own. Any differences that may exist among those involved in science development should be laid aside. Nobody can claim to have *the* recipe for science development; any energetic and experienced person who wants to try a different approach should be allowed and encouraged to do so. It seems ridiculous to argue about problem- versus program-oriented approaches and institutional versus problematic development when the problems are so numerous and the challenges so large. Theoretical discussions are appropriate, but they must not interfere with the quickest and most extensive action possible.

What is needed for the future? The problems have been clarified; the work has been marked out. What is needed is conviction, enthusiasm, energy, and persistence on the part of many more people. Hopefully, this book has brought you a step closer to participating in science development.

References

ACS 1966 American Chemical Society and American Physical Society. *Information on International Scientific Organizations, Services, and Programs.* Washington, D.C.: American Chemical Society, 1966.

ADAMS 1968 Adams, Walter, ed. *The Brain Drain.* New York: Macmillan Co., 1968.

ADAMS 1970 Adams, Scott. *Proposals for Establishing Communication Linkage for an Argentine National Science Information Network.* Washington, D.C.: National Academy of Sciences, 1970.

ADISESHIAH 1969 Adiseshiah, Malcolm S. "Unemployment of Engineers in India." *Impact* 19:1 (1969): 63.

AID 1970 Agency for International Development. *Survey Report on the Establishment of the Korea Advanced Institute of Science.* Washington, D.C.: AID, 1970.

AID 1972a Agency for International Development. *Technical Cooperation with Iran: A Case Study of Opportunities and Policy Implications for the United States.* Washington, D.C.: AID, 1972.

AID 1972b Agency for International Development. *Science and Technology for International Development: A Selected List of Information Sources in the United States* TA/OST 72-7. Washington, D.C.: AID, 1972.

AID 1973a Agency for International Development. *Policies and Programs in Selected Areas of Science and Technology* TA/OST 73-18. Washington, D.C.: AID, 1973.

AID 1973b Agency for International Development. Preliminary data provided by the US Government in response to a questionnaire from the Organization for Economics Cooperation and Development (OECD) relating to an inventory of projects and resources devoted to research and experimental development for the benefit of developing countries by OECD member countries. Washington, D.C.: AID, 1973.

AID 1973c Agency for International Development. *Appropriate Technologies for International Develop-*

ment: *Preliminary Survey of Research Activities*
TA/OST 72-11. Washington, D.C.: AID, 1972,
pp. 42ff.

AITKEN 1968   Aitken, Norman D. "The International Flow of
Human Capital: Comment." *The American
Economic Review* 58 (1968): 539.

ALLENDE 1972   Allende, Salvador G. "Science in Chile's Development Programme." *Impact* 22:1/2
(1972): 29.

ALLISON 1960   Allison, Samuel K. "Physics in Egypt: A New
Type of Lend-Lease." *Bulletin of the Atomic
Scientists* 16 (1960): 317.

ALONSO 1969   Alonso, Marcelo. *Integration of Science and
Education: A Survey of the Situation and Problems in Latin America.* Israel: Rehovot Conference, 1969.

ALTER 1968   Alter, Charles. *University Resources for International Development.* Washington, D.C.:
Agency for International Development, June
1968.

APTER 1961   Apter, David E. "New Nations and the Scientific Revolution." *Bulletin of the Atomic
Scientists* 17 (February 1961): 60.

ARGENTINA 1966   Argentina. *Comision Nacional de Energia Ato-
mica.* Published for "Visita de la delegacion
de la Comision Chilena de Energia Nuclear."
Buenos Aires: Comision Nacional de Energia
Argentina, 1966.

ASAIHL 1964   Association of Southeast Asian Institutions of
Higher Learning. *Seminar on Mathematical Education in Southeast Asia.* Bangkok: ASAIHL,
1964.

ASAIHL 1967   Association of Southeast Asian Institutions of
Higher Learning. *Seminar on Mathematics and
the Physical and Natural Sciences.* Bangkok:
ASAIHL, 1967.

ASAIHL 1969   Association of Southeast Asian Institutions of
Higher Learning. *Basic Sciences in Southeast
Asian Universities.* Bangkok: ASAIHL, 1969.

ASIA 1971   Asia Foundation. "Improving the Environment
for Science." *Program Quarterly* Spring/Summer
1971.

ASIA 1972a   Asia Foundation. *1971 President's Review.* San
Francisco: Asia Foundation, 1972.

ASIA 1972b   Asia Foundation. "Reducing the Information

Gap." *Asia Foundation Program Quarterly* Summer 1972.

BALDWIN 1970 — Baldwin, George. "Brain Drain or Overflow?" *Foreign Affairs* 48 (1970): 358.

BANAGE 1967 — Banage, W.B. "The Development of Science in East Africa." *Scientific World* 11 (1967): 15.

BARANSON 1969 — Baranson, Jack. "Role of Science and Technology in Advancing Development of Newly Industrialized States." *Socio-Economic Planning of Science* 3 (1969): 351.

BASALLA 1967 — Basalla, George. "The Spread of Western Science." *Science* 156 (1967): 611.

BAZIN 1972a — Bazin, Maurice. "Lasers into Pruning Hooks: Science for the People." *Ramparts* 11:2 (August 1972): 26.

BAZIN 1972b — Bazin, Maurice. "Science, Scientists, and the Third World." *Science for the People* 4:3 (1972): 3.

BAZIN 1973 — Bazin, Maurice. "La 'Science Pure,' Outil de L'imperialisme Culturel: Le Cas du Chile." *Les Temps Modernes* 29 (March 1973): 1593.

BFS 1971 — Board of Foreign Scholarships. *A Quarter Century.* Washington, D.C.: Board of Foreign Scholarships, 1971.

BFS 1972 — Board of Foreign Scholarships. *Reports on Exchanges: Tenth Annual Report.* Washington, D.C.: Board of Foreign Scholarships, 1972.

BHABHA 1966a — Bhabha, H.J. "Science and the Problems of Development." *Science* 151 (1966): 541.

BHABHA 1966b — Bhabha, H.J. "Indian Science: Two Methods of Development." *Science and Culture* 32 (1966): 333.

BHATHAL 1969 — Bhathal, R.S. "Science in Singapore." *New Scientist* 44 (1969): 514.

BHATHAL 1970 — Bhathal, R.S. "Physics for the Arts Students at the University of Singapore." *Technology and Society* 6:2 (1970): 72.

BHATHAL 1971a — Bhathal, R.S. "Science and Technical Education in Asia." *New Scientist and Science Journal* (June 1971): 729.

BHATHAL 1971b — Bhathal, R.S. "Science and Government in Singapore." *Bulletin of the Atomic Scientists* 27 (1971): 20.

BHATHAL 1971c — Bhathal, R.S. "Science, Religion, and Society." *Journal of the Political Science Society* Singapore (November 1971): 8.

BHATHAL 1971d   Bhathal, R.S. "Science Policy in the Developing Nations." *Nature* 232 (1971): 227.

BLACKETT 1963   Blackett, P.M.S. "Planning for Science and Technology in Emerging Countries." *New Scientist* 17 (1963): 345.

BLACKETT 1967   Blackett, P.M.S. "The Ever Widening Gap." *Science and Culture* 33 (1967): 303.

BLACKETT 1968   Blackett, P.M.S. "Science and Technology in an Unequal World." *Science and Culture* 34 (1968): 16.

BLANPIED 1970   Blanpied, William, and Strassenburg, Arnold. *The Indo-U.S. Conference on Physics Education and Research*. Unpublished. Copies available from the authors.

BLANPIED 1972   Blanpied, William. "Satyendranath Bose: Co-Founder of Quantum Statistics." *American Journal of Physics* 40 (1972): 1212.

BLOUNT 1965   Blount, B.K. "Consejo Superior de Investigaciones Cientificas, Spain." *Nature* 205 (1965): 340.

BOK 1948   Bok, Bart J. "UNESCO and the Physical Sciences." *Bulletin of the Atomic Scientists* 4 (1948): 343.

BONFIGLIOLI 1972   Bonfiglioli, Alberto. "Physics and Politics in Latin America." *Bulletin of the Atomic Scientists* (28 February 1972): 4, 48.

BOOKS 1973   Books for Asia Program. *Annual Report 1973*. San Francisco: Books for Asia Program, 1973.

BOSE 1965   Bose, N.K. "The Language Problem." *Science and Culture* 31 (1965): 391.

BOWDEN 1964   Bowden, Lord B.V. "The Migrant Scientist." *New Scientist* 21 (1964): 594.

BRADY 1973   Brady, Edward L. to Michael Moravcsik, April 1973, concerning the role of the National Bureau of Standards in building science in less advanced countries. An abbreviated edition is available: Harrison Brown and Theresa Tellez, International Development Programs of the Office of the Foreign Secretary, National Academy of Sciences, Washington, D.C., 1973.

BRAZIL 1971   Government of Brazil. *First National Development Plan 1972/74.* Brasilia: Government of Brazil, 1971.

BRODA 1964   Broda, Engelbert. "When Exchange is Not Really Exchange." *Bulletin of the Atomic Scientists* 20 (November 1964): 23.

BROOKS 1967   Brooks, Harvey. "Applied Research: Definitions, Concepts, Themes." In *Applied Science and Technological Progress.* Report by the National Academy of Sciences to the Committee on Science and Astronautics, 1967, 21-55.

BULLETIN 1950   "Science and Foreign Relations: Berkner Report to the U.S. Department of State." *Bulletin of the Atomic Scientists* 6 (1950) :293.

BULLETIN 1964   "UNESCO Science and Technology." *Bulletin of the Atomic Scientists* 20 (November 1964): 31.

BULLETIN 1972   "East African 'Center of Excellence': The International Centre of Insect Physiology and Ecology." *Bulletin of the American Academy of Arts and Sciences* 25:6 (1972): 3.

BURKHARDT 1966   Burkhardt, G. "Science Education in Africa." *Bulletin of the Atomic Scientists* 22 (1966): 46.

BUZZATI 1965   Buzatti-Traverso, Adriano. "Scientific Research: The Case for International Support." *Science* 148 (1965): 1440.

BYUNG 1972   Byung, Min Kil. *Problems in and Needs for Industry: Academic Collaboration in Korea.* Seoul: Report, Korean Consultant Group, 1972.

CALDER 1960   Calder, Ritchie. "Science and the New States." *New Scientist* 8 (1960): 526.

CARDENAS 1970   Cardenas, Rodolfo Jose. *Ciencia y Technologia.* Caracas: Oficina Central de Informacion, Imprenta Nacional, 1970.

CELASUN 1972   Celasun, Merih. "Technological Advance as a Factor in the Turkish Development Planning: Some Observations and Suggestions." In *Management of Research and Development.* Proceedings of the Istanbul Seminar on Research and Development Management. Paris: OECD, 1972, 11-32.

CEN 1970   "Program Sends Young Faculty to Brazil."

Chemical and Engineering News 48 (1970): 32.

CERNUSCHI 1971
Cernuschi, Felix. *Educacion, Ciencia, Technica y Desarrollo.* Montevideo: Universidad de la Republica, 1971.

CFA 1970
US House of Representatives Committee on Foreign Affairs. *Science, Technology, and American Diplomacy.* Selected Annotated Bibliography. Washington, D.C.: Library of Congress, 1970.

CHANG 1969
Chang, Parris H. "China's Scientists in the Cultural Revolution." *Bulletin of the Atomic Scientists* 25 (May 1969): 19.

CHATTERJI 1968
Chatterji, S.K. "Testament of a Veteran Educationalist." *Science and Culture* 34 (1968): 313.

CHENG 1965
Cheng, Chu-yuan. *Scientific and Engineering Education in Communist China.* Washington, D.C.: National Science Foundation, 1965.

CHINA 1972
Republic of China, National Science Council. *Science Development in the Republic of China.* Taipei: National Science Council, 1972.

CIBA 1972
CIBA Foundation. *Civilization & Science—In Conflict or Collaboration.* Amsterdam: Elsevier, 1972.

CIMT 1970a
Committee on the International Migration of Talent. *Modernization and the Migration of Talent.* New York: Education and World Affairs, 1970.

CIMT 1970b
Committee on the International Migration of Talent. *International Migration of High-Level Manpower.* New York: Praeger, 1970.

CLAF 1971
Centro Latino Americano de Fisica. *Final Report of the Evaluation Panel.* Rio de Janeiro: CLAF, 1971.

CLARKE 1971
Clarke, Robin. *The Great Experiment: Science and Technology in the Second United Nations Decade.* New York: UN Centre for Economic and Social Information, 1971.

COOPER 1971
Cooper, Charles. "Science, Technology and Development." *Economic and Social Review* 2 (1971): 165.

COOPERATION 1973
Cooperation Canada. "Aid Flows During 1972." *Cooperation Canada.* November/December 1973, p. 12.

COPISAROW 1970   Copisarow, Alcon. "The Issues." Keynote address at the Conference on Role of Science and Technology in Economic Development at the California Institute of Technology, 1970. (Reprints available)

CRAWFORD 1966   Crawford, Malcolm. "Thought on Chemical Research and Teaching in East Africa." *Minerva* 4 (1966): 170.

CREOLE 1966   Creole Foundation (Fondacion Creole). *The First Decade.* Caracas: Creole Foundation, 1966.

CSA 1967   US House of Representatives, Committee on Science and Astronautics. *Science, Technology, and Public Policy During the 89th Congress.* Washington, D.C.: US Government Printing Office, 1967.

CSA 1968   US House of Representatives, Committee on Science and Astronautics. *Policy Issues in Science and Technology.* Washington, D.C.: US Government Printing Office, 1968.

CSA 1971a   US House of Representatives, Committee on Science and Astronautics. *International Science Policy.* Compilation of papers prepared for the 12th Meeting of the Panel on Science and Technology. Washington, D.C.: US Government Printing Office, 1971.

CSA 1971b   US House of Representatives, Committee on Science and Astronautics. "International Science Policy." *Proceedings of the 12th Meeting of the Panel on Science and Technology.* January 1971.

CST 1969   Committee on Science and Technology (Delhi). *Report on Science and Technology (1969).* New Delhi: Committee on Science and Technology, 1969.

CST 1970   Committee on Science and Technology (India). "Science and Technology 1969-70." *Annual Report.* New Delhi: Committee on Science and Technology, 1970.

DANFORTH 1972   Danforth Foundation. *Annual Report 1971/72.* St. Louis: Danforth Foundation, 1972.

DARIEN 1973   Darien Books Aid Plan to Moravcsik, 1973, concerning outline of program.

DART 1963   Dart, Francis. "The Rub of Cultures." *Foreign Affairs* 41 (1963): 360.

DART 1966 — Dart, Francis. "Science as a Second Culture." *East-West Review.* June 1966, p. 17.

DART 1967 — Dart, Francis, and Pradhan, Panna Lal. "Cross-Cultural Teaching of Science." *Science* 155 (1967): 649.

DART 1971a — Dart, Francis, and Moravcsik, Michael J. *The Physics Graduate Student in the United States (A Guide for Prospective Foreign Students).* New York: American Institute of Physics, 1971.

DART 1971b — Dart, Francis. "Science Teaching for a Developing Nation." *U.P.N.G. News,* no. 26 (October 1971).

DART 1972 — Dart, Francis. "Science and the Worldview." *Physics Today* 25 (1972): 48.

DART 1973a — Dart, Francis. "Readiness in Abstraction." In *Education in Developing Countries of the Commonwealth.* London: Commonwealth Secretariat, 1973.

DART 1973b — Dart, Francis. "The Cultural Context of Science Teaching." *Search* 4 (1973): 322.

DEDIJER 1957 — Dedijer, Stevan. "Research and Freedom in Underdeveloped Countries." *Bulletin of the Atomic Scientists* 13 (1957): 238.

DEDIJER 1958 — Dedijer, Stevan. "The Birth and Death of a Myth." *Bulletin of the Atomic Scientists* 14 (May 1958): 164.

DEDIJER 1959 — Dedijer, Stevan. "Windowshopping for a Research Policy." *Bulletin of the Atomic Scientists* 15 (1959): 367.

DEDIJER 1960 — Dedijer, Stevan. "Scientific Research and Development: A Comparative Study." *Nature* 187 (1960): 458.

DEDIJER 1962 — Dedijer, Stevan. "Research: The Motor of Progress." *Bulletin of the Atomic Scientists* 18 (June 1962): 4.

DEDIJER 1963 — Dedijer, Stevan. "Underdeveloped Science in Underdeveloped Countries." *Minerva* 2:1 (1963): 61. Reprinted in Shils, Edward. *Criteria for Scientific Development: Public Policy and National Goals.* Cambridge, Mass.: MIT Press, 1968.

DEDIJER 1964a — Dedijer, Stevan. "International Comparisons of Science." *New Scientist* 21 (1964): 461-64.

DEDIJER 1964b | Dedijer, Stevan. "Migration of Scientists: A World-Wide Phenomenon and Problem." *Nature* 201 (1964): 964.

DEDIJER 1966 | Dedijer, Stevan, and Rahman, A. *Research Potential and Science Policy of the People's Republic of China (A bibliography)*. New Delhi: Research Policy Program, and Lund, Sweden: Research Survey and Planning Organization, 1966.

DE HEMPTINNE 1963 | De Hemptinne, Y. "The Science Policy of States in Course of Independent Development." *Impact* 13:3 (1963): 233.

DE HEMPTINNE 1972 | De Hemptinne, Y. *Governmental Science Policy Planning Structures* (UNESCO SC/WS/488), Paris, 1972.

DESSAU 1969 | Dessau, Jan. "Social Factors Affecting Science and Technology in Asia." *Impact* 19:1 (1969): 13.

DHARAMPAL 1971 | Dharampal. *Indian Science and Technology in the 18th Century*. Delhi: Impex, 1971.

DILLON 1966 | Dillon, Wilton S. "The Flow of Ideas Between Africa and America." *Bulletin of the Atomic Scientists* 22 (1966): 23.

DJERASSI 1968 | Djerassi, Carl. "A High Priority: Research Centers in Developing Nations." *Bulletin of the Atomic Scientists* 24 (January 1968): 22.

DVORIN 1965 | Dvorin, Eugene. "The Chile-California Experiment." *Bulletin of the Atomic Scientists* 21 (November 1965): 35.

ECHEVERRIA 1972 | Echeverria, Luis. "To Harness What Nature Gives Us." *Impact* 22:1/2 (1972): 43.

EKUBAN 1973 | Ekuban, E.E. "Technical Assistance to West Africa 1945-1968: A Conservative Review of British and American Policies." In *Education in Developing Countries of the Commonwealth*. London: Commonwealth Secretariat, 1973.

EL-SAID 1969 | El-Said, M.E.M. "A Study of National Science Policy Making Bodies of 61 Countries and a Brief Account of the Historical Development of the Science Council of U.A.R." Unpublished, n.d. (Copies available from the author at 101, Kasr El-Eini Street, Cairo, UAR.)

ENG. ED. 1970 | "Open Forum: Are We Mistreating Our Foreign

Graduate Students?" *Engineering Education* 61:3 (1970): 272.

ESPOSITO 1972   Esposito, Bruce J. "Science in Mainland China." *Bulletin of the Atomic Scientists* 28 (January 1972): 36.

FALICOV 1970   Falicov, L.M. "Physics and Politics in Latin America: A Personal Experience." *Bulletin of the Atomic Scientists* 26:11 (November 1970): 8.

FEDEROV 1963   Federov, E.K. "Some Problems Relating to Developing Countries." *Impact* 13:4 (1963): 273.

FLEMING 1967   Fleming, Launcelot. "Living With Progress." *New Scientist* 36 (1967): 166.

FORD 1971   Ford Foundation. *Annual Report 1971.* New York: Ford Foundation, 1972.

FORGE 1971   FORGE. *Fund for Overseas Research, Grants and Education.* Stanford, Conn.: FORGE, 1971.

FRANKLIN   Franklin Book Programs. *Franklin Book Program —Books Translated 1952-1970.* New York: Franklin Book Programs, Inc., n.d.

FRANKLIN 1971   Franklin Book Programs. *Annual Report 1970.* New York: Franklin Book Programs, Inc., 1971.

FREEMAN 1969a   Freeman, Christopher. *The Measurement of Scientific and Technological Activities: Proposals for the Collection of Statistics on Science and Technology on an Internationally Uniform Basis.* (UNESCO Statistical Reports and Studies no. 15), Paris, 1969.

FREEMAN 1969b   Freeman, Christopher. *Measurement of Output of Research and Experimental Development: A Review Paper.* (UNESCO Statistical Reports and Studies no. 16), Paris, 1969.

GANDHI 1969   Gandhi, Indira. "Moving Asia Forward." *Impact* 19:1 (1969): 3.

GARCIA 1966   Garcia, Rolando V. "Organizing Scientific Research." *Bulletin of the Atomic Scientists* 22 (September 1966): 12.

GARDNER 1964   Gardner, John W. *AID and the Universities.* Washington, D.C.: AID, 1964.

GARVEY 1972   Garvey, William, and Griffith, Belver C. "Communication and Information Processing within Scientific Disciplines: Empirical Findings for Psychology." *Information Storage Retrieval* 8 (1972): 123.

GASPARINI 1969   Gasparini, Olga. *La Investigacion en Venezuela:*

Condiciones de su Desarrollo. Caracas: IVIC, 1969.

GHANA 1971 — Council for Scientific and Industrial Research (Ghana). *Scientific Research in Ghana.* Accra: CSIR, 1971.

GHANA 1973 — Council for Scientific and Industrial Research (Ghana). *Workshop on the Role of the Council for Scientific and Industrial Research in Determining Science Policy and Research Priorities.* Ghana: CSIR, 1973.

GLASS 1968 — Glass, Bentley. "Pugwash Interest in Communication." *Science* 159 (1968): 1328.

GLYDE 1972 — Glyde, Henry R. *Institutional Links in Science and Technology: The Case of the United Kingdom and Thailand.* Technical Report 55/5. Bangkok: Applied Scientific Research Corporation, 1972.

GLYDE 1973 — Glyde, Henry R. "On Science and Technology in Thailand." *Science* (Thailand) 27:1 (1973): 19.

GOWON 1972 — Gowon, Yakubu. "Science, Technology, and Nigerian Development." *Impact* 22:1/2 (1972): 55.

GREENE 1971 — Greene, Michael. *Physics in Latin America: Peru and Chile.* Technical Report No. 72-050. College Park: Department of Physics, University of Maryland, 1971.

GRESFORD 1964 — Gresford, G.B. "Regional Organization of Research in Australia and South-East Asia." *Nature* 204 (1964): 432.

GRIFFITH 1972 — Griffith, Belver C., and Mullins, Nicholas C. "Coherent Social Groups in Scientific Change." *Science* 177 (1972): 959.

GRIFFITH 1973a — Griffith, Belver C.; Small, Henry G.; Stonehill, Judith A.; and Malin, Morton V. "Mapping Scientific Literatures." *Proceedings of the Information Science Advanced Study Institute.* Aberytwyth, Wales: 1973.

GRIFFITH 1973b — Griffith, Belver C.; Small, Henry G.; Stonehill, Judith A.; and Dey, Sandra. "The Structure of Scientific Literature II: Toward a Macro- and Microstructure for Science." Forthcoming.

GRUBEL 1966 — Grubel, Herbert G., and Scott, Anthony. "The International Flow of Human Capital." *The American Economic Review* 56 (1966): 268.

GRUBEL 1968a — Grubel, Herbert G. "The International Flow of

Human Capital: Reply." *American Economic Review* 58 (1968): 545.

GRUBEL 1968b — Grubel, Herbert G. "Foreign Manpower in the U.S. Sciences." *Rural Income and Wealth* 14 (March 1968): 57.

GRUBEL 1968c — Grubel, Herbert G. "The Reduction of the Brain Drain: Problems and Policies." *Minerva* 6 (1968): 541.

GRUBER 1961 — Gruber, Ruth, ed. *Science and the New Nations.* New York: Basic Books, 1961.

HAFNER 1967 — Hafner, Everett. "An Institute in North Bengal." *Physics Today* 20:6 (1967): 44.

HAMBRAEUS 1972 — Hambraeus, Gunnar. "Science and Technology in China after the Cultural Revolution." *IVA* 43: 4 (1972): 149.

HARARI 1968 — Harari, Roland. "The Long March of Chinese Science." *Science Journal* 4 (April 1968): 78.

HARBISON 1965 — Harbison, Frederick, and Myers, Charles A. *Manpower and Education: Country Studies in Economic Development.* New York: McGraw Hill Book Co., 1965.

HAWKES 1971 — Hawkes, Nigel. "Chile: Planning for Science Faces Obstacles Old and New." *Science* 174 (1971): 1217.

HERRERA 1970 — Herrera, Amilcar O., ed. *America Latina: Ciencia y Tecnologia en el Desarrollo de la Sociedad.* Santiago, Chile: Editorial Universitaria, SA, 1970.

HOWE 1974 — Howe, James, et al. *The U.S. and the Developing World Agenda for Action 1974.* New York: Praeger, 1974.

HUDDLE 1970 — Huddle, Franklin P. *The Evolution of International Technology.* Washington, D.C.: US Government Printing Office, 1970.

IAEA 1972 — International Atomic Energy Agency. *International Atomic Energy Agency Publications.* Vienna: IAEA, 1972.

IAEA 1973a — International Atomic Energy Agency. *Annual Report, 1 July 1972–30 June 1973* (IAEA GC [XVII] / 500), Vienna: IAEA, 1973.

IAEA 1973b — International Atomic Energy Agency. *The Provision of Technical Assistance by the Agency with Special Reference to 1972* (IAEA GC [XVII] /INF/142), Vienna: IAEA, 1973.

IAEA 1973c	International Atomic Energy Agency. *IAEA Services and Assistance.* Vienna: IAEA, 1973.
IDRC 1971	International Development Research Centre. *Annual Report 1970-71.* Ottawa: IDRC, 1971.
IIE 1971	Institute of International Education. *Teaching Abroad.* New York: IIE, 1971, mimeographed.
IIE 1972	Institute of International Education. *Open Doors.* New York: IIE, 1972.
INDIA 1969	University Grants Commission, India. *Chemistry: Design for Innovation.* New Delhi: UGC, 1969.
INDIA 1970	University Grants Commission and National Council for Science Education. *Physics in India: Challenges and Opportunities.* Proceedings of the Conference on Physics Education and Research. New Delhi: UGC, 1970.
INDONESIA 1969	Government of Indonesia. *The First Five-Year Development Plan (1969/70-1973/74).* Six Volumes. (See particularly Vol. 2c.) Djakarta: Government of Indonesia, 1969.
INDONESIA 1971	Government of Indonesia. *Indonesian Institute of Sciences (Lembaga Ilma Pengetahuan Indonesia).* Djakarta: LIPI, 1971.
INTERAMERICAN 1969	Banco Interamericano de Desarrollo. *Fomento de la Educacion, la Ciencia y la Tecnologia por el Banco Interamericano de Desarrollo.* Washington, D.C.: Interamerican Bank, 1969, mimeographed.
IVIC 1971	Instituto Venezolano de Investigaciones Cientificas. *Centro de Investigaciones Technologicas.* Caracas: Instituto Venezolano de Investigaciones Cientificas, 1971.
JAPAN 1972	Science and Technology Agency, Japan. *Summary, Fiscal Year 1972: White Paper on Science and Technology.* Tokyo: Science and Technology Agency, 1973.
JEQUIER 1970	Jequier, Nicolas. *Le defi industriel Japonais.* Lausanne: Centre de recherches europeennes, 1970.
JOHNSON 1965	Johnson, Harry G. "The Economics of the 'Brain Drain': The Canadian Case." *Minerva* 3 (1965): 299; 4 (1966): 273; 6 (1967): 105.
JONES 1970	Jones, Burton W. *General Principles of International Collaboration in Mathematical Educa-*

tion. Washington, D.C.: Conference Board of the Mathematical Sciences, 1970.

JONES 1971

Jones, Graham. *The Role of Science and Technology in Developing Countries.* Oxford: Oxford University Press, 1971.

JOSHI 1967

Joshi, A.C. "The Education of the Abler Students." *Science and Culture* 33 (1967): 299.

KARVE 1963

Karve, D.D. "The Universities and the Public in India." *Minerva* 1 (1963): 263.

KARVE 1965a

Karve, D.D. "On the Improvement of the Indian Universities." *Minerva* 3 (1965): 159.

KARVE 1965b

Karve, D.D. "Language and Democracy." In *Studies in Indian Democracy.* Edited by S.P. Aiyar and R. Srinavasan. Bombay: Allied Publishers Private, Ltd., 1965.

KARVE 1967

Karve, D.D. "Universities and the Language Question." *Quest.* Special no. 32 (March 1967).

KELLOGG 1972

Kellogg Foundation. *1971 Annual Report.* Battle Creek, Mich.: Kellogg Foundation, 1972.

KHAN 1969

Mohammed Ali Khan. "Education and Research in Pakistan." *Impact* 19:1 (1969): 85.

KIM 1969

Kim, Kee-Hyong. "Korea's Strategy for Science and Technology." *Impact* 19:1 (1969): 93.

KING 1957

King, Alexander. "UNESCO's First Ten Years." *New Scientist* 2 (1957): 15.

KOPECZI 1972

Kopeczi, Bela. "Az akademiai intezetek fiatal kutatoinak helyzete." *Magyar Tudomany* 17 (1972): 669.

KOREA 1970

Government of the Republic of Korea, Ministry of Science and Technology. *The Long-Term Plan for Scientific and Technological Development (Summary).* Seoul: Ministry of Science and Technology, 1970.

KOREA 1971a

Government of the Republic of Korea. *The Third Five-Year Economic Development Plan, 1972-76.* Seoul: Government of Korea, 1971.

KOREA 1971b

Government of the Republic of Korea, Ministry of Science and Technology. *The Third Five-Year Manpower Development Plan.* Seoul: Ministry of Science and Technology, 1971.

KOREA 1972a

Government of the Republic of Korea, Ministry of Science and Technology. *Handbook of Science and Technology, 1972.* Seoul: Ministry of Science and Technology, 1972.

KOREA 1972b   Government of the Republic of Korea, Ministry of Science and Technology. *The Ministry of Science and Technology Report.* Seoul: Ministry of Science and Technology, 1972.

KOVDA 1963   Kovda, Victor A. "Index of Prosperity: S.T. P." *UNESCO Courier* 16 (July-August 1963): 19.

KOVDA 1968   Kovda, Victor A. "Search for a U.N. Science Policy." *Bulletin of the Atomic Scientists* 24 (March 1968): 12.

LARWOOD 1961   Larwood, H.J.C. "Science and Education in India Before the Mutiny." *Annals of Science* 17 (June 1961): 81.

LEWIS 1961   Lewis, Arthur W. "Needs of New States: Science, Men, and Money." *Bulletin of the Atomic Scientists* 17 (February 1961): 43.

LEWIS 1962   Lewis, Arthur W. "Education for Scientific Professions in the Poor Countries." *Daedalus* 91 (1962): 310.

LINDBECK 1969   Lindbeck, John M.H. "An Isolationist Science Policy." *Bulletin of the Atomic Scientists* 25 (February 1969): 66.

LOCKARD 1972   Lockard, J. David. *Eighth Report of the International Clearinghouse on Science and Mathematics Curricular Development.* College Park: University of Maryland Press, 1972.

LONSDALE 1968   Lonsdale, Dame Kathleen. "Science and the Good Life." *New Scientist* 39 (1968): 370.

LONSDALE 1969   Lonsdale, Dame Kathleen. "Developing Nations and Scientific Responsibility." *Bulletin of the Atomic Scientists* 25 (November 1969): 27.

LOPES 1966   Lopes, J. Leite. "Science for Development: A View from Latin America." *Bulletin of the Atomic Scientists* 22 (September 1966): 7.

LOW 1967   Low, Ian. "The Land They Leave." *New Scientist* 34 (1967): 404.

LUBKIN 1972   Lubkin, Gloria. "Physics in China." *Physics Today* 25:12 (1972): 23.

MACKAY 1973   Mackay, Lindsay. "An Experimental Evaluation of Some Aspects of Secondary School Science Curriculum in Papua, New Guinea." In *Education in Developing Countries of the Commonwealth.* London: Commonwealth Secretariat, 1973.

MAHEU 1963   Maheu, Rene. "330 Million Brains for a New

Era." *UNESCO Courier* 16 (July-August 1963): 25.

MALECKI 1963 — Malecki, I. "Some Problems Concerning Organization of Scientific Research in the Developing Countries." *Impact* 13 (1963): 181.

MARTIN 1970 — Martin, N.R. *Nigeria: The National Science Policy Machinery.* (UNESCO Serial No. 2247/BMS. RD/SCP), Paris, 1970.

MATHUR 1947 — Mathur, K.N. "The National Physical Laboratory of India." *Nature* 159 (1947): 184.

MCBAIN 1954 — McBain, Evelyn. "India Turns to Science." *Chemical and Engineering News* 32 (1954): 604.

MENDELSOHN 1960 — Mendelsohn, Kurt. "Science in China." *The New Scientist* 8 (1960): 1261.

MEXICO 1970 — Instituto Nacional de la Investigacion Cientifica. *Politica Nacional y Programas en Ciencia y Tecnologia.* Mexico: INIC, 1970.

MEXICO 1971 — CONACYT (Mexico). *CONACYT.* Ciudad de Mexico: CONACYT, 1971.

MIRABOGLU 1972 — Miraboglu, M. *Aspects of the Turkish Brain Drain.* (UNESCO Document SC.72/CONF.3/3, Annex 24[a]), Paris, 1972.

MITCHIE 1968 — Mitchie, Allan A. *Higher Education and World Affairs.* New York: Education and World Affairs, 1968.

MITCHISON 1960 — Mitchison, Naomi. "Science in Egypt." *The New Scientist* 7 (1960): 1073.

MORAVCSIK 1964a — Moravcsik, Michael J. "Fundamental Research in Underdeveloped Countries." *Physics Today* 17:1 (1964): 21.

MORAVCSIK 1964b — Moravcsik, Michael J. "Fundamental Research in Developing Countries." *International Atomic Energy Agency Bulletin* 6:2 (1964): 8.

MORAVCSIK 1964c — Moravcsik, Michael J. "Technical Assistance and Fundamental Scientific Research in Underdeveloped Countries." *Minerva* 2 (1964): 197. Reprinted in Shils, Edward, ed. *Criteria for Scientific Development: Public Policy and National Goals.* Cambridge, Mass.: MIT Press, 1968; and in Shah, A.B., ed. *Education, Scientific Policy and Developing Societies.* Manaktalas, 1967.

MORAVCSIK 1965a — Moravcsik, Michael J. "Private and Public Communications in Physics." *Physics Today* 18:3 (1965): 25.

MORAVCSIK 1965b	Moravcsik, Michael J. "A Case of a Scientist in Pakistan's Social Order—A Different View." *The Nucleus* 2:1 (1965): 19.
MORAVCSIK 1966a	Moravcsik, Michael J. "Scientists In Politics and Out." *Bulletin of the Atomic Scientists* 22:1 (1966): 32.
MORAVCSIK 1966b	Moravcsik, Michael J. "The Physics Information Exchange: A Communication Experiment." *Physics Today* 19:6 (1966): 62.
MORAVCSIK 1966c	Moravcsik, Michael J. "Some Practical Suggestions for the Improvement of Science in Developing Countries." *Minerva* 4 (1966): 381; Reprinted in Shils, Edward, ed. *Criteria for Scientific Development: Public Policy and National Goals.* Cambridge, Mass.: MIT Press, 1968.
MORAVCSIK 1970a	Moravcsik, Michael J. "Reflections on National Laboratories." *Bulletin of the Atomic Scientists* 26:2 (1970): 11.
MORAVCSIK 1970b	Moravcsik, Michael J. *A Summary of the Discussion Meeting of Problems of Physics in the Developing Countries.* College Park: University of Maryland Press, 1970.
MORAVCSIK 1971a	Moravcsik, Michael J. "Some Modest Proposals." *Minerva* 9 (1971): 55.
MORAVCSIK 1971b	Moravcsik, Michael J. "The Research Institute and Scientific Aid." *International Development Review* 13:3 (1971): 17.
MORAVCSIK 1971c	Moravcsik, Michael J. "On the Brain Drain in the Philippines." *Bulletin of the Atomic Scientists* 27:2 (1971): 36.
MORAVCSIK 1972a	Moravcsik, Michael J. "Aspects of Science Development." In *Management of Research and Development.* Paris: OECD, 1972, pp. 189-240.
MORAVCSIK 1972b	Moravcsik, Michael J. "Physics in Developing Countries." *Physics Today* 25:9 (1972): 40.
MORAVCSIK 1972c	Moravcsik, Michael J. *Science Development in the Framework of International Relations.* Santa Monica: Southern California Arms Control and Foreign Policy Seminar, 1972.
MORAVCSIK 1972d	Moravcsik, Michael J. "The Committee on International Education in Physics." *American Journal of Physics* 41 (1973): 309, 608; *Physics Teaching* 25:9 (1972): 40.
MORAVCSIK 1972e	Moravcsik, Michael J. "The Physics Interview-

ing Project." *International Educational and Cultural Exchange.* Summer 1972, p. 16.

MORAVCSIK 1973a   Moravcsik, Michael J. "A View on Foreign Assistance Policy." In *Views on Foreign Assistance Policy.* US Senate, Committee on Foreign Relations. Washington, D.C.: US Government Printing Office, 1973, pp. 235-40.

MORAVCSIK 1973b   Moravcsik, Michael J., and Nelson, William M. *Pursuit of Science in Less Developed Countries (A Bibliography).* Washington, D.C.: AID, 1973, mimeographed.

MORAVCSIK 1973c   Moravcsik, Michael J. "Science Education for Foreign Graduate Students." *International Educational and Cultural Exchange.* Summer 1973, p. 45.

MORAVCSIK 1973d   Moravcsik, Michael J. "The Transmission of a Scientific Civilization." *Science and Public Affairs* 29:3 (1973): 25.

MORAVCSIK 1973e   Moravcsik, Michael J. "Desarrollo de la Ciencia." *Acta Cientifica Venezolana* 29:4 (1973).

MORAVCSIK 1973f   Moravcsik, Michael J. "American Scientists in Developing Countries: What Can They Do?" Unpublished.

MORAVCSIK 1973g   Moravcsik, Michael J. *Science and Technology in National Development Plans: Some Case Studies.* Washington, D.C.: AID, May 1973.

MORAVCSIK 1973h   Moravcsik, Michael J. "Measures of Scientific Growth." *Research Policy* 2:3 (1973): 256.

MORAVCSIK 1973i   Moravcsik, Michael J. "A Chance to Close the Gap?" *Science and Culture* 39:5 (1973): 205.

MORAVCSIK 1974a   Moravcsik, Michael J. "Scientists and Artists —Motivations, Aspirations, Approaches and Accomplishments." *Leonardo* 7:2 (1974).

MORAVCSIK 1974b   Moravcsik, Michael J. "New Directions in Scientific and Technological Assistance." *Science Policy* 2:2 (1973): 179.

MORAVCSIK 1974c   Moravcsik, Michael J. "Communication in the Worldwide Scientific Community." *Science and Culture* 41:1 (1975): 10.

MORAVCSIK 1974d   Moravcsik, Michael J. "A Refinement of Extrinsic Criteria for Scientific Choice." *Research Policy* 3:1 (1974).

MORAVCSIK 1974e   Moravcsik, Michael J. "The Limits of Scientific Knowledge." Unpublished.

MORAVCSIK 1974f   Moravcsik, Michael J. "Scientific Aid in Local Currency." Unpublished.

MOREHOUSE 1967   Morehouse, Ward. "Confronting a Four-Dimensional Problem: Science, Technology, Society, and Tradition in India and Pakistan." *Technology and Culture* 8 (1967): 363.

MOREHOUSE 1968   Morehouse, Ward, ed. *Science and the Human Condition in India and Pakistan.* New York: Rockefeller University Press, 1968.

MOSHARRAFA 1946   Mosharrafa Pasha, A.M. "The Egyptian Academy of Sciences." *Nature* 157 (1946): 573.

MULLINS 1973   Mullins, Nicholas C. "A Sociological Theory of Normal and Evolutionary Science." In *Determinants and Controls of Scientific Development.* Edited by Karin D. Knorr, Hermann Strasser, and H.G. Zillian. Boston, Mass.: D. Reidel Publishing Co., 1975.

MURIEL 1970   Muriel, Amador. "Brain Drain in the Philippines." *Bulletin of the Atomic Scientists* 26 (1970): 38.

NADER 1969   Nader, C., and Zahlan, A.B., eds. *Science and Technology in Developing Countries.* Cambridge, Mass.: Cambridge University Press, 1969.

NAS 1965a   National Academy of Sciences, *Report by the Study Group on Animal Diseases in Africa.* Washington, D.C.: NAS, 1965.

NAS 1965b   National Academy of Sciences. *Summary Report, Workshop on Science and Nigerian Development.* Washington, D.C.: NAS, 1965.

NAS 1966   National Academy of Sciences. *The Role of Science and Technology in Peruvian Economic Development.* Workshop Report. Paracas: NAS, 1966.

NAS 1967   National Academy of Sciences. *Applied Science and Technological Progress.* Report to the Committee on Science and Astronautics, Washington, D.C.: NAS, 1967.

NAS 1968a   National Academy of Sciences. *Institutions of Higher Education, Research, and Planning in Colombia.* Washington, D.C.: NAS, 1968.

NAS 1968b   National Academy of Sciences. *Industrial Research as a Factor in Economic Development.* Report of the Joint Study Group on Industrial Research, US, Brazil Science Cooperation Program. Washington, D.C.: NAS, 1968.

NAS 1968c   National Academy of Sciences. *Science and Bra-*

	zilian Development Report of the Second Work-shop on Contribution of Science and Technology to Development. Washington, D.C.: NAS, 1968.
NAS 1968d	National Academy of Sciences. *Final Report of the Meeting on Research in Peru.* Peru: Ancon, 1968.
NAS 1969a	National Academy of Sciences. *The Future of U.S. Technical Cooperation with Korea.* A Report to AID. Washington, D.C.: NAS, November 1969.
NAS 1969b	National Academy of Sciences. *Report to the AID Mission in Colombia Technical Assistance Project.* Washington, D.C.: NAS, 1969.
NAS 1969c	National Academy of Sciences. *Report of the Argentine-U.S. Workshop on Science and Technology in Economic Development, Mar del Plata.* Washington, D.C.: NAS, 1969.
NAS 1970a	National Academy of Sciences. *Semiannual Progress Report on the Brazil-U.S. Chemistry Program.* Washington, D.C.: NAS, 1970, 1971.
NAS 1970b	National Academy of Sciences. *Argentine-U.S. Panel on Scientific Information: Report of the First Meeting.* Washington, D.C.: NAS, 1970.
NAS 1970c	National Academy of Sciences. *Program to Stimulate Graduate Education and Research in Colombian Universities.* Washington, D.C.: NAS, 1970.
NAS 1971a	National Academy of Sciences. *The International Development Institute. A Report of an Ad Hoc Committee of the Board in Science and Technology for International Development.* Washington, D.C.: NAS, 1971.
NAS 1971b	National Academy of Sciences. *Research Priorities and Problems in the Execution of Research in Ghana. Proceedings of the Workshop.* Accra: NAS, 1971.
NAS 1971c	National Academy of Sciences. *East Pakistan Land and Water Development as Related to Agriculture.* NAS report prepared for AID. Washington, D.C.: NAS, 1971.
NAS 1971d	National Academy of Sciences. *The International Development Institute.* Washington, D.C.: NAS, 1971.
NAS 1971e	National Academy of Sciences. *Report on Colciencias-NAS Panel Study of Graduate Education*

and Research in Mathematics in Colombia. Washington, D.C.: NAS, 1971.

NAS 1971f   National Academy of Sciences. *Report of a Colciencias-NAS Panel Study of Graduate Education and Research in Chemistry in Colombia.* Bogota, Colombia: NAS, 1971.

NAS 1972a   National Academy of Sciences. *Solar Energy in Developing Countries: Perspectives and Prospects.* Washington, D.C.: NAS, 1972.

NAS 1972b   National Academy of Sciences. *Semiannual Progress Report, Brazil-U.S. Chemistry Program, July-December 1971.* Washington, D.C.: NAS, 1972.

NAS 1973a   National Academy of Sciences. *U.S. International Firms and R, D, and E in Developing Countries.* Washington, D.C.: NAS, 1973.

NAS 1973b   National Academy of Sciences. *Interim Progress Report, CNPq-NAS Chemistry Program.* Washington, D.C.: NAS, September 1973.

NAS 1973c   National Academy of Sciences. *National Academy of Sciences: International Development Programs of the Office of the Foreign Secretary. Summary and Analysis of Activities, 1961-1971.* Washington, D.C.: NAS, 1973.

NAS 1973d   National Academy of Sciences. *Annual Report of the Board on Science and Technology for International Development.* Washington, D.C.: NAS, 1973.

NAS 1973e   National Academy of Sciences. *NAS-CNPq Science Cooperation Program.* Washington, D.C.: NAS, 1973.

NATURE 1955   "Council of Scientific and Industrial Research, India." *Nature* 175 (1955): 23.

NATURE 1964a   "Pros and Cons of International Research Centres." *Nature* 203 (1964): 454.

NATURE 1964b   "Organization and Administration of Indian Science." *Nature* 204 (1964): 528.

NATURE 1964c   "Science Planning, Development and Cooperation in the Countries of the Middle East and North Africa." *Nature* 189 (1964): 362.

NATURE 1968   "Science After the Cultural Revolution." *Nature* 217 (1968): 1196.

NAUDE 1959   Naude, S.M. "The South African Council for Scientific and Industrial Research." *Nature* 183 (1959): 853.

NAYUDAMMA 1967   Nayudamma, Y. "Promoting the Industrial Application of Research in an Underdeveloped Country." *Minerva* 5 (1967): 323.

NBS 1971   National Bureau of Standards. *Metrology and Standardization in Less-Developed Countries: The Role of a National Capability for Industrializing Economies.* Special Publication No. 359. Washington, D.C.: National Bureau of Standards, 1971.

NBS 1972   National Bureau of Standards. *A Report on a Survey in Ecuador on Standardization and Measurement Services in Support of Industrialization Goals.* Report No. 10 881. Washington, D.C.: National Bureau of Standards, 1972.

NBS 1973   National Bureau of Standards. *Collaborative Research Program between NBS and Indian Scientific Institutions, Special Foreign Currency Program—1973 Status.* Technical Note 798. Washington, D.C.: National Bureau of Standards, 1973.

NEEDHAM 1948   Needham, Joseph. "Practical Steps for International Cooperation Among Scientists." *UNESCO Courier* 1 (February 1948): 2.

NICHOLLS 1969   Nicholls, Frank G., and Pradisth, Cheosakul. "Harnessing Science to Development in Thailand." *Impact* 19:1 (1969): 75.

NIGERIA 1970a   Nigerian Council for Science and Technology. *First Annual Report.* Lagos: NCST, 1970.

NIGERIA 1970b   Government of Nigeria. *Second National Development Plan 1970-74.* Lagos: NCST, 1970.

NIXON 1970   Nixon, Richard M. "Foreign Assistance for the Seventies." Message to Congress, September 15, 1970. Washington, D.C.: Agency for International Development, 1970.

NIXON 1971   Nixon, Richard M. "The Foreign Assistance Program." Annual Report to the Congress for Fiscal Year 1970. Washington, D.C.: US Government Printing Office, 1971.

NOYES 1957   Noyes, W. Albert Jr. "Do We Need a Foreign Policy in Science?" *Bulletin of the Atomic Scientists* 13 (1957): 234.

NORTHROP 1965   Northrop, Eugene P. "Improving Science Education in Turkey." *Yeni Ortaogretim (New Secondary Education)* no. 5 (February 1965).

NSF 1973   National Science Foundation. *Science Educa-*

tion Improvement Project February 1967-June 1973. Project Completion Report. New Delhi: NSF Science Liaison Staff, 1973.

OAS 1970 — Organization of American States. *Proyectos Multinacionales del Programa Regional de Desarrollo Cientifico y Technologico de la OEA.* Washington, D.C.: OAS, February 1970.

OAS 1971 — Organization of American States. *Services Provided to the Member States, Fiscal Year 1970-71.* Washington, D.C.: OAS, undated.

OAS 1972 — Organization of American States. *OAS Programs Related to Science and Technology.* (OEA/Ser.K/XVIII.1), August 1972.

ODHIAMBO 1967 — Odhiambo, Thomas. "East Africa: Science for Development." *Science* 158 (1967): 876.

OECD 1963 — Organization for Economic Cooperation and Development. *Proposed Standard Practice for Surveys of Research and Development.* Paris: OECD, 1963.

OECD 1965 — Organization for Economic Cooperation and Development. "Relating Science and Technology to Economic Development—A Five-Country Experiment." *OECD Observer* 15 (1965): 8.

OECD 1968a — Organization for Economic Cooperation and Development. *Science and Development. Pilot Teams Project. Evaluation Conference.* Paris: OECD, 1968.

OECD 1968b — Organization for Economic Cooperation and Development. *National Reports of the Pilot Teams. Spain: Science and Development.* Paris: OECD, 1968.

OECD 1968c — Organization for Economic Cooperation and Development. *National Reports of the Pilot Teams. Greece: Science and Development.* Paris: OECD, 1968.

OECD 1969 — Organization for Economic Cooperation and Development. *Scientific Research and Technology in Relation to the Economic Development of Turkey. Directorate of Scientific Affairs: Pilot Teams' Project on Science and Economic Development.* Paris: OECD, 1969.

OECD 1971a — Organization for Economic Cooperation and Development. *Science, Growth, and Society: Report of the Secretary General's Ad Hoc Group on New Concepts of Science Policy.* Paris: OECD, 1971.

OECD 1971b   Organization for Economic Cooperation and De-
                    velopment. *Politicas Nacionales de la Ciencia—
                    Espana.* Madrid: OECD, 1971.

OECD 1971c   Organization for Economic Cooperation and De-
                    velopment, Committee for Science Policy. *The
                    Goals of R & D in the 1970's.* Paris: OECD,
                    1971.

OECD 1972a   Organization for Economic Cooperation and De-
                    velopment. *Development Cooperation: Efforts
                    and Policies of the Members of the Development
                    Assistance Committee, 1972 Review.* Report pre-
                    pared by Edwin M. Martin, Chairman, DAC. Paris:
                    OECD, 1972.

OECD 1972b   Organization for Economic Cooperation and De-
                    velopment. *Analytical Methods in Government
                    Science Policy: An Evaluation.* Paris: OECD,
                    1972.

OLDHAM 1966   Oldham, C.H.G. "Science and Education." *Bul-
                    letin of the Atomic Scientists* 22 (June 1966):
                    40.

OLDHAM 1968   Oldham, C.H.G. "Science in China's Develop-
                    ment." *Advancement of Science* 24 (1968):
                    481.

ORLEANS 1972   Orleans, Leo. "How the Chinese Scientist Sur-
                    vives." *Science* 177 (1972): 864.

OTIENO 1967   Otieno, N.C. "Today's Schools Prepare Tomor-
                    row's African Scientists." *UNESCO Courier* 20
                    (June 1967): 33.

PAKISTAN 1968   National Research Council. *Pakistan Report on
                    the Organization of Scientific Research.* Kara-
                    chi: National Research Council, 1968.

PARTHASARATHI 1966 Parthasarathi, Ashok. " 'Aid' Science: Help
                    or Hindrance?" *New Scientist* 32 (1966): 642.

PARTHASARATHI 1969 Parthasarathi, Ashok. "Appearance and Reality
                    in Indian Science Policy." *Nature* 221 (1969):
                    909.

PERES 1969   Peres, Leon. "Scientific Research Institu-
                    tions in Asia." *Impact* 19:1 (1969) 25.

PERU 1970   Consejo Nacional de Investigacion. *Plan Na-
                    cional de Desarrollo Cientifico y Tecnologico
                    1971-1975.* Lima: Consejo Nacional de Investi-
                    gacion, 1970.

PHILIPPINES 1966   *Second U.S. Philippines Workshop on Coopera-
                    tion in Science and Technology.* Philippines:
                    National Science Development Board, 1966.

PHILIPPINES 1969a   *Philippines-U.S. Workshop on Industrial Research, Part I.* Baguio City: National Science Development Board, 1969.

PHILIPPINES 1969b   *Philippines-U.S. Workshop on Industrial Research, Part II.* Working Papers. Baguio City: National Science Development Board, 1969.

PIRIE 1967   Pirie, N.W. "Science and Development." *Political Quarterly* 38 (1967): 62.

PRICE 1963   De Solla Price, Derek J. *Little Science, Big Science.* New York: Columbia University Press, 1963.

PRICE 1964a   De Solla Price, Derek J. "The Science of Science." In *The Science of Science.* Edited by M. Goldsmith and A.L. Mackay. London: Souvenir Press, 1964. Published in USA as *Society and Science.* New York: Simon and Schuster, 1964, pp. 195-208. Pelican edition, London, 1966. Russian edition, Moscow, 1966.

PRICE 1964b   De Solla Price, Derek J. "Ethics of Scientific Publications." *Science* 144 (1964): 655.

PRICE 1964c   De Solla Price, Derek J. *Distribution of Scientific Papers by Country and Subject—A Science Policy Analysis.* Unpublished.

PRICE 1965a   De Solla Price, Derek J. "Is Technology Historically Independent of Science? A Study in Statistical Historiography." *Technology and Culture* 6 (1965): 553-68.

PRICE 1965b   De Solla Price, Derek J. "The Science of Science." Edited by John R. Platt. In *New Views of the Nature of Man.* Chicago: University of Chicago Press, 1965.

PRICE 1965c   De Solla Price, Derek J. "The Scientific Foundations of Science Policy." *Nature* 206 (1965): 233.

PRICE 1965d   De Solla Price, Derek J. "Networks of Scientific Papers." *Science* 149 (1965): 510.

PRICE 1966   De Solla Price, Derek J. "The Science of Scientists." *Medical Opinion and Review* 1:10 (1966): 88.

PRICE 1968   De Solla Price, Derek J. "The Difference Between Science and Technology." Address at the International Edison Birthday Celebration, Thomas Alva Edison Foundation, February 1968.

PRICE 1969a   De Solla Price, Derek J. "Measuring the Size of Science." *Proceedings of the Israel Acad-*

emy of Sciences and Humanities 4 (1969): 98.

PRICE 1969b   De Solla Price, Derek J. "Who's Who in the History of Science: A Survey of a Profession." *Technology and Society* 5:2 (1969): 52.

PRICE 1969c   De Solla Price, Derek J. "Policies for Science?" *Melbourne Journal of Politics* 2 (1969):1.

PRICE 1969d   De Solla Price, Derek J. "The Structure of Publication in Science and Technology." In *Factors in the Transfer of Technology.* Edited by William H. Gruber and D.R. Marquis. Cambridge, Mass.: MIT Press, 1969, pp. 91-104.

PRICE 1970   De Solla Price, Derek J. "Citation Measures of Hard Science, Soft Science, Technology, and Non-Science." Paper delivered at the Conference on Communication Among Scientists and Technologists, October 1969. Lexington: Heath & Co., 1970.

PRICE 1972a   De Solla Price, Derek J. *The Relations Between Science and Technology and Their Implications for Policy Formation.* (Report: FOA P Rapport B 8018-M5),FOA (Research Institute of National Defense), Sweden, 1972.

PRICE 1972b   De Solla Price, Derek J., and Gursey, Suha. "The Dynamics of Scientific Authorship." Unpublished.

PRINCE 1968   Prince, J.R. "Science Concepts Among School Children." *South Pacific Bulletin* 4th quarter (1968): 21.

QUBAIN 1966   Qubain, Fahim I. *Education and Science in the Arab World.* Baltimore: Johns Hopkins Press, 1966.

RAHMAN 1964   Rahman, A. et al. "National Laboratories in India." *Nature* 203 (1964): 582.

RAHMAN 1973   Rahman, A.; Bhargava, R.N.; Qureshi, M.A.; and Sudarshan, Pruthi. *Science and Technology in India.* New Delhi: Indian Council for Cultural Relations, 1973.

RAHNEMA 1969   Rahnema, Majid. "Iran: Science Policy for Development." *Impact* 19:1 (1969): 53.

RAM 1968   Ram, Atna. "Science in India: Some Aspects." *Science and Culture* 34 (1968): 5.

RANGANATHAN 1959   Ranganathan, A. "Science in Modern India." *Impact* 9 (1959): 210.

RANGARAO 1966	Rangarao, B.V. "Science in China." *Science and Culture* 32 (1966): 342.
RANGARAO 1967	Rangarao, B.V. "Scientific Research in India: An Analysis of Publications." *Journal of Scientific and Industrial Research* 26 (1967): 166.
RAO 1966	Rao, K.N. "Goals for Science and Technology Development in Latin America." Unpublished.
RAO 1967	Rao, K.N. *Financing Graduate Education and Research in Science and Engineering in Latin America.* Caracas: First Pan-American Conference on Postgraduate Education in Engineering, 1967.
RAO 1970	Rao, K.N. "Innovation, Adaptation, and Diffusion of Reforms in Science Teaching in Latin America." Paper delivered at the 137th AAAS meeting, 1970.
RAY 1967a	Ray, P. "A National Policy of Education." *Science and Culture* 33 (1967): 247.
RAY 1967b	Ray, A.C. "Scientific and Technological Research in the Country and Their Problems." *Science and Culture* 33 (1967): 7.
RAY 1969	Ray, Kamalesh. "Research in the Third World." *New Scientist* 42 (1969): 420.
RETTIG 1964	Rettig, Richard. *Bibliography on Science and World Affairs.* Washington, D.C.: Foreign Service Institute, US Department of State, 1964.
RIAZUDDIN 1970	Riazuddin. "Higher Education as an Essential Part of the Scientific Effort of a Developing Country and International Cooperation." Address at the British Association Meeting, Durham, Summer, 1970. (Reprint copies available.)
RICHARDSON 1969	Richardson, Jacques. "UNESCO: Super-Ministry with Problems." *Science Journal* 5A:7 (August 1969).
RIDEAL 1950	Rideal, Eric K. "The Spanish Higher Council for Scientific Research." *Nature* 165 (1950): 790.
ROCHE 1966	Roche, Marcel. "Social Aspects of Science in a Developing Country." *Impact* 16:1 (1966): 51.
ROCKEFELLER 1971	Rockefeller Foundation. *President's Ten-Year Review & Annual Report, 1971.* New York: Rockefeller Foundation, 1972.

ROCKEFELLER 1972 Rockefeller Foundation. *The President's Review and Annual Report, 1972.* New York: Rockefeller Foundation, 1973.

RODERICK 1962 Roderick, Hilliard. "The Future Natural Sciences Programme of UNESCO." *Nature* 195 (1962): 215.

ROESSNER 1968 Roessner, J. David. "Science Policy and Economic Growth in Underdeveloped Countries, with Special Reference to Sub-Saharan Africa." National R&D Assessment Program, National Science Foundation, 1968.

ROMO 1973 Romo, Jesus to Moravcsik, 1973, concerning comments on the Institute of Chemistry.

ROYAL 1968 Royal Society. *Conference of Commonwealth Scientists.* London: Royal Society, 1968.

RPP 1966 Research Policy Program. *An Attempt at a Bibliography of Bibliographies in Science of Science.* Lund,Sweden: RPP, 1966.

RPP 1967 Research Policy Program. *Brain Drain and Brain Gain: A Bibliography on Migration of Scientists, Engineers, Doctors, and Students.* Lund, Sweden: RPP, 1967.

RYDER 1969a Ryder, Walter D. "Politics of Science in Cuba." *New Scientist* 44 (1969): 436.

RYDER 1969b Ryder, Walter D. "How Cuba Manages Its Science." *New Scientist* 44 (1969): 339.

SAAVEDRA 1969 Saavedra, Igor. "El Problema del Desarrollo Cientifico en Latin America." *Cuadernos de la Realidad Nacional* 1 (1969): 32.

SAAVEDRA 1973 Saavedra, Igor. "Scientific Development in an Underdeveloped Country: The Case of Chile." *Buturi (Journal of the Physical Society of Japan)* 28 (1973): 436.

SABATO 1963 Sabato, Jorge A. "Metallurgy at the Argentine Atomic Energy Commission." *The Metallurgist,* July 1963.

SABATO 1968 Sabato, Jorge A. "Atomic Energy in Argentina." *Estudios Internacionales* 2:3 (1968).

SABATO 1970 Sabato, Jorge A. "Quantity versus Quality in Scientific Research (I): The Special Case of Developing Countries." *Impact* 20 (1970): 183.

SABATO 1973 Sabato, Jorge A. "Atomic Energy in Argentina: A Case History." *World Development* 1:8 (1973): 23.

SALAM 1963	Salam, Abdus. "Diseases of the Rich and Diseases of the Poor." *Bulletin of the Atomic Scientists* 19 (1963): 3.
SALAM 1964a	Salam, Abdus. "The Less-Developed World: How Can We Be Optimistic?" *New Scientist* 21 (1964): 139.
SALAM 1964b	Salam, Abdus. "Science and Technology in the logical Development." *Bulletin of the Atomic Scientists* 20 (March 1964): 2.
SALAM 1965a	Salam, Abdus. "The International Centre for Theoretical Physics." *Physics Today* 18:3 (1965): 52.
SALAM 1965b	Salam, Abdus. "A New Center for Physics." *Bulletin of the Atomic Scientists* 21:43 (December 1965).
SALAM 1965c	Salam, Abdus. "Science and Technology in the Emerging Nations." *Science in the Sixties.* Edited by David Arm. Albuquerque: University of New Mexico Press, 1965, p. 32.
SALAM 1966	Salam, Abdus. "The Isolation of the Scientist in Developing Countries." *Minerva* 4 (1966): 461. Reprinted in Shils, Edward, ed. *Criteria for Scientific Development: Public Policy and National Goals.* Cambridge, Mass.: MIT Press, 1968, p. 200.
SALAM 1968	Salam, Abdus. "The United Nations and the International World of Physics." *Bulletin of the Atomic Scientists* 24 (February 1968): 14.
SALAM 1970a	Salam, Abdus. "Memorandum on a World University." *Bulletin of the Atomic Scientists* 21 (March 1970): 38.
SALAM 1970b	Salam, Abdus. *Towards a Scientific Research and Development Policy for Pakistan.* Karachi: National Science Council of Pakistan, 1970.
SALCEDO 1972	Salcedo, Juan Jr. "Scientists and Progress in the Philippines." *Impact* 22:1/2 (1972): 175.
SALOMON 1971	Salomon, Jean-Jacques. "A Science Policy for the 1970's." *OECD Observer* no. 53 (August 1971).
SCHROEDER 1973	Schroeder-Gudehus, Brigitte. *Canada, Science, and International Affairs.* Ottawa: Science Council of Canada, 1973.
SCHWEITZER 1972	Schweitzer, Glenn. "Toward a Methodology for Assessing the Impact of Technology in Developing Countries." In *Technology and Economics*

	in International Development. (Report TA/OST 72-9), Washington, D.C.: Office of Science and Technology, Agency for International Development, 1972.
SEN 1949	Sen, S.N. "Scientific Strides of Modern India." *UNESCO Courier* 2 (May 1949): 7.
SESHACHAR 1967	Seshachar, B.R. "Problems of Indian Science Since Nehru." *Impact* 22:1/2 (1972): 133.
SHAH 1967	Shah, A.B.,ed. *Education, Scientific Policy, and Developing Societies.* Bombay: Manaktalas, 1967.
SHIBER 1973	Shiber, Hilda G., and Zahlan, A.B. *An Assessment of Arab Doctorates Earned in the United States and the United Kingdom and of Arab Intellectual Output and Conference on Crises of Cultural Change in the Arab World.* Kuwait, April 1974. (Copies available from the author at Box 8815, Beirut, Lebanon.)
SHILS 1961	Shils, Edward. "Scientific Development in the New States." *Bulletin of the Atomic Scientists* 17 (February 1961): 48.
SHURCLIFF 1967	Shurcliff, Alice W. "Exporting PhD's: Is It Profitable?" *Science* 157 (1967): 138.
SID 1973	Society for International Development. "Performance Facts About Assistance Flows to the Developing Countries by Member Countries of the OECD Development Assistance Committee, 1961-1971." *Survey of International Development* 10:1 (1973).
SIDA 1972a	Swedish International Development Authority. *Support to Research Programmes of Benefit to Developing Countries from Swedish Aid Funds During the Fiscal Year 1971/72.* Stockholm: SIDA, October 1972.
SIDA 1972b	Swedish International Development Authority. *Faktablad* 2:5A (November 1972): 1.
SIDA 1973a	Swedish International Development Authority. *Reply by Sweden to International Inventory of Projects and Resources Devoted to Research and Experimental Development for the Benefit of Developing Countries by OECD Member Countries.* (DD-271; DAS/SPR/72.17), January 1973, mimeographed.
SIDA 1973b	Swedish International Development Authority.

Courses and Seminars, 1973/74. Stockholm: SIDA, 1973.

SIDDIQI | Siddiqi, M. Shafqat Husain. *Statement from Pakistan on Organization and Management of Research and the Difficulties Experienced.* Karachi: National Research Council, n.d.

SINGH 1965 | Singh, Jagit. "Scientific Research in India." *Bulletin of the Atomic Scientists* 21 (February 1965): 41.

SINHA 1967 | Sinha, Purnima. "Social Obstacles to Science in India." *Science and Culture* 33 (1967): 326.

SKOLNIKOFF 1967 | Skolnikoff, Eugene B. *Science, Technology, and American Foreign Policy.* Cambridge, Mass.: MIT Press, 1967.

SMALL 1973 | Small, Henry G., and Griffith, Belver C. *The Structure of Scientific Literatures I: Identifying and Graphing Specialties.* Philadelphia: Drexel University Press, 1973.

SNOW 1964 | Snow, C.P. *Two Cultures and a Second Look.* Cambridge, Mass.: Cambridge University Press, 1964.

SPAEY 1969 | Spaey, Jacques et al. *Le developpement par la Science.* Paris: UNESCO, 1969. Published in English, 1971.

STAKMAN 1952 | Stakman, E.C. "The Natural Science Program in UNESCO." *AIBS Bulletin* 2 (1952): 12.

STATE 1971 | US Department of State. *A Statistical Profile of the US Exchange Program 1971.* Washington, D.C.: Bureau of Educational and Cultural Affairs, Department of State, 1972.

SWAMINATHAN 1954 | Swaminathan, V.S. "Scientific and Industrial Research in India." *American Scientist* 42 (1954): 625.

SZASZ 1970 | Szasz, Paul C. *The Law and Practices of the International Atomic Energy Agency.* (IAEA Legal Series no. 7, STI/PUB/250). Vienna: IAEA, 1970.

TASK 1970 | Task Force on International Development. *U.S. Foreign Assistance in the 1970s: A New Approach.* Report to the President. Washington, D.C.: US Government Printing Office, 1970.

TELLEZ 1966 | Tellez, Theresa. "The Crisis of Argentine Science." *Bulletin of the Atomic Scientists* 22 (December 1966): 32.

TELLEZ 1968 — Tellez, Theresa. "Mexican Science: A New Era?" *Bulletin of the Atomic Scientists* 24 (April 1968): 46.

THOMAS 1967 — Thomas, Brinley. "The International Circulation of Human Capital." *Minerva* 5 (1967): 479.

THOMPSON 1963 — Thompson, H.W. "Science in China." *International Science and Technology* 18 (1963): 86.

THOMPSON 1972 — Thompson, Kenneth W. "Higher Education for National Development: One Model for Technical Assistance." Occasional Paper No. 5. New York: International Council for Educational Development, 1972.

THONG 1968 — Thong Saw Pak. "Malaysia: Problems of Science and Technology in Malaysia." In *Conference of Commonwealth Scientists*. London: Royal Society, 1968, p. 364.

TURKELI 1972 — Turkeli, A. *Doctoral Training Environments and Post-Doctoral Productivity of Turkish Physicists.* UNESCO Document SC.72/CONF.3/3, Annex 24 (b). Ankara, 1972.

TURKEY 1969 — Government of Turkey. *Second Five Year Development Plan 1968-72.* Ankara: Central Bank of the Republic of Turkey, 1969.

UFFEN 1972 — Uffen, Robert J. "How Science Policy is Made in Canada." *Science Forum* 30 (December 1972): 3.

UN 1968 — United Nations General Assembly. *Outflow of Trained Professional and Technical Personnel at All Levels from the Developing to the Developed Countries, Its Causes, Its Consequences and Practical Remedies for the Problems Resulting From It* (UN Document A/7294). New York, 1968.

UN 1969 — United Nations, Economic and Social Council. *World Plan of Action for the Application of Science and Technology to Development* (UN-E/AC.52/L.68). New York, October 1969.

UN 1970a — United Nations, ACASTD. *Science and Technology for Development—Porposal for the Second UN Development Decade.* New York: United Nations, 1970.

UN 1970b — United Nations. *World Plan of Action for the Application of Science and Technology to Development Part I. Science and Technology Poli-*

cies and Institutions (Sector No. I) (UN-E/AC.52/R.13) (1970). Prepared by UNESCO.

UN 1971a — United Nations, Advisory Committee on the Application of Science and Technology to Development for the Second United Nations Development Decade. *World Plan of Action for the Application of Science and Technology to Development* (E/4962/Rev.1, ST/ECA/146), 1971.

UN 1971b — United Nations. *The Application of Computer Technology for Development* (UN-E/4800,ST/ECA/136), 1971.

UN 1973a — United Nations. *Report on the First Session of the Committee on Science and Technology for Development* (UN-E/5272), 1973.

UN 1973b — United Nations. *Multinational Corporations in World Development* (UN ST/ECA/190), 1973.

UNESCO 1961 — UNESCO. *Besoin et Ressources de Dix Pays d'Asie en Personnel Scientifique et Technique* (Statistical Reports and Studies, no. 6), Paris, 1961.

UNESCO 1964a — UNESCO. *Final Report of the Lagos Conference.* Paris, 1964.

UNESCO 1964b — UNESCO. *Science and Technology in UNESCO.* (UNESCO/NS/ROU/43), Paris, 1964.

UNESCO 1964c — UNESCO. *Outline of a Plan for Scientific Research and Training in Africa.* Paris, 1964.

UNESCO 1964d — UNESCO. *The Teaching of Sciences in African Universities.* Paris, 1964.

UNESCO 1965a — UNESCO. *National Science Policies in Countries of South and South-East Asia* (Science Policy Studies and Documents no. 3), Paris, 1965.

UNESCO 1965b — UNESCO. *Lagos Conference: Selected Documents.* Paris, 1965.

UNESCO 1966a — UNESCO. *Scientific Research in Africa—National Policies, Research Institutions.* Paris, 1966.

UNESCO 1966b — UNESCO. *World Directory of National Science Policy-Making Bodies.* 4 vols. Paris, Forthcoming.

UNESCO 1967a — UNESCO. *Structural and Operational Schemes of National Science Policy* (Science Policy Studies and Documents no. 6), Paris, 1967.

UNESCO 1967b — UNESCO. *Principles and Problems of National Science Policies* (Science Policy Studies and Documents no. 5), Paris, 1967.

UNESCO 1968   UNESCO. *Activities of UNESCO in the Field of Promoting Scientific and Technical Cooperation* (UNESCO/NS/ROU/172), Paris, 1968.

UNESCO 1969a   UNESCO. *Bilateral Institutional Links in Science and Technology.* Prepared by Daisy Loman. Paris, 1969.

UNESCO 1969b   UNESCO. *The Promotion of Scientific Activity in Tropical Africa* (Science Policy Studies and Documents no. 11), Paris, 1969.

UNESCO 1969c   UNESCO. *La Politica Cientifica en America Latina* (Estudios y Documentos de Politica Cientifica no. 14), Paris, 1969.

UNESCO 1969d   UNESCO. *UNESCO Machinery for Dealing with Science and Technology* (UNESCO/NS/SP/ROU/177), Paris, 1969.

UNESCO 1969e   UNESCO. *Proceedings of the Symposium on Science Policy and Biomedical Research* (Science Policy Studies and Documents no. 16), Paris, 1969.

UNESCO 1970a   UNESCO. *Science and Technology in Asian Development* (New Delhi Conference, 1968), Paris, 1970.

UNESCO 1970b   UNESCO. *The Role of Science and Technology in Economic Development* (Science Policy Studies and Documents no. 18), Paris, 1970.

UNESCO 1970c   UNESCO. *World Summary of Statistics on Science and Technology* (Statistical Reports and Studies no. 17), Paris, 1970.

UNESCO 1970d   UNESCO. *Manual for Surveying National Scientific and Technological Potential* (Science Policy Studies and Documents no. 15), Paris, 1970.

UNESCO 1970e   UNESCO. *National Science Policy and Organization of Research in the Philippines* (Science Policy Studies and Documents no. 22), Paris, 1970.

UNESCO 1970f   UNESCO. *Politica Cientifica y Organisacion Cientifica en la Argentina* (Science Policy Studies and Documents no. 20), Paris, 1970.

UNESCO 1970g   UNESCO. *Directory of Educational Research Institutions in the Asian Region.* Bangkok: UNESCO Regional Office, 1970.

UNESCO 1971a   UNESCO. *Summary Review of UNESCO's Activities in Connection with Transfer of Technology* (UNESCO/NS/ROU/216), Paris, 1971.

UNESCO 1971b   UNESCO. *Science Policy Research and Teaching Units* (Science Policy Research and Teaching no. 28), Paris, 1971.

UNESCO 1972a   UNESCO. *Impact of UNESCO Assistance to Developing Countries for the Establishment of National Science Policy Bodies* (UNESCO/NS/ROU/209 [Rev.1]), Paris, 1972.

UNESCO 1972b   UNESCO. *A Functional Description of UNESCO's Science Policy Programme* (UNESCO/NS/ROU/270), Paris, 1972.

UNESCO 1973a   UNESCO. *Programs for Natural Sciences and Their Application to Development* (UNESCO SP/801/26/1086), Paris, 1973.

UNESCO 1973b   UNESCO. *Report of the Ad Hoc Working Group of the United Nations Advisory Committee on the Application of Science and Technology to Development (UNACAST) on UNESCO's Science Policy Programmes* (UNESCO/93/EX/14), Paris, 1973.

USMANI 1964   Usmani, I.H. "Search for Research." *CENTO Symposium* (November 1964).

USMANI 1969   Usmani, I.H. "Developing Countries and IAEA." Paper delivered at 13th Session of the General Conference of IAEA, Vienna, 1969.

USMANI 1970   Usmani, I.H. "International Atom in the Seventies." Speech at the 14th General Conference of the IAEA, Associated Printers and Publishers, Karachi, Pakistan, 1970.

USMANI 1971   Usmani, I.H. *Organization and Financing of Scientific Research in Pakistan.* Karachi: Pakistan Atomic Energy Commission, 1971.

VARSAVSKY 1967   Varsavsky, Oscar. "Scientific Colonialism in the Hard Sciences." *The American Behavioral Scientist* 10:22 (June 1967).

VIOLINO 1973   Violino, P. "L'insegnamento della Fisica nelle universita dell'Africa Centrale." *Giornale de Fisica* 13 (1972): 248.

WATANABE 1969   Watanabe, S. "The Brain Drain from Developing to Developed Countries." *International Labor Review* 99 (1969): 401.

WEINBERG 1963   Weinberg, Alvin. "Criteria for Scientific Choice." *Minerva* 1 (1963): 159.

WEINBERG 1967   Weinberg, Alvin. *Reflections on Big Science.* Cambridge, Mass.: MIT Press, 1967.

WEISS 1973   Weiss, Charles. "The World Bank Group and

Science and Technology." Unpublished internal paper. Washington, D.C., 1973.

WHITE 1966   White, Stanley. "Status Symbol or Stimulus?" *New Scientist* 30 (1966): 542.

WILLIAMS 1964   Williams, B.R. "Research and Economic Growth— What Should We Expect?" *Minerva* 3:1 (1964): 57. Reprinted in Shils, Edward, ed. *Criteria for Scientific Development: Public Policy and National Goals.* Cambridge, Mass.: MIT Press, 1968, p. 92.

WILSON 1972   Wilson, Mitchell. *Passion to Know—The World's Scientists.* New York: Doubleday, 1972.

WON 1972   Won Ki Kwon. *Skilled Manpower Planning in Korea.* Seoul: Ministry of Science and Technology, 1972.

WORTHINGTON 1948   Worthington, E.B. "Research Services in East Africa." *Nature* 162 (1948): 554.

WORTHINGTON 1960   Worthington, E.B. "Science in Africa." *The New Scientist* 7 (1960): 151.

WU 1970   Wu, Yuan-li, and Sheeks, Robert B. *The Organization and Support of Scientific Research and Development in Mainland China.* New York: Praeger, 1970.

ZACHARIAH 1973   Zachariah, Mathew. "The Impact of Long-Term Educational Advisory Experts on the Development of New Nations." In *Education in Developing Countries of the Commonwealth.* London: Commonwealth Secretariat, 1973.

ZAHEER 1968   Zaheer, S. Husain. "The Development of Science and Technology in Underdeveloped Countries." *Scientific World* 12 (1968): 9.

ZAHLAN 1967   Zahlan, A.B. "Science and Backward Countries." *Scientific World* 11:6 (1967): 5.

ZAHLAN 1968   Zahlan, A.B. "The Brain Drain: The American University of Beirut and the Arab World." *al-Kulliyah* (Spring 1968).

ZAHLAN 1969a   Zahlan, A.B. "The Acquisition of Scientific and Technological Capabilities by Arab Countries." *Bulletin of the Atomic Scientists* 25 (November 1969): 7.

ZAHLAN 1969b   Zahlan, A.B. "Migrations of Scientists and the Development of Scientific Communities in the Arab World." (For copies write to the author at Box 8815, Beirut, Lebanon.)

ZAHLAN 1970   Zahlan, A.B. "Science in the Arab Middle
                     East." *Minerva* 8:1 (1970): 8.

ZAHLAN 1972a   Zahlan, A.B. "The Lebanese Brain Drain."
                     Conference on the Lebanese Brain Drain, Leba-
                     nese Ministry of Information, Beirut, Lebanon,
                     May 1972. (Copies available from the author at
                     Box 8815, Beirut, Lebanon.)

ZAHLAN 1972b   Zahlan, A.B. "The Arab Brain Drain." *Middle
                     East Studies Association Bulletin.* 6:3
                     (1972): 1.

ZAHLAN 1972c   Zahlan, A.B. "National Science Policies (For
                     Arab Middle Eastern Countries)." In *UN Eco-
                     nomic and Social Office in Beirut, Elements
                     for a Regional Plan for the Application of
                     Science and Technology to Development in Se-
                     lected Countries of the Middle East* (ESOB/ST/
                     WP.1 Sept. 1972 or ESOB/HR/72/31), Beirut,
                     1972.

ZAHLAN 1972d   Zahlan, A.B. "Science and Technology Educa-
                     tion (For Arab Middle Eastern Countries)." In
                     *UN Economic and Social Office in Beirut, Ele-
                     ments for a Regional Plan for the Application
                     of Science and Technology to Development in
                     Selected Countries of the Middle East* (ESOB/
                     ST/WP.1 September 1972 or ESOB/HR/72/31),
                     Beirut, 1972. (Final title: *National Planning
                     for Education in Science and Technology.*)

ZAHLAN 1973   Zahlan, A.B. "Science and Higher Education in
                     the Arab World." *New Edinburgh Review* no. 23
                     (1973): 12.

ZIMAN 1969   Ziman, John. "Some Problems of the Growth and
                     Spread of Science into Developing Countries."
                     Proceedings of the Royal Society A 311 (1969):
                     349.

ZIMAN 1971   Ziman, John. "The 'Winter College' Format."
                     Science 171 (1971): 352.

ZIMAN 1973   Ziman, John. "Internationalism Is Not
                     Enough." *Physics Bulletin* 24 (May 1973): 274.

ZOPPO 1971   Zoppo, Ciro E. "Toward a U.S. Policy on Nu-
                     clear Technology Transfer to the Developing
                     Countries." Southern California Arms Control
                     and Foreign Policy Seminar, July 1971.

ZWEMER 1957   Zwemer, Raymund L. "The UNESCO Program for
                     Scientific Research." *AIBS Bulletin* 7 (1957): 8.

The bibliography contains entries dating before the end of 1973. A few additional items that have come to my attention after that date and which appear relevant are listed below. These references, however, do not appear in the text.

Blanpied, William A. "Notes for a Study on the Early Scientific Work of the Asiatic Society of Bengal." *Japanese Studies in the History of Science* 12 (1973): 121.

Blanpied, William A. "The Movement for Popular Science in Early Nineteenth Century Bengal." *Proceedings of the XIV International Congress of the History of Science.* Tokyo, 1974.

US House of Representatives, Committee on Foreign Affairs. *U.S. Scientists Abroad: An Examination of Major Programs for Non-Governmental Scientific Exchange.* Washington, D.C.: US Government Printing Office, 1974.

US House of Representatives, Committee on Science and Astronautics, Subcommittee on Science, Research, and Development. *The Participation of Federal Agencies in International Scientific Programs.* Washington, D.C.: US Government Printing Office, 1967.

Library of Congress, Congressional Research Service, Foreign Affairs Division. *Brain Drain: A Study of the Persistent Issue of International Scientific Mobility.* Washington, D.C.: US Government Printing Office, 1974.

Suttmeier, Richard P. *Research and Revolution.* Lexington, Mass.: D.C. Heath & Co., 1974.

In addition, the July-September 1974 issue of *Impact of Science on Society*, which deals with "A new look at the earth's resources," has some scientific implications. Similarly relevant issues of *Impact* are the April-June 1974 issue ("Science and food for man") and the October-December 1973 issue ("Appropriate technology"). The April-June 1973 issue, "Science and the Sub-Sahara," contains an article by Odhiambo on planning and teaching of science.

Suggested Initial Readings

I found the following references particularly interesting or pertinent: ADAMS 1968, ALONSO 1969, BASALLA 1967, BAZIN 1972b, BHABHA 1966 a or b, BLACKETT 1968, CARDENAS 1970, CERNUSCHI 1971, CIMT 1970b, DART 1963, DART 1967, DEDIJER 1964b, DE HEMPTINNE 1963, DJER-ASSI 1968, FREEMAN 1969b, GARCIA 1966, GASPARINI 1969, GLYDE (undated), GREENE 1971, GRIFFITH 1973a, GRUBER 1968, JONES 1970, KARVE 1963, KOREA 1972a, KOVDA 1968, LARWOOD 1961, MORAV-CSIK 1972a, MORAVCSIK 1972c, MORAVCSIK 1973c, MORAVCSIK 1974b, NADER 1969, NAS 1965b, NAS 1967, NAS 1973a, NAS 1973c, OAS 1972, OECD 1968a, OLDHAM 1966, PERES 1969, PIRIE 1967, PRICE 1963, PRICE 1969a, PRICE 1972a, QUBAIN 1966, RAM 1968, RANGARAO 1966, RANGARAO 1967, ROCHE 1966, RODERICK 1962, ROESSNER 1968, SABATO 1970, SABATO 1973, SALAM 1966, SHILS 1961, UN 1968, UN 1970b, UNESCO 1969a, UNESCO 1970a, UNESCO 1970c, WATANABE 1969, WU 1970, ZAHALN 1970, ZAHLAN 1972c, ZIMAN 1969.

Subject Index

Academy of Sciences (People's Republic of China), 111
Africa: regional assistance in, 170
Agency for International Development: description of, 165; programs supported by, 182-84; bilateral program of, 196
Applied research, 33-34, 96, 105-106, 137
Applied science, 22, 32-33
Argentina, 143
Asia Foundation, 188
Atomic Energy Commission (AEC), 166, 184
Atomic Energy Laboratory (India), 158

Basic Research, 95-97; arguments for and against in LDCs, 106-107; statistics on funds for in various countries, 107-109
Bilateral links, 78, 173-74, 196-97; Glyde study in Britain and Thailand, 90-91; University of California-University of Chile, 197
"Book aid" organizations, 87
Books for Asia (Asia Foundation), 87
Brain drain, 44, 52, 81; education and, 29, 37, 46; arguments in favor of, 46-47, 53-54; detrimental effects of, 47-48, 54-55; statistics on from LDCs, 55-56; severity of in various countries, 59-60; counteraction to in India, 61-62; counteraction to in the People's Republic of China, 61; to the US, 56-57; to Canada, 57-58; to France, 58; to and from Britain, 58
Brazilian chemistry program, 62-63, 185-86
Britain, 58

Canada: migration of scientists to, 57-58; International Development Research Centre, 168, 186
Centers of excellence, 35-36, 101, 115-16; examples of, 115
Centre European pour la Recherche Nucleaire (CERN), 178, 189-90
Centro Latino Americano de Fisica, 91, 119, 170, 191
Change: attitude toward in LDCs, 5-6; science as a producer of, 12
China, the People's Republic of. See People's Republic of China
Civil service system, 51, 102, 118, 156; in the UN, 171
"Colonial science," 26-27
Communication, 7; among scientists, 43, 51, 73-74; between scientists and government, 74-75, 131; of research results, 86
Computer: use of in LDCs, 72
Conselho Nacional de Pesquisas (CNP) chemistry project, 185-86
Cooperative Science Program in Latin America (National Science Foundation), 167
Corruption in administrative structures, 148
Council of Scientific and Industrial Research (CSIR), 158
"Critical mass," 44, 73, 84, 132
Cultural imperialism, 9
Cultural traditions: relationship of science to in LDCs, 20, 27-28; in Nepal, 18; in Papua New Guinea, 18; in Japan, 20-21; in France, 28
Customs offices in LDCs, 132-33, 159

Darien Book Aid Plan, 87
Department of Scientific Affairs (Organization of American States), 170, 190-91

Education: function of, 17. *See also* Science education
Equipment, laboratory: availability of in LDCs, 101, 116
Examinations: in LDCs, 21, 31
Exceptional people, 50, 100-101, 160; loss of in LDCs, 47, 54-55; needed as policy-makers, 134

Financing science in LDCs, 127-31; role of private capital in, 4, 168-69, 187-89; "overhead payments," 128-29; GNP as a guideline for expenditures, 129; support of individual merit in various LDCs, 147-48; statistics for individual countries, 150-51; cost of research per scientist in various countries, 152; financial targets of various countries, 155
Florence agreement, 159
Ford Foundation, 187-88
Foundations, private: role of in science development, 169, 187-89
France, 28, 58, 168-69
Franklin Book Program, 32, 83, 87
Frascati manual, 138, 149
Fund for Overseas Research Grants and Education (FORGE), 115-16, 189

Gardner report, 183-84
Grants, individual merit, 128

Harbison-Myers index, 63-64
History, philosophy, and methodology of science, 23, 32, 63, 122

India, 10, 15; education in, 21, 22, 32; centers of excellence, 35-36; scientists' pool in, 61, 61-62; manpower statistics for, 65; science policy organizations in, 157; governmental laboratories in, 158; construction of nuclear reactors in, 206
Indigenous science: importance of in LDCs, 11
Industrial research: in LDCs, 99-100, 113-14, 132; in the Philippines, 114
Industry, private: involvement of in science development, 186-87. *See also* Industrial research
Infighting in LDCs, 44-45, 134
Instituto Venezolano de Investigaciones Cientificas (IVIC), 158
Interamerican Bank, 170
International Atomic Energy Agency (IAEA), 92, 119, 172-73, 195-96; travel program of, 89; training fellowships of, 90; arranged international scientific meetings, 91
International Centre for Insect Physiology and Ecology (ICIPE), 79, 179
International Centre for Theoretical Physics (ICTP), 173, 196; description of, 78-79; location of, 91
International Development Institute (IDI), 166, 180-81
International Development Research Center (Indiana University), 88
International Development Research Centre (Canada), 168, 186
International Rice Research Institute, (IRRI), 113
International Science Foundation (ISF), 179
International scientific assistance. *See* Scientific assistance, international
"Invisible college," 70, 82
Isolation of scientists in LDCs, 48, 70-71, 80-81, 82

Japan, 20-21, 42, 110
Journals: arguments for and against publishing, in LDCs, 71, 82-83; access to in LDCs, 75, 85-86

Korea Advanced Institute of Science (KAIS), 182-83
Korea Institute of Science and Technology (KIST), 183
Korea, Republic of. *See* Republic of Korea

Laboratories, governmental, 113; as a location for research, 100; organization in, 157-58; in the US which aid LDCs, 168
Laboratories, international: involving LDCs, 178
Language: as an educational problem in LDCs, 25-26, 29
Latin America: regional assistance in, 170
Libraries and library science in LDCs, 72, 83-84, 117; tools for information retrieval and classification, 76, 86; in the People's Republic of China, 83
Lysenko affair, 142-43

Manpower, 41; planning for, as long-term project, 42; quality of in LDCs, 42, 51; claimed surpluses of, 49-50; retention of, 44-45, 60-63; statistics on researchers per million population in various countries, 66; development of in ple's Republic of China, 49, statistics for the US, the Republic of Korea, the People's Republic of China, India, and Turkey, 64-66
Mexico: steroid chemistry program, 35, 62
Microfiche, 76, 86
Microfilm, 76, 86
Military strength: as a motivation for developing science in LDCs, 16
Morale, 4-5, 48, 202-205
Motivations to do science, 199-201

National Academy of Sciences (NAS), 119, 185-86; description of, 167; NAS-CNP chemistry project, 62-63, 185-86
National Bureau of Standards (NBS), 168
National Science Foundation (NSF): Office of International Programs, 166-67; Science Education Improvement Project in India, 184
Nationalism and science, 19-20, 207
Nepal, 18
Nigeria, 108
Nonproliferation agreement on nuclear weapons, 8
Nuclear reactor programs: in LDCs, 115; in the People's Republic of China, 113; in India, 206

Oak Ridge National Laboratory, 168
Office of International Programs (National Science Foundation), 166-67
Organization of American States (OAS), 119; travel program of, 89; fellowships awarded by, 92; regional programs of, 92, 190-91; Department of Scientific Affairs, 190
Organization for Economic Cooperation and Development (OECD), 170
"Overhead payments," 128-29

Pakistan, 14, 109
Papua New Guinea, 18
Papyrocentric/papyrophobic, 81, 104
Patents: as a measure of technological activity, 102
People's Republic of China, 61, 110, 175; "red and expert" scheme, 30-31, 36; manpower in, 49, 65; libraries in, 83; Academy of Sci-

ences, 111; University of Science and Technology, 112; nuclear program in, 113; relationship of science and politics in, 15-16, 141; prizes for scientific work in, 207

Peru, 142

Peterson report, 166, 180

Philippines, 114

Physics Interviewing Project (Committee on International Education in Physics), 24

Politics: political interference with science, 45, 141-43; relationship of science to, 73, 140-41; separation of science policy from, 124-25; subjugation of science to in the People's Republic of China, 15-16, 141; political interference with science in the People's Republic of China, 142-32; political interference with science in Peru, 142; separation of science from, in Argentina, 143

Premature specialization, 21-22, 30; example of in the People's Republic of China, 30-31

Preprints and research reports, 75-76, 86, 164

President's Science Advisory Committee (PSAC), 165, 180

Professional scientific societies, 73, 84, 178-79

Public Law 480 funds, 166-67, 168, 174

Publication and citation counts, 55, 70, 81-82, 122-23, 137-38

Publications, scientific, 81; in LDCs, 82-83; as a measure of scientific activity, 102

Project Physics at Harvard University, 35

Provincialism: science as an antidote to, 19-20

"Red and expert" scheme (People's

Republic of China), 30-31, 36

Regional science development, 169-70, 189-91

Republic of Korea, 4, 46, 65; Korea Advanced Institute of Technology (KAIS), Korea Institute of Science and Technology (KIST), 182-83

Research, scientific, 93; recommended spending for, 96-97; location of, 97-100; estimates of the cost of, 104; in Pakistan, 109; in the People's Republic of China, 110-11; in the Philippines, 114. *See also* Applied research; Basic research; Industrial research

Rockefeller Foundation, 187-88; favors centers of excellence, 35

Sakharov affair, 143

Salaries of scientists, 130-31, 155

Science education, 2-3, 17, 21, 28-29; foreign, 21, 23-25, 36-37, 39, 46; shortcomings of in LDCs, 21-23, 30-32; the importance of quality in, 25, 36; language of, 25-26, 29; statistics on funds for in various countries, 38; enrollment statistics, 38-39; educating policy-makers, 135; organizations involved in, 189; in the People's Republic of China, 30-31; in India, 32, 35

Science Education Improvement Project in India (National Science Foundation), 35

Science policy, 123-24, 125-27, 138-40, 146-47; creators of, 4, 48, 63, 74, 133-35, 146, 159-60; access to material on in LDCs, 76, 86-87; education concerning, 134-35, 136; evaluation of, 135, 137; in the Republic of Korea, 4; in India, 15

Science and technology: benefits of,

2, 3; relationship between, 10-11, 69-70, 81, 93-95, 104-105. *See also* Transfer of science and technology

Scientific assistance, international, 161-65, 177, 210-11; regional projects, 169-70; associate expert scheme, 173; statistics on in Percentage of GNP, 192-93; from the US, 164-68, 179-80; from Canada, 168-69; from France, 168-69; from Sweden, 186; to the People's Republic of China, 175. *See also* Financing Science in LDCs

"Scientific colonialism," 109, 114

Scientific community, indigenous: importance of, 1-2, 6, 10; nature of in LDCs, 23; need for international participation in, 82; as a policy-maker, 126-27

Scientific conferences, international, 79-91

"Scientific size" of country: correlated with GNP, 12, 152-54

Scientists and Engineers in Economic Development (SEED), 89, 167

Specialization, premature, 21-22, 30-31

Steroid chemistry program in Mexico, 35, 62

Sweden: international scientific assistance in, 186

Swedish International Development Authority (SIDA), 186

Technology. *See* Science and technology

Telephone: in LDCs, 74, 85

Telex, 76, 83, 86

Textbooks in LDCs, 32; production of, 71-72

Transfer of science and technology, 2, 97, 110-11; in Japan, 110; in the People's Republic of China, 110-11

Translations, 72, 83

Turkey, 66

Unemployment of scientists in LDCs, 66

Union of Soviet Socialist Republics: Lysenko affair, 142; Sakharov affair, 143

United Nations, 170-73; civil service system of, 171; agencies of involved with science development, 171-73; expenditures on science, 192; World Plan, 171, 192-94. *See also* specific agencies within the United Nations

United Nations Development Programme (UNDP), 172

United Nations, Educational, Scientific, and Cultural Organization (UNESCO), 91, 92, 172, 194-95

United States of America: foreign students in, 23-24; brain drain to, 56-57; manpower statistics for, 64-65; international scientific assistance from, 164-68, 180

Universities: as a location for research, 33-34, 97-98, 111-12; function of science in, 98-99; in LDCs, 132

University of Science and Technology in the People's Republic of China, 112

Venezuela: research in, 108; Instituto Venezolano de Investigaciones Científicas (IVIC), 158

Visiting speakers, 73-74

Volunteers for International Technical Assistance (VITA), 179

West Pakistan, 3

World Plan. *See* United Nations: World Plan

World University, 179

Author Index

Adiseshiah, Malcolm, 30
Aitken, Norman, 54
Allende, Salvador, 110; on
    research, 106, 109, 115;
    on science and politics,
    140, 141
Alonso, Marcelo, 145
Alter, Charles, 183-84
Apter, David, 28
Ashby, Eric, 36
Auger, P., 105

Baldwin, George, statistics
    on foreign education, 39;
    on manpower in LDCs,
    49; on the brain drain,
    53, 54, 56, 57, 58, 59,
    61-62
Basalla, George, 15, 26-27,
    82, 207
Bazin, Maurice, 141
Bethe, Hans, 32
Bhabha, H.J., 33, 111, 176,
    206
Bhathal, R.S., 30
Blackett, P.M.S., 50-51, 107,
    110
Blanpied, William, 111-12
Blount, B.K., 127
Brooks, Harvey, 34, 137
Brown, Harrison, 157
Burkhardt, G., 177
Buzzati-Traverso, Adriano,
    176

Cardenas, Rodolfo Jose, 15,
    143
Cernuschi, Felix, 38, 39
Chandrashekar, B.S., 112
Chou En-lai, 15
Clark, Robert, 49
Clarke, Robin, 12-13, 37-38,

206-207; estimates size
    of brain drain, 56; on
    research, 103, 119
Cooper, Charles, 104
Copisarow, Alcon, 196

Dart, Francis, 28, 36-37
de Hemptinne, Y., 11, 66,
    104, 140
de Solla Price, Derek, 136,
    137, 160, 206; on science
    and technology, 10-11,
    104-105; correlates the
    "scientific" and economic
    size of countries, 12, 153-
    54; on exceptional scien-
    tists, 55; on manpower,
    64-67; on communication,
    81-82; on research, 103,
    114, 117, 157-58; on the
    communication of research
    results, 86; favors centers
    of excellence, 116
Dedijer, Stevan, 81, 82, 106;
    on indigenous science,
    12; on planning for science,
    136, 144, 147; on politics,
    140, 142; mathematically
    relates R&D expenditure
    and GNP per capita, 153,
    154, 155
Dessau, Jan, 27, 30
Djerassi, Carl, 62; on centers
    of excellence, 35, 178

Freeman, Christopher, 137, 149
Friedman, Bruno, 141

Garcia, Rolando: on science
    in universities, 12, 111;
    on research, 34, 103

Gasparini, Olga: survey on
the Venezuelan scientific
community, 138, 207-208
Glyde, Henry: on bilateral
links, 90-91, 196-97
Greene, Michael, 82, 115
Griffith, Belver, 55
Grubel, Herbert, 54

Hambraeus, Gunnar, 108,
141, 143
Harari, Roland, 142
Hardy, William, 106
Herrera, Amilcar, 144
Holton, Gerald, 15, 35, 137
Houssay, Nernard, 53

Jones, Burton, 203
Jones, Graham, 12, 30, 110,
112, 190, 206; on research,
33-34, 109, 115; on science
policy, 136, 138

Kee-Hyong, Kim, 190
Kepler, Johannes, 136
King, Alexander, 189-90, 194
Kothari, D.S., 144
Kovda, Victor, 119; measures
scientific potential, 115,
137; on UN programs,
191-92

Larwood, H.J.C., 27
Lewis, Arthur: on education,
29,51; on the UN, 192
Long, Franklin, 196
Lopes, J. Leite, 9, 114, 140-41
Low, Ian, 51-52
Lubkin, Gloria, 108

Ma Hsu-lun, 106
Malecki, I., 114

Mathur, K.N., 117
Mendelsohn, Kurt, 155
Merton, Robert, 116
Miraboglu, M., 55
Moravcsik, Michael, 15, 108,
208; on education, 28-29,
30, 33, 37; on communica-
tion, 80, 84, 89; on bilateral
links, 119, 181; favors
separation of science and
politics, 140, 143; favors
international scientific
assistance, 175; on morale,
205-206
Morehouse, Ward, 61,145
Mosse, Robert, 28
Myint, Hla, 54

Nader, C., 9
Nayudamma, Y., 10, 109
Nehru, Jawharwahl, 10, 29

Odhiambo, Thomas, 29, 179
Oldham, C.H.G., 115

Parthasari, Ashok, 157, 176
Peres, Leon: statistics on
research in Asia, 108, 111,
113
Piganiol, Pierre, 142
Pirie, N.W., 29, 51, 103
Prothro, Provost, 12

Ram, Atna, 103, 156
Rangarao, B.V., 117, 138
Rao, K.N., 28
Ray, A.C., 112
Ray, Kamalesh, 104, 153, 154
Richardson, Jacques, 194
Roche, Marcel, 10, 13; on
scientific communication
in Venezuela, 207; statis-
tics on types of research

in Venezuela, 108
Roderick, Hillard, 194
Roessner, J. David, 144, 160
Ryder, Walter, 141, 142

Saavedra, Igor, 13, 86, 114, 196
Sabato, Jorge, 51, 138, 159;
    on research, 103, 118; ap-
    proves nuclear technology
    in LDCs, 115; on planning
    for science in LDCs, 146
Salam, Abdus, 14, 116, 202;
    on the brain drain, 54-55;
    Director of International
    Centre for Theoretical
    Physicists, 78-79, 173;
    his isolation in Lahore,
    82; on UN activities in
    science, 119, 192
Salcedo, Juan, 143
Salomon, Jean-Jacques, 139
Seshachar, B.R., 141-42, 146,
    156; manpower statistics
    for India, 65; on excep-
    tional people, 160
Shils, Edward, 144, 156
Siddiqi, M., Shafqat Husain,
    50, 110
Siffin, William, Director of the
    International Development
    Research Center, 88
Singer, Milton, 28
Skolnikoff, Eugene, 180
Skyes, Gerald, 205, 207
Snow, C.P., 14, 28, 206

Teller, Edward, 30
Tellez, Theresa, 52, 142
Thompson, Kenneth, 175-76,
    196
Thong Saw Pak, 114
Turkeli, A., 115

Usmani, I.H., 105, 107

Varsavsky, Oscar, 9, 109

Watanabe, S.: on manpower
    in ACs, 51; on the brain
    drain, 54, 57, 58, 61
Weinberg, Alvin, 11, 14-15
Weiss, Charles, 107
Wharton, Clifton, 50
Whitehead, Alfred North, 26
Williams, B.R., 153, 154

Yuan-li, Wu, 15-16, 104, 146;
    on manpower shortage in
    the People's Republic of
    China, 49; on publications
    and libraries in the People's
    Republic of China, 83; on
    technology transfer to the
    People's Republic of China,
    110, 175; on political in-
    terference, 206

Zachariah, Mathew, 177
Zaheer, S. Husain, 146, 194
Zahlan, A.B., 52, 84, 86, 89,
    103, 177, 196, 206; on
    education in Arab countries,
    32, 51; on the brain drain,
    53, 54, 56, 57, 58-59, 59-
    60; on manpower, 66; on
    research, 107, 109; on
    scientific activity in Arab
    countries, 117, 137; on
    UNESCO, 144-45, 194-
    95; on planning for
    science in LDCs, 146
Zhmudsky, A.Z., 146
Ziman, John, 28, 34, 89, 105,
    106, 196
Zoppo, Ciro, 175

Michael J. Moravcsik, born in Budapest, Hungary, on 25 June 1928, was educated at the Lutheran Gymnasium in Budapest (1938-46), the University of Budapest (1946-48) and the Eotvos College (1946-48), majoring in mathematics and physics. After immigrating to the US in 1948, he received the AB degree (cum laude) in physics from Harvard University (1951) and the PhD in theoretical physics from Cornell (1956). He has served as research associate at Brookhaven National Laboratory (1956-58) and Head of the Elementary Particle and Nuclear Theory Group, Theoretical Division of the Lawrence Radiation Laboratory, University of California, Livermore (1958-67). In 1967 he joined the Department of Physics (as Professor) and the Institute of Theoretical Science (as Research Associate) at the University of Oregon, Eugene. He served as Director of the Institute from 1969 to 1972.

Professor Moravcsik has served as a Visiting Professor, lecturer, and speaker at various institutions and programs throughout the world. In 1974 he received a Scientists and Engineers in Economic Development grant and a NATO Senior Fellowship in Science. He is a member of Sigma Xi and Phi Kappa Phi, the American Association of Physics Teachers, and was the originator of the Physics Interviewing Project, now operated by the AAPT Committee on International Education in Physics. He has served a three-year term on the Advisory Committee on East Asia of the Committee on International Exchange of Persons, is a consultant to the Los Alamos Meson Physics Facility (Los Alamos, New Mexico), on the Grants Advisory Panel of the Fund for Overseas Research Grants and Education, Inc., and a Fellow of the American Physical Society. He is the author of one other book, *The Two-Nucleon Interaction* (1963), and some 130 articles dealing with nuclear and elementary particle physics, the "science of science," and science organization and policy, particularly in the context of less developed countries.